Global Power Shift

Ample empirical evidence points to recent power shifts in multiple areas of international relations taking place between industrialized countries and emerging powers, as well as between states and non-state actors. However, there is a dearth of theoretical interpretation and synthesis of these findings, and a growing need for coherent approaches to understand and measure the transformation. The central issues to be addressed include theoretical questions and empirical puzzles: How can studies of global power shift and the rise of 'emerging powers' benefit from existing theories, and which alternative aspects and theoretical approaches might be suitable? How can the meanings, perceptions, dynamics, and consequences of global power shift be determined and assessed? This edited series will include highly innovative research on these topics. It aims to bring together scholars from all major world regions as well as different disciplines, including political science, economics and human geography. The overall aim is to discuss and possibly blend their different approaches and provide new frameworks for understanding global affairs and the governance of global power shifts.

All titles in this series are peer-reviewed.

This book series is indexed in Scopus.

Jon-Arild Johannessen

The AI Battleground Between the USA and China

Technological Innovation, Strategic Containment, and the New Silk Roads

Springer

Jon-Arild Johannessen
Communication, Leadership and Marketing
Campus Kristiania
Oslo, Oslo, Norway

ISSN 2198-7343 ISSN 2198-7351 (electronic)
Global Power Shift
ISBN 978-3-032-10137-2 ISBN 978-3-032-10138-9 (eBook)
https://doi.org/10.1007/978-3-032-10138-9

This Springer imprint is published by the registered company Springer Nature Switzerland AG
The registered company address is: Gewerbestrasse 11, 6330 Cham, Switzerland

Preface

In the context of the Fourth Industrial Revolution, artificial intelligence (AI) is viewed as one of the most important technological innovations. The ground-breaking technological developments have depended on knowledge first being generated through education and then being applied in innovative and entrepreneurial ways. With the aim of equipping its population with the skills necessary to develop high technology, following the end of the Cultural Revolution, China started to invest heavily in mass education from the late 1970s. As a result, China's technological competence is now on a par with that of the world's leading industrial nations, especially in artificial intelligence.

Between 1976 and 2011, several million students travelled from China to study at Western universities. In the United States alone, more than one million Chinese students graduated between 1978 and 2013. Many of these students gained degrees in fields such as engineering, computer sciences, and the natural sciences.[1] When these students returned to China, many started businesses that were based on innovative technologies. Along with many of their contemporaries who had remained in China to study, they went on to become tech entrepreneurs in large cities such as Shanghai.

As time went on, Chinese tech start-ups became serious competitors for Western tech companies. For example, in 2022, China's Huawei held around 14 percent of all patents worldwide relating to 5G technology. If Huawei were to get the opportunity to participate in the expansion of Western 5G networks, China would strengthen its competitive position vis-à-vis the United States in the development of digital systems. In order to prevent Huawei from competing with Western companies, issues relating to national security were raised. As a result, many Chinese tech companies were banned from the United States and a number of European countries.

[1] https://ebrary.net/120924/business_finance/chinese_international_students_united_states_1978.

Core Message

The combination of the building of three New Silk Roads and the emergence of a Chinese middle class has put China into a favourable position in high technology generally, and AI in particular. This is an important justification for the USA's grand strategy towards China-Technological containment, trade wars and military alliances. This position began with the Obama administration, continued with Trump I, and was continued by the Biden administration, and is reinforced under Trump II.

Statement of Aims

Briefly, what is your book about?

Chinese technological innovation has also become vital for China's expansion along the three New Silk Roads: the land-based and maritime routes (together the BRI or the 'Belt and Road Initiative') and a digital 'silk road'. The three New Silk Roads can be understood as ways for China to invest in minerals and the future production of green energy. At the same time, the three New Silk Roads are an important social mechanism for China's growing middle class. It is because of China's investments around the world that many graduates from Chinese universities, and Chinese graduates from universities in the United States, the UK, France, Germany, and so on, can secure lucrative jobs. Accordingly, if the building of the three New Silk Roads were to be obstructed, it seems reasonable to assume that the employment prospects of Chinese students would be adversely affected. If such a situation were to arise, it would affect the growth and expectations of the Chinese middle class.

In 2011, the United States started to develop an important new strategy towards China. We can describe this strategy as one of technological containment. We see the first signs of this new strategy in the article, "America's Pacific century", published in *Foreign Policy* in 2011 by Hillary Clinton, who was then the US Secretary of State. China's response to the US policy of containment was to develop various economic strategies, such as the "Dual Circulation Development Paradigm"; "Made in China 2025"; and "China Standards 2035". In order to become less dependent on the Western world, China also joined the world's largest free trade area, RCEP, on 1 January 2022.

What Are Its Main Themes and Objectives?

We investigate two topics in this book: the three New Silk Roads and the emergence of the Chinese middle class. These two topics are systemically linked. In practice, this means that although each topic is distinct, they are linked by factors relating to technological innovation and the development of innovative entrepreneurship. Innovative entrepreneurship has been particularly important in promoting the development of high technology in general, and AI in particular.

Why Is Your Book Different, More Innovative or Better Than Existing Books?

Our book is different in four respects.

1. We focus on the increasing significance of AI, especially in relation to the intensification of tensions between the United States and China.
2. We investigate the growth of China's tech competence during 1978–2011, which was the result, among other things, of the influx of Chinese students to American and other Western universities. China's burgeoning competence was an important factor in subsequent US-China tensions concerning competition in the high-tech sector.
3. We use conceptual generalization as our method for investigating the general issue explored in this book (see Chap. 5).
4. We use systemic thinking (see Chap. 5) to link the growth of the Chinese middle class to the three New Silk Roads, which are crucial underlying social mechanisms for China's leading position in AI.
5. We use six case letters to describe and explain the question investigated (see Chapter 5).

Oslo, Norway Jon-Arild Johannessen

Contents

Chapter 1
The Underlying Factors for China's Progress in Artificial Intelligence

Core Idea
China's soft power, i.e. the competence nurtured by its higher education policies, has put China in a leading position within high technology in general, and AI in particular.

Key points

- Since around 1976, China's mass education policies have put the country's technological competence on a par with that of the world's leading industrial nations.
- From around 2011, the United States started to develop a new 'grand strategy' towards China. We can describe this strategy as one of technological containment.
- China's response to this US policy has been to develop various economic strategies, such as the "Dual Circulation Development Paradigm", "Made in China 2025"; and "China Standards 2035".
- In order to reduce its dependence on the West, China has joined the world's largest free trade area, the RCEP.
- In 2022, the Chinese company Huawei held around 14 percent of all patents worldwide relating to 5G technology.
- If Huawei were to get the opportunity to participate in the expansion of Western 5G networks, China would strengthen its competitive position vis-à-vis the United States in the development of digital systems.
- Arguments about national security were used in order to prevent Huawei from out-competing Western companies.

The original version of the chapter has been revised. A correction to this chapter can be found at https://doi.org/10.1007/978-3-032-10138-9_6

J. Johannessen, *The AI Battleground Between the USA and China*, Global Power Shift,
https://doi.org/10.1007/978-3-032-10138-9_1

Introduction

In this book, we will examine China's increasing geo-economic influence, especially related to the development of artificial intelligence (Johannessen 2021a, b, c). In the context of the Fourth Industrial Revolution, artificial intelligence (AI) is viewed as one of the most important technological innovations (Schwab 2016, 2018; Johannessen 2020a, b, 2020a, b, 2023d). This technology is the driving force in the emerging innovation economy.[1] In China's case, it is the emergence of the middle class, which has enabled the country to gain a leading position in the development of high technology (Li 2021). It is both the development of knowledge through the education system and the application of knowledge through innovative entrepreneurship that has been decisive for the development of high-tech innovations and thus also artificial intelligence (Li 2010a, b; Jain 2021). China has developed technological innovations in many areas, especially related to the semiconductor industry, infrastructure and infostructure,[2] which has become vital for China's expansion along the three Silk Roads: the land-based and maritime routes, and the digital 'Silk Road'. The ground-breaking technological developments, and especially artificial intelligence, have depended on knowledge first being generated through education and then being applied in innovative and entrepreneurial ways (Li 2010a, b; Jain 2021). The three New Silk Roads can be understood as ways for China to invest in minerals and the future production of green energy. At the same time, the three New Silk Roads are an important social mechanism for China's growing middle class. It is because of China's investments around the world that many graduates from Chinese universities, and Chinese graduates from universities in the United States, the UK, France, Germany, and so on, can secure lucrative jobs (Hannum et al. 2008). In other words, the development of the three New Silk Roads is facilitating the growth and prosperity of the Chinese middle class.

It is the investment in mass education, and especially in higher technological education, that laid the foundation for Chinese technological development (Jain 2021; Knight et al. 2013). This step was not a clear strategy from day one, following the Chinese Revolution in 1949. It can instead be understood against the background of the anti-intellectual Cultural Revolution in 1966–76. During the Cultural Revolution, intellectuals came under strict government control, and many were sent out into the countryside to do hard agricultural work, while many schools and universities were closed, resulting in a loss of expertise and competence amongst the general population (Vogel 2011). Consequently, it wasn't until after 1976 that investment in education was put on the political agenda. This initiative was primarily due to the efforts of Deng Xiaoping (Deng 1994; Vogel 2011).

---

[1] Carou et al. (2022), Johannessen (2020a, 2021a, b, c, 2022a, 2022b, 2023a, b, c, d, e), Marr (2021), Schwab (2016, 2018).

[2] Info-structure refers to all the information and communication processes that are necessary to make a digital economy work.

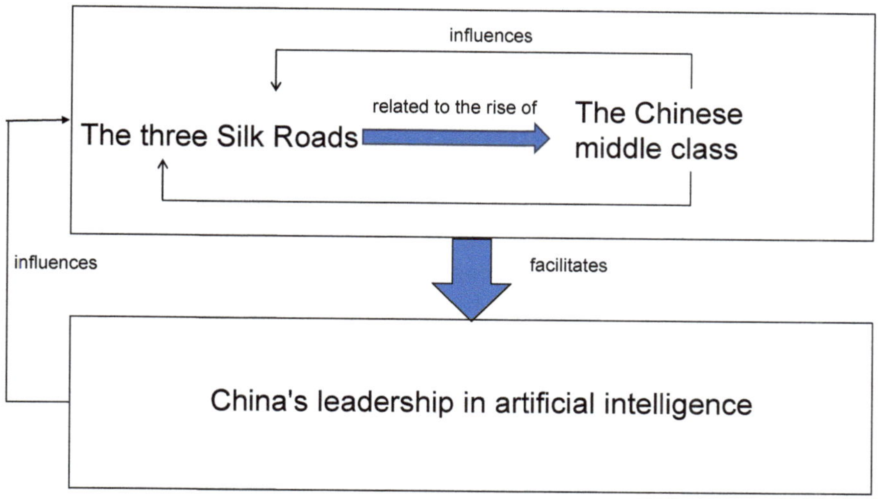

Fig. 1.1 The prerequisites for the development of artificial intelligence in China

Working from this brief introduction, we will investigate the following general research problem: How has China become a threat to the United States with regard to the development of AI?

There are many different perspectives and approaches to this question. However, this book focuses mainly on the three Silk Roads and the Chinese middle class, and in particular the relationship between these elements. We have therefore formulated two research questions to address the general research problem:

1. How have the three New Silk Roads influenced China's role in the development of AI?
2. What has been the role of China's middle class in the development of AI?

We have developed a conceptual model in Fig. 1.1, in order to show figuratively the general research problem, the research questions, and the relationship between them. This model also shows how the book is structured.

Narratives

Case letter 1 The United States' new grand strategy towards China: Technological containment

The threat posed by China to many Western countries is illustrated by the so-called 'chip war', which is the result of many countries' attempts to contain China's ability to develop advanced technologies. The most high-profile cases have perhaps been those involving TikTok and Huawei. In July 2023, the Dutch government entered the field by putting Dutch producers of advanced chips and chip-making tools under similar export restrictions to those imposed by the United States on American companies involved in chip manufacturing.[3] The Dutch move revealed a split within the EU, as France is more inclined towards the idea of a Europe that is strategically independent of both the United States and China. Moreover, the new Dutch rules clash with Germany's geo-economic reality: since 2021, China has been Germany's biggest export market. For Germany, increased decoupling in the global economy, with heightened tensions between China and the West, could spark an economic crisis. Given that Germany is the economic engine room of Europe, the 'chip war' has the potential to create tensions within the EU, as well as between China and the West.

Of course it is interesting that European countries are aligning themselves with the United States' policy of containment: basically, containing China's capability to develop advanced technology by restricting its access to advanced or intelligent chips, and also the machines and processes used to manufacture them. Advanced or intelligent chips are chips that use intelligent algorithms for various practical purposes. These purposes or functions can include surveilling human behaviour, weapons manufacture, the manufacture of medical products, the management and control of industrial production and so on. Most interesting of all, however, is the fact that the United States now sees itself as being forced to deviate from a four-decades-old economic policy that began with a secret visit by Henry Kissinger (President Nixon's security adviser) to China in 1971 and the 'Nixon in China' presidential visit the following year. As far as the United States was concerned, there were two important consequences. On the one hand, American investments in China resulted in an enormous amount of capital being accumulated by a tiny number of individuals. On the other hand, millions of traditional industrial jobs in the United States were unable to survive competition with low-paid Chinese workers.

The policy regarding US investment in China showed signs of becoming problematic around 2011. This became evident in relation to the article "America's Pacific century", published in *Foreign Policy* in 2011 by Hillary Clinton, who was then the US Secretary of State. Since 2011, there have been increasing tensions between the US and China. These became visible when President Trump launched a trade war, and later, when President Biden escalated this conflict in several other areas. What we can see emerging around 2022–2023 is a new US 'grand strategy', involving the technological containment of China, which, amongst other things, is focused on impeding China's further development of artificial intelligence.

It is against this background that it is interesting to consider the strategic initiatives that the Chinese leadership has implemented in order to respond to US policies aimed at limiting China's technological development. We can use Clinton's (2011) article, mentioned above, as a marker for the start of a historical timeline in relation to the rising tensions between the US and China over the last ten years and earlier. Two years after Clinton's article, in 2013, Xi Jinping, the newly elected leader of the Chinese Communist Party, proposed the New Silk Road initiative at a meeting in Kazakhstan.[4]

---

[3] https://www.japantimes.co.jp/news/2023/07/01/business/asml-new-china-export-restrictions/

[4] https://www.iris-france.org/112196-kazakhstan-must-look-beyond-the-belt-and-road/

In the period from 2013 to 2023, the year that the Netherlands joined what we have termed the US 'technological containment policy' of China, the New Silk Road had become three Silk Roads. These Silk Roads run from China to South America, Europe, Southeast Asia and Africa. The Silk Roads can be viewed as China's response to the American-led containment policy. In addition, the American decoupling from China since 2011 has led to Chinese leaders launching new economic strategies, such as the "Dual Circulation Development Paradigm", aimed at reorienting the country's economy by focusing more on domestic consumption, as well as on international trade. Domestic consumption can be increased due to the growing Chinese middle class, which already numbers 700 million according to some metrics.[5] To put this into perspective, the American middle class numbers approx. 150–200 million and is in sharp decline. We can also mention here that the Chinese government has initiated other economic strategies, partly in response to American policies; these are: "Made in China 2025" and "China Standards 2035" (Johannessen 2021a, b, c, 2022a, 2023b). In other words, from 2013 onwards, China has developed various strategies in response to American attempts to block Chinese technological development.

Case letter 2: The Chip War Has Diplomatic and Political Dominance As Its Strategic Intent

Taiwan Semiconductor Manufacturing Company (TSMC) has been called the world's most important company. Amongst its most important customers are AMD, Apple, Nvidia, and others. Contributing to the tensions between the US and China, especially over Taiwan, is the fact that TSMC currently makes computer chips used in US Lockheed-Martin F-35 Lightning II fighter jets, Javelin missiles and other crucial military equipment.

Against this background, if China were to invade Taiwan, the United States would have to respond by taking military action. China is, of course, aware of this probability. Therefore, it is unlikely that China will launch a large-scale attack on Taiwan, in order to gain control of Taiwan's advanced technology, and not least the components needed for the further development of artificial intelligence.

The above description partly explains the increasing intensification of tensions between the United States and China, regarding the battle between the two nations for tech supremacy, especially in relation to the development of artificial intelligence, and the production of components needed for this development.

China has explicitly stated that its strategic goal is to become the world leader in artificial intelligence by 2030.[6] This goal and plan involve the use of AI in various areas, such as the military and smart cities. The Chinese leaders believe that artificial intelligence will be the core technology that drives future economic development. In plain language, they believe that the Fourth Industrial Revolution, which is underway, will be driven by AI technology.

---

[5] https://chinapower.csis.org/china-middle-class/#:~:text=Based%20on%20Pew%27s%20income%20band,of%20the%20population)%20in%202018.

[6] https://www.cnbc.com/2017/07/21/china-ai-world-leader-by-2030.html.

As noted, in 2017, China explicitly stated that its strategic goal is to become a world leader in artificial intelligence by 2030. Since then, China has had artificial intelligence, and all the various aspects of this technology, as its strategic focus in many areas of the economy.[7]

China is developing artificial intelligence in the following areas: the construction industry, pandemic prevention, integration of industrial production, climate-related issues, health, art, carbon capture, digital systems, the infostructure, and also 5G and 6G networks. Moreover, artificial intelligence applications are also being developed in the following: innovative entrepreneurship, the auto industry, the police service, the military, surveillance, the financial sector, the banking sector, human–computer interfaces, social services, drone technology, the aircraft industry, etc. This long list, which is in no way exhaustive, indicates that China aims to become the global leader in many areas, not only in high tech. Tech supremacy only functions as a means to an end. In reality, China seeks to take the global lead in other areas, such as the political and diplomatic domains, the military, and the economy.

The Chinese leaders also aim to develop 6G networks, utilizing artificial intelligence. So what is a 6G network? In brief, 6G is the successor to 5G and will be able to use higher frequencies than 5G networks, providing substantially higher capacity, and will be able to facilitate large improvements in various areas, by working in conjunction with artificial intelligence. In other words, these new networks will increase the speed of information transfers, making them more secure, as well as increasing the quality of the transfer of information. In addition, new technology will be able to continuously monitor the exchange of information, so that many new applications will become possible with the development of these networks. One area of application will most probably be the further development of telesurgery, that will be able to utilize robotic technology and 6G networking to connect patients and surgeons who are geographically distant from each other. For example, the surgeon could be located in New York, but will be able to carry out surgery remotely, by using robotic technology and 6G networking, in distant areas, such as in the rural areas of Uganda or the Congo. The point here is that such future technology within healthcare will have enormous potential for improving people's health in ways that could hardly be envisioned before. How will this affect China if it becomes a world leader in the development of AI by 2030? The answer is that the countries that can help underdeveloped countries, such as countries in Africa and South America, by solving some of their healthcare problems, will also gain political and diplomatic influence there.

Description: Is China Taking the Lead in AI?

In the following, we will give a brief description of the two elements in Fig. 1.1. The two elements are: the three Silk Roads and the growth of the Chinese middle class.

[7] Ibid.

The Three New Silk Roads

In 2012, Xi Jinping was elected leader of the Chinese Communist Party. It was from this point onward that the New Silk Road started to take shape, first as an idea, and then as a reality.[8] The formal name is the Belt and Road Initiative (BRI). The BRI is basically a complex system of infrastructure projects, where China, through various forms of investment, can initiate the construction of roads, railways, ports, and airports, in the various BRI countries. The New Silk Road is believed to be Xi Jinping's most important foreign policy strategy (Angang 2014; Xing 2019). One of the strategic intentions is to enable China to assume a stronger global position. The BRI was officially launched at a meeting held by Xi Jinping in November 2012 in Kazakhstan (Batzhan et al. 2020).

The New Silk Road was originally conceived as an infrastructure project running through Central Asia. As the initiative took shape, the goals also changed. Today, there are various BRI projects in Asia, Europe, Africa, and South America. The Maritime Silk Road also took shape, and was established as a trade route to Europe, the Middle East, and Africa, but also as a means of safeguarding Chinese trade with the West (Yuzhu 2020). There are many examples of completed projects, as well as those planned for the future. Amongst the completed projects are the China-Laos railway; the Hambantota International Port in Sri Lanka, leased to China on a 99-year lease; and the Port of Doraleh, an extension of the Port of Djibouti, west of Djibouti City, located in the Horn of Africa. The latter port also functions as an intermediate port for Chinese ships travelling through the Red Sea and the Suez Canal on their way to Piraeus, the main port of Athens.

The BRI is considered to be a fundamental element within China's foreign policy and was thus incorporated into the CCP's constitution in 2017.

The BRI has a target completion date of 2049, coinciding with the centenary of the Chinese Revolution of 1949, and the creation of the People's Republic of China. There are many countries opposed to the uncontrolled further development of the New Silk Road, and the United States is one of the most sceptical. The US views the New Silk Road as an attempt by China to take control of international trade routes, and thus achieve strategic dominance in many areas that the US previously considered to be its own spheres of interest (Mahbubani 2018, 2020). Against this background, one can understand the US naval presence in the South China Sea, and its signing of the AUKUS agreement, the security partnership for the Indo-Pacific region between Australia, the UK, and the US. Similarly, the Biden administration's international infrastructure development project, the Blue Dot Network, may be viewed as a means of offsetting Chinese influence. In other words, the Blue Dot Network (BDN), involving cooperation between the United States, Japan, and Australia, has the aim of developing new infrastructure projects around the world, with the target of matching the projects along the New Silk Road. However, the New Silk Road has been operational since 2013, whereas the Blue Dot network was first established in

[8] Macaes (2020), Batzhan et al. (2020), Berlie and Hung (2020), Feng and Liang (2019), Vangeli (2018, 2019), Pan (2020), Zou (2018).

2019, six years later. In other words, China has a head start. A report from CEBR has calculated that by 2040 the BRI projects will have lifted global economic growth by US$ 7.1 trillion per year.[9] This economic growth will most probably have a locomotive effect on the further development of the New Silk Road. In this context, it is probable that the US objections to the New Silk Road will fall on deaf ears in those countries that benefit economically.

The Rise of the Chinese Middle Class

One of the main policies of the leadership of China's Communist Party is to lift the middle class (Brown 2019). It may also be said that the 'Chinese Dream' is to raise everyone in China to a middle class income through collective effort (Brown 2018). The Chinese leaders view the middle class as a key factor if China is to move into socio-political modernization (Li 2021; Rocca 2018). In order to promote the growth of the middle class in terms of size and income, it will be necessary to expand the higher education sector (Liu 2021). The growth of the middle class also promotes economic inequality in China (Liu 2016). It might be said, that the growth of the Chinese middle class also results in this social class developing its own identity, attitudes and behaviour, which in turn promotes the aim of Chinese leaders to make China into a dynamic economy that can compete with the leading global economies (Miao 2019). It also seems reasonable to assume that the growth of the Chinese middle class is associated with the strengthening of Chinese nationalism, which will also serve the interests of the Chinese leaders (Rocca 2018). This assumption can be explained by the growing tensions emerging between the United States and China. In other words, the Chinese leaders anticipate that nationalism, and defending the interests of the nation, will be viewed as synonymous with defending the interests of middle class families, in relation to their economic well-being, and the future higher educational opportunities for young Chinese people at Chinese or foreign universities.

China's middle class constitutes around 700 million people, calculated according to income. This is an enormous growth of approx. 80 million since 2002.[10] The growing Chinese middle class will also ensure that the new economic strategies, such as the "Dual Circulation Development Paradigm", will be able to maintain domestic demand, which will also create a multiplier effect in the Chinese economy. Figuratively, the middle class will become the locomotive of the Chinese economy, pulling the other carriages (other sections of society) behind it in the pursuit of economic progress. This 'locomotive effect' can become extremely important at a time when Chinese high-tech companies, such as Huawei, are struggling in global

[9] The Centre for Economics and Business Research (CEBR) supplies economic forecasting and analysis to private firms and public organisations. https://cebr.com/reports/belt-and-road-initiative-to-boost-world-gdp-by-over-7-trillion-per-annum-by-2040/.

[10] https://www.statista.com/statistics/875874/middle-class-population-in-china/.

markets, because they have been excluded from Western markets over so-called security concerns, a policy spearheaded by the Biden administration.[11]

Narratives Related to the Three Silk Roads and the Middle Class

Case letter 1: National Security and Digital Solutions

China has invested heavily in the development of 5G networks, and is also investing in the development of 6G, which is related to the development of artificial intelligence (AI). By 2022, China had taken the global lead in the number of 5G patents, totalling 40 percent of the globally registered patents.[12] The development of 5G technology is crucial for the growth of China's Digital Silk Road. By 2022, approx. 210,000 5G patents had been registered. The fact that China has such a large share of these patents also says something about the future development of the Chinese economy. The growth of the Chinese economy, especially in relation to high-tech, is also bound up with the growth of the middle class, due to the fact that the high-tech employees are mainly middle class. The US is second to China in the number of registered 5G patents, with approx. 34 percent, and South Korea, third, with approx. nine percent.[13]

High-tech patent data, especially 5G, also reveals something about the US-China tech competition. In other words, the United States and China are competing with each other to deploy fifth-generation (5G), wireless networks. This competition has also resulted in various political and economic policy measures being implemented. As mentioned above, the US and its allies have barred Huawei from operating in their 5G networks, claiming that Huawei represents a risk to national security.[14] However, it has not been proven that Huawei's technology would pose any risk to US and European security. Nevertheless, the danger to national security is such an overarching and pervasive argument that it has not been deemed necessary to present hard facts, before implementing political measures banning Huawei. Perhaps more relevant in this case is that in 2022, Huawei alone registered approximately 6583 5G patents, representing around 14 percent of all worldwide patents relating to 5G technology.[15] This information puts the Huawei case into a completely new perspective.

---

[11] https://www.reuters.com/technology/biden-signs-legislation-tighten-us-restrictions-huawei-zte-2021-11-11/.

[12] https://www.mondaq.com/china/patent/1203776/china-takes-global-lead-in-number-of-declared-5g-patents#:~:text=China%20owns%20nearly%2040%20percent,involving%20almost%2047%2C000%20patent%20families.

[13] Ibid.

[14] https://www.reuters.com/business/media-telecom/us-fcc-bans-equipment-sales-imports-zte-huawei-over-national-security-risk-2022-11-25/.

[15] https://www.mondaq.com/china/patent/1203776/china-takes-global-lead-in-number-of-declared-5g-patents#:~:text=China%20owns%20nearly%2040%20percent,involving%20almost%2047%2C000%20patent%20families.

If Huawei were to have the opportunity to participate in the development of the 5G networks in the West, this would have strengthened China in the tech competition with the US regarding the development of 5G networks. Against this background, it is understandable that the US would do everything within its means to get rid of a 'troublesome competitor'. If we look further into the data regarding 5G patents, the following picture emerges: among the top 15 corporate applicants for patents, seven were Chinese companies, and two from each of the United States, Japan, Europe, and South Korea.[16] This is an indication of the possible future global competition, regarding the development of digital technology. In this context, it can be mentioned that the Biden administration has banned approvals of all new telecommunications equipment from Huawei, because they pose a risk to US national security.[17] In other words, this can be viewed as a further strengthening of the US's containment of China's high-tech sector, which seems to be part of the US's new 'grand strategy' towards China, at least as far as technological competition is concerned.

Sub-conclusion: Is China Taking the Lead in AI?

In this chapter, we have considered the general research problem: How has China become a threat to the United States with regard to the development of AI? We have chosen two aspects to focus on: the three Silk Roads and the Chinese middle class. These two aspects will be more thoroughly reviewed in Chaps. 2 and 3. The two aspects are distinct but are also systemically linked. The answer to the general research problem, which we have examined in this chapter, and which will be further elaborated upon throughout the book, is that China has been able to transform its economy from being a supplier of cheap goods to the West, into becoming a high-tech industrial country, with a focus on the development of artificial intelligence. China managed to do this by focusing on the systemic connections between various social mechanisms that have promoted the development of artificial intelligence. This book will examine two of these systemically linked social mechanisms. In the remaining part of the book, we will also examine these two social mechanisms related to China's aim of gaining global leadership in the development of artificial intelligence.

References

Angang H (2014) Silk road economic belt: strategic considerations, positioning and implementation routes. J Xinjiang Norm Univ 2:1–10

---

[16] Ibid.

[17] https://www.reuters.com/business/media-telecom/us-fcc-bans-equipment-sales-imports-zte-huawei-over-national-security-risk-2022-11-25/.

Batzhan A, Alpysbayeva S, Kapsalyamova Z (2020) The belt and road initiative: Case of Kazakhstan. In: Chay YW, Menkhoff T, Low L (eds) Chinas belt and road initiative: Understanding the dynamics of a global transformation. World Scientific, London, pp 71–97
Berlie JA, Hung S (2020) The greater Bay area and the role of Hong Kong and Macau SARs in the Belt and Road initiative. In: Berlie JA (ed) China's globalization and the belt and road initiative. Palgrave, London, pp 77–100
Brown K (2018) China's dream. Polity, London
Brown K (2019) The world according to Xi, I. B. Tauris, London
Carou D, Sartal A, Darim JP (2022) Machine learning and artificial intelligence with industrial applications: From big data to small data. Springer, London
Clinton H (2011) America's Pacific century. Foreign Policy 189
Deng X (1994) Selected works of Deng Xiaoping, Vol III (1982–1992). Foreign Language Press, Beijing
Feng DH, Liang HM (2019) Belt and road initiative: Chinese version of Marshall Plan. World Scientific, London
Hannum EJ, Behrman M, Wang M, Liu J (2008) Education in the reform era. In: Brandt L, Rawski TG (eds) China's great economic transformation. Cambridge University Press, Cambridge, pp 215–249
Johannessen J-A (2020a) The workplace of the future. Routledge, London
Johannessen J-A (2020b) Automation, innovation and economic crises: survival in the fourth industrial revolution. Routledge, London
Jain R (2021a) China's soft power and higher education in South Asia. Routledge, London
Johannessen J-A (2021b) China's innovation economy: artificial intelligence and the new silk road. Routledge, London
Johannessen J-A (2021b) Artificial intelligence, automation and ethics in the innovation economy. Routledge, London
Johannessen J-A (2021c) Communication as social theory: the social side of knowledge management. Emerald, London
Johannessen J-A (2022a) The new silk road and the innovation economy in China: four driving forces. Routledge, London
Johannessen J-A (2022b) Artificial intelligence and creativity: implications for automation in the innovation economy. Routledge, London
Johannessen J-A (2023a) The fourth industrial revolution and the labour market: future-proofing work in the innovation economy. Routledge, London
Johannessen J-A (2023b) Feudal capitalism and the innovation economy. Routledge, London
Johannessen J-A (2023c) Consciousness and creativity in artificial intelligence: the cognitive side of knowledge management. Emerald, London
Johannessen J-A (2023d) Creativity, innovation and the fourth industrial revolution: the Da Vinci strategy. Routledge, London
Johannessen J-A (2023e) De-globalization. Routledge, London
Knight J, Sicular T, Ximing Y (2013) Educational inequality in China: the intergenerational dimension. In: Shi L, Sato H, Sicular T (eds), Rising inequality in China. Cambridge University Press, Cambridge, pp 142–197
Li C (2010a) China's emerging middle class beyond economic transformation. Brookings Institution Press, Washington
Li C (2010b) Introduction: the rise of the middle class in the Middle Kingdom. China's emerging middle class beyond economic transformation. Brookings Institution Press, Washington, pp 3–31
Li, C. (2021). Middle class Shanghai: reshaping U.S.-China engagement. Brookings Institution Press, Washington, DC
Liu S (2021) Neoliberalism, globalization and "Elite" education in China, Becoming international. Routledge, London
Liu Y (2016) Higher education, meritocracy and inequality in China. Springer, London

Macaes B (2020) Belt and road: A Chinese world order. C. Hurst &, London
Mahbubani K (2018) Has the west lost. Allen Lane, New York
Mahbubani K (2020) Has China won? PublicAffairs, London
Marr B (2021) Data strategy: how to profit from a world of big data, analytics and artificial intelligence. Kogan Page, New York
Miao Y (2019) Being middle class in China: identity, attitudes and behaviours. Routledge, London
Pan Z (2020) Strategic linkages: China's Belt and Road Initiative and power through global value chain. In: Chay YW, Menkhoff T, Low L (eds) China's belt and road initiative: understanding the dynamics of a global transformation. World Scientific, London, pp 221–241
Rocca J-L (2018) The making of the Chinese middle class: small comfort and great expectations. Palgrave, London
Schwab K (2016) The fourth industrial revolution. World Economic Forum, Geneva
Schwab K (2018) Shaping the fourth industrial revolution. World Economic Forum, Geneva
Vangeli A (2018) Normative foundation of the belt and road initiative. In: Wenhua S, Nuotio K, Zhang K (eds) Normative readings of the belt and road initiative. Springer, London, pp 59–83
Vangeli A (2019) A framework for the study of one belt one road initiative as a medium of principle diffusion. In: Xing L (ed) Mapping China's one belt one road initiative. Palgrave Macmillan, London, pp 57–89
Vogel EF (2011) Deng Xiaoping and the transformation of China. Harvard University Press, Cambridge, Mass
Xing L (ed) (2019) Mapping China's one belt one road initiative. Palgrave, London
Yuzhu W (2020) New regional cooperation and integration strategy and the 21st-Century maritime silk road initiative. In: Jianglin (ed) 21st-Century Maritime Silk Road Initiative, Aims and objectives, implementation strategies and policy recommendations. World Scientific, London, pp 211–225
Zou L (2018) The political economy of China's Belt and Road Initiative. World Scientific, Singapore

Chapter 2
The Three Silk Roads

Core Idea
The purpose of the three New Silk Roads is to strengthen the periphery in order to secure the centre (China).

Key Points

- Stability in the centre and dynamism in the periphery seems to be a formula for Chinese economic growth going into the future.
- There are three Silk Roads: the land-based, the maritime, and the digital.
- There are five areas that are driving the New Silk Roads. These are: economic policy, national security, the political sphere, technology, and diplomacy.
- The New Silk Roads can be used by China to re-design the global value chains.
- The new global value chain can be viewed as networks of rivers, canals, roads and maritime routes, crossing and interconnecting countries and continents.
- The Silk Roads can function as a security architecture for China's 'grand strategy', so that China will be able to achieve global domination in the Fourth Industrial Revolution, economically, politically, technologically, and culturally.
- The three Silk Roads can be viewed as the tentacles of an octopus, which provide the nourishment necessary for survival and growth. The tentacles have rows of suckers. The octopus's suckers are powerful, and once they have grasped something, are very difficult to remove.
- The competition between China and the US is increasingly focused on becoming the leader in the development of new technological innovations.
- The three silk roads are being used by China as a crowbar to achieve global influence.
- History does not repeat itself, but history sends signals to today's decision-makers, which can affect how the future takes shape.

J. Johannessen, *The AI Battleground Between the USA and China*, Global Power Shift,
https://doi.org/10.1007/978-3-032-10138-9_2

Introduction

We will examine the following question: How have the three New Silk Roads influenced China's role in the development of AI?

The Belt and Road Initiative (BRI), China's global infrastructure development strategy, was launched in 2013. It was originally announced by Xi Jinping as the new "Silk Road", an economic belt referring to the proposed land-based and maritime trade routes, which constitute the first two Silk Roads. Today, the third Silk Road concerns the development of global digital networks. The "New Silk Roads" can be compared analogously to the historical Silk Road, due to the emphasis on international trade.

The land-based Belt and Road Initiative links China with Central Asia and many other regions. The Initiative is also comprised of a Maritime Silk Road, a sea route linking China to regions towards the south, and the west, which we can term the Second New Silk Road. The northern route, which is not yet fully developed, heads to the north of Japan and into the Bering Strait towards the Barents Sea and then towards the European continent. The southern route runs through the Straits of Malacca towards the port of Sri Lanka and then towards the port of Djibouti, where it splits into two. The first part goes via the Suez Canal into the Mediterranean, where the port of Athens, Piraeus, has become an important trading node for China. The other part from Djibouti heads towards the south in Africa, via the development of roads and railways (Zou 2018; Feng and Liang 2019). The third Silk Road is what we refer to here as the Digital Silk Road. This Silk Road has been made possible through the development of digital technology and networks along the first two Silk Roads (Hillman 2021; Johannessen 2021).

Narratives

Case Letter 2 The Silk Road as the Chinese Economic Crowbar

Between 2013 and 2020, the cumulative value of trade in goods between China and the BRI countries reached $10.4 trillion.[1] The efficient logistics services, as well as improved digital competencies, have yielded fruitful results for China and the participating BRI countries (Yuzhu 2020). The benefits for the countries participating in the BRI projects have been so great that the US, under the Biden administration, has launched the Blue Dot Network, as a counterweight to the new Silk Road, or more correctly the three Silk Roads. The Blue Dot Network is an initiative aimed at building an alliance of various countries, and business interests, in order to develop global infrastructure projects that can compete with the new Silk Road. Moreover, in order to meet Chinese competition, the US has imposed various sanctions on China in an effort

[1] http://en.qstheory.cn/2021-12/02/c_686845.htm.

to prevent Chinese technology companies from competing with Western companies.[2] It is particularly evident that the Chinese development of artificial intelligence, and the trade and digital relations that are being developed along the new Silk Road, are perceived as a threat by the US.

China's ability to improve its logistics performance helps it to develop trade along the new Silk road, as well as in other contexts, such as in the re-designing of the global value chain. There are many indications that the global value chain will be redesigned in the future. The rationale for such a development is that China's leaders have clearly expressed the view that the US is trying to stem China's economic, technological, diplomatic and political development (Mahbubani 2018, 2020). This has resulted in, as we have described previously, China developing institutional innovations to cope with the perceived containment. For example, China has implemented the so-called Dual Circulation Development Paradigm, in order to reorient the country's economy by focusing more on domestic consumption as well as on international trade. Domestic consumption can be increased due to the growing Chinese middle class, which already numbers around 700 million people, depending on how it is measured.[3] At the same time, although there is still a focus on international trade with the West, this will most probably be toned down in the future, not least because the US has imposed sanctions on Chinese companies doing business in the US, as previously mentioned in the case of Huawei, where the US government imposed trading restrictions on the company. The increase in domestic consumption, and the reduced focus on trade with the West, will most probably result in a re-designing of the global value chain, so that it will be more adapted to trade with the countries along the new Silk Road. Moreover, the goods exported to the West will become more expensive. The rationale is that increased domestic demand in China will put pressure on Chinese wages and thus increase prices. In addition, the reduction in the Western import of cheap Chinese goods will be in part replaced by more expensive goods from countries with higher costs, which will increase prices in the West. Therefore, it is quite conceivable that the American containment policy may be likened to making a rod for your own back; in other words, the containment policy will most probably be unsuccessful, and create more problems for the US in the future, not least because the policy will most probably fuel continuous inflation. Another element in the redesign of the global value chain will be China's greater emphasis on trade and production in the Asian area, which can be facilitated through its membership in the Regional Comprehensive Economic Partnership (RCEP), the world's largest free trade organization.

The sum of these measures in the emerging innovation economy may soon result in China focusing more on re-designing production, distribution, and consumption towards the Chinese domestic market, which is three times larger than the EU market.

---

[2] https://rules.house.gov/sites/democrats.rules.house.gov/files/BILLS-117HR4521RH-RCP117-31.pdf.

[3] https://www.chinausfocus.com/2022/wp-content/uploads/Part+02-Chapter+07.pdf.

Where it has become evident that the US, and some European countries, have implemented measures restricting the development of Chinese technology, it is very probable, that Chinese companies will then focus on the areas where they have free access, without being hindered both by various laws and measures, and by arguments claiming that Chinese companies pose a threat to the US national security, and the national security of other nations. If such a development as outlined above is allowed to develop freely, this will not necessarily result in a new cold war, but rather in the emergence of two major global alliances that will implement various protectionist measures in order to protect their own economic interests.

For Chinese consumers, such a development can be positive, because more small and medium-sized enterprises will emerge, primarily focusing on Chinese consumers. For Western consumers, the picture is more complex. On the one hand, it seems reasonable to assume that more companies will produce for the Western market, which will result in more jobs, and a thriving labour market. On the other hand, increasing labour costs in Europe and the United States will lead to accelerating price inflation.

Case Letter 3 The Reasons for the Growth of the New Silk Road

China was an underdeveloped country in the 1980s, when it opened up to foreign investment, especially US investment. China sought help from the United States against what the Chinese leaders believed was an aggressive Soviet Union. In the 1980s, Chinese economic reforms also included establishing special economic zones (SEZs) in order to boost the economy. In 1989, the student protest in Tiananmen Square in China was brutally put down in such a way that shocked the US and the rest of the world. The demise of Communist regimes in Eastern Europe and the collapse of the Soviet Union also occurred around this time (1989–1992). Consequently, the US no longer needed to ally itself with China against the Soviet Union. Although the American political rhetoric was negative towards China after 1989, American business leaders were strong stakeholders in the political arena that lobbied for a continued increase of trade and investment in China. President George Bush officially denounced the actions in Tiananmen Square, but the Bush administration and US business leaders would not allow the Chinese government's bloody crackdown to upset the economic partnership between the United States and China. In other words, the US government ensured that investment and trade were maintained between the United States and China (Doshi 2021). In the 1990s, the Chinese leaders were also interested in China remaining the "most favoured nation" (MFN) in relation to the United States. China's MFN status meant that China was given preferential treatment with regard to trade and access to the American market, with favourable conditions in terms of customs duties, taxes, and investment opportunities. China's MFN status was maintained by the US Congress every year from 1989 onwards, despite the fact that there was much opposition to this from within the US (Doshi 2021). In 1999, despite continued opposition, the US Congress maintained China's MFN status.[4]

The questions that began to be asked were whether the companies that were partly owned by the PLA (People's Liberation Army) could be included in the MFN status. The debate intensified, focusing on human rights' abuses, China's nuclear weapons program, and the PLA's possible shares in technological companies that operated in the US, such as Huawei; such arguments were used with the aim of terminating China's MFN status. However, China was granted permanent MFN status in 2001. China also became a member of the World Trade Organization in the same year. This meant that China was no longer dependent on maintaining the MFN status in order to further expand trade. Although China was granted permanent MFN status, the US government placed restrictions on Chinese companies, citing national security concerns. In this context, Huawei is a good case in point. By referring to the company's connections to the PLA and Chinese government, the US restricted Huawei from working with American companies. Later, the company was also excluded from entering into contracts with many of the US's allies, for example, in some of the European countries. The MFN status, however, had another function for China. Several hundred thousand Chinese students were able to study at colleges and universities in the United States. Many of these students were able to start new businesses when they returned to China, in large cities such as Shanghai (Li 2021).

Another major event occurred in 2001 that had significance for the relationship between China and the United States. This was the September 11 terrorist attacks against the World Trade Center and the Pentagon, and its aftermath, the US "War on Terror" and the US invasion of Afghanistan. The US's war on terror was prioritized by all the US presidents from 2001 until 2021, when Jo Biden withdrew the last US forces from Afghanistan. The US and China were able to cooperate in the war against terror in the wake of the 9/11 terror attacks. China was especially interested in preventing a spillover of terror activities from Afghanistan into the Xinjiang Region.

Two years after the US invasion of Afghanistan, another major event occurred which caused the Chinese leaders to rethink their strategy vis-à-vis the United States. This was the US invasion of Iraq in 2003. The Chinese leaders had in no way imagined that the US could so easily defeat Iraq. The technological superiority and capabilities of the US military completely overwhelmed the conventional Iraqi forces. China's military strategy had up until this point focused on building up conventional forces with little technological capabilities. In other words, the US's rapid defeat of Iraq changed the entire Chinese military strategy, leading to a greater focus on advanced technology.

In 2012, Xi Jinping was elected as the new leader of the Chinese Communist Party. One of the first things he did was to launch the Belt and Road Initiative (BRI), or in popular parlance, the New Silk Road. The purpose was, among other things, to strengthen the periphery in order to secure the centre (Doshi 2021). This was to be done by developing infrastructure that could strengthen and connect China's neighbours more closely. From this point on, China focused on creating economic

---

[4] https://www.everycrsreport.com/reports/RL30225.html.

growth in the periphery, i.e. China's neighbouring countries. Metaphorically, this may be understood as building walls and fortifications around the centre, i.e. the Middle Kingdom (China), by strengthening the economic and technological foundations of its neighbours. If China was able to implement this strategy, then it would become less dependent on the United States and its allies in terms of trade.

Since Xi Jinping announced the strategy of the "New Silk Road" during an official visit to Kazakhstan in 2013, 130 countries or more have signed up to BRI projects, which also include major international organizations. China has issued large loans in order to finance the numerous BRI infrastructure projects. The name "New Silk Road" is a misnomer, because it is not one single road, but rather a network of roads passing through different countries and also along sea routes; moreover, China's Digital Silk Road is also a vital component of its New Silk Road (Belt and Road Initiative).

With the perspective that we have presented in this case letter, it can be said that the US laid the foundation for Chinese economic growth. It can also be said that the American decoupling of China with regard to trade and business, especially concerning the US government's restrictions on Chinese technology companies doing business with American companies, during the Obama and Trump administrations, has created uncertainty and scepticism in China as to whether American trade relations can be trusted. The trade war introduced by the Trump administration resulted in the Chinese leaders becoming even more determined to strengthen trading relations with other countries both through the New Silk Road, and also other global trading possibilities, such as trading within the world's largest free trade area RCEP (1 January 2022).

Description of the Three Silk Roads

There are at least five areas common to the three Silk Roads.

Firstly, investment is being made in an extensive development of the infrastructure in most of the countries that are part of the Belt and Road Initiative (BRI). This concerns the construction of roads, such as between China and Kazakhstan (Batzhan et al. 2020); the building of railways, such as between China and Laos (Berlie and Hung 2020); port development, such as in Sri Lanka, Djibouti, and Piraeus (Chay et al. 2020; Feng and Liang 2019). In addition, information systems (infostructures) are being developed, so that the digitization of the BRI countries' economies is being improved (Hillman 2021). Bridges, airports and other physical structures are also being built that improve logistics and the value chain for trade between the BRI countries (Lauridsen 2019).

Secondly, which we cannot stress enough, is the fact that the economic consequences of the Silk Road projects are changing the dynamics of the global economy into an innovation-driven economy (Vangeli 2018). For China, this means a transition from economic growth based on cheap labour, to a country that can increasingly compete on technology and innovation (Xing 2019). However, this is in contrast to many of the countries with which China trades along the New Silk Road, whose economies are to a great extent based on cheap labour; these countries are providing cheap goods for Chinese consumers, as well as cheap inputs for Chinese production. This concerns countries such as Laos and Kazakhstan, as well as several countries in Africa (Yu 2020). This entire transformation in economic relations will necessarily lead to changes in the global value chains. The assumption here is that even if China has benefitted from economic growth based on cheap labour, and the production of cheap consumer goods exported to the West, as well as the export of technological innovations, this is changing due to circumstances beyond China's control. The US strategy of imposing various trading sanctions on Chinese technology companies will, of necessity, result in China reducing its trade to the US and other countries in the West, while increasing trade with the BRI countries, as well as within the RCEP, the world's largest free trade organization. In this way, the American strategy of imposing sanctions on China may very easily backfire, and have an opposite and adverse effect to what was intended. The explanation here is quite straightforward. When the global value chains change, the prices of goods for consumers and inputs for American industry will increase. The assumption here, of course, is that the US will not be able to replace the cheap imports from China with cheap imports from other low-cost countries. There are many indications that this will be difficult, because many of the low-cost countries are now part of the New Silk Road.

Thirdly, the New Silk Road will lead to economic growth in both China and in the countries that are participating in the various infrastructure and infostructure projects.[5] In some countries, this economic growth will be possible because they have a labour reserve that can be rapidly deployed in response to the needs of the various projects, such as road and tunnel construction and railways construction, as well as the construction projects in the various Silk Road ports. In other words, the unskilled part of the respective workforces of the BRI countries can be utilized to increase economic growth. In the slightly longer term, high-tech competences will be needed to develop other areas of the various economies, such as the digital sectors, and not least in relation to the application of new AI solutions. In this way, the unskilled part of the labour force and the highly skilled workers will over time support each other in relation to boosting the economic growth of the respective countries.

Fourthly, trade between the countries will increase. As we have described above in Case Letter 1, the New Silk Road has already resulted in increased trade and incomes for the BRI countries. This has promoted the development of small and medium-sized enterprises (SMEs) (Yuan 2019). In other words, both businesses and wage earners have benefitted from the various projects. On the other hand, if the only focus had been on the digital sectors of the various economies, the unskilled part of the respective labour forces would not have benefitted from the economic development, which could easily have led to social tensions and unrest.

The fifth area common to the three Silk Roads is the development of diplomatic and political relations between China and many of the countries included in the BRI projects. For example, we have already seen this in the case of Ukraine, where Ukraine

[5] The info-structure projects are all the projects that are connected to the Digital Silk Road.

abstained from voting on the UN Human Rights Council resolution condemning Uyghur people's rights violations. We also see that there is a development of the New Silk Road towards South America, such as in Colombia. These developments will further affect the diplomatic and political relations with the United States.

We have developed a conceptual model for the three Silk Roads, based on the above narratives and description.

In the following, we will briefly describe each of the five elements in Fig. 2.1.

New Investments in Infrastructure

After the financial crisis in 2008, it became evident to the Chinese leaders that the US had major economic challenges. These challenges resulted in China changing its global strategy from "hiding its strength, and biding its time" to a more assertive policy, challenging American hegemony, as stated by the leader of the Communist Party at the time, Hu Jintao (Doshi 2021). In other words, the era of "hiding one's strength", which had been a strategy since the leadership of Deng Xiaoping, was now over (Fewsmith 2008). The new era was characterized by China's new strategy of developing its infrastructure as a foundation for a completely new 'grand strategy' (Doshi 2021). This infrastructure development had received attention during the leadership of Hu Jintao, but first materialized as a strategic concept under Xi Jinping. This strategic concept, the Belt and Road Initiative, also known as the New Silk Road, became one of China's axes in its new 'grand strategy'. Some of the other axes of China's new 'grand strategy', which we will not elaborate upon further in this book, are:

- Chinese efforts to move away from the dollar as the world's reserve currency.
- The expansion of Chinese naval capabilities, in order to protect its investments along the three New Silk Roads.
- China's focus on developing technological innovations, in order to be able to compete with the US, especially related to the development of artificial intelligence.
- Participation in, and development of, global institutions to ensure China's economic growth, such as its membership of the RCEP, the world's largest free trade area.

The investments along the New Silk Road were secured through the development of the Asian Infrastructure Investment Bank (AIIB). The bank started operation on 25 December 2015, after ratifications were received from 10 member states. As of May 2022, the AIIB has 105 member countries. The UN has stated that this bank can improve economic development in many developing countries around the world. The bank was first proposed by China in 2013, but first came into operation in 2015, two years later. Since its inception, the AIIB has become a potential rival to the World Bank and the International Monetary Fund. In this context, we should be aware of the fact that China, through various statutes and relationships, controls the AIIB,

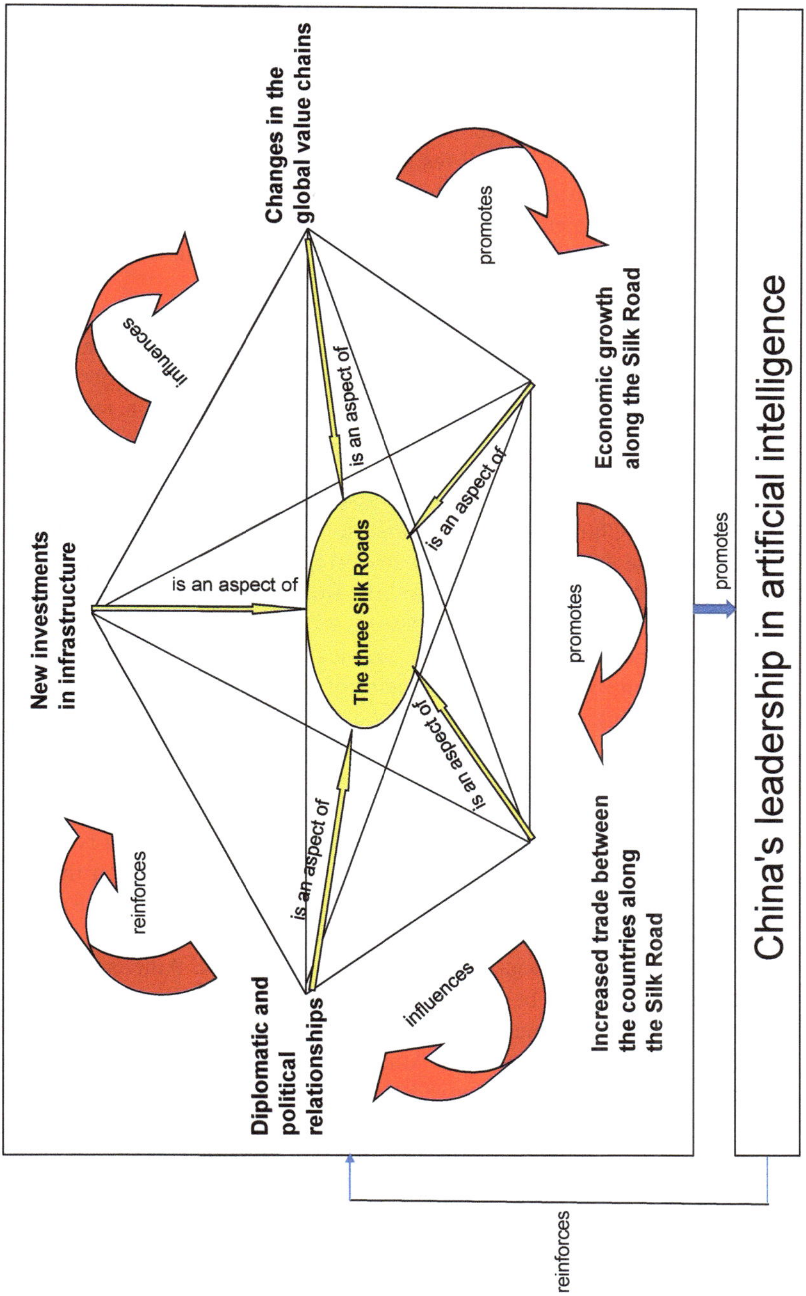

Fig. 2.1 The three Silk Roads: a conceptual model

while the United States exerts considerable control of the International Monetary Fund (IMF) and the World Bank. China has a 30% stake in the AIIB, and thus veto power.[6] Against this background, the New Silk Road, with its financial superstructure AIIB, already has the potential for increasing the ongoing rivalry between the US and China. The *Foreign Policy* magazine, in an article dated 31 March 2015, writes that the AIIB is a threat to US global economic governance.[7] This is perhaps evident if we take into consideration the huge investments in the various projects along the New Silk Road that are controlled by China, and also the fact that the financial superstructure makes the implementation of these projects possible. In other words, the BRI and AIIB are, according to Zhao (2020: 1–2), part of China's new global strategy, what we here refer to as China's new 'grand strategy'.

China emerged as a global power, like a butterfly emerging from its cocoon. However, this transformation was partly due to the relative decline of the United States, especially after the financial crisis. In this context, it is probably more correct to say that it was China's perception of the US's weakened global position, rather than the fact that the US suffered any serious military, political or diplomatic setbacks after the financial crisis. The bottom line, however, was that China believed its time had come, and that it now had to be more globally assertive. Thus, taking into account chaos theory, when the Chinese butterfly started to flap its wings, this resulted in overwhelming consequences at other places around the globe. This was also what occurred with the development of the New Silk Road. After the financial crisis of 2008, China emerged as a new global power. As early as 2011, this threat to American hegemony became evident in the article, "America's Pacific Century" (*Foreign Policy*), written by the former Secretary of State, Hillary Clinton (during the Obama administration), where she wrote about the Chinese threat to the United States supremacy in the Asia–Pacific (Clinton 2011).

Huge investments in global infrastructure, such as roads, bridges, ports, and airports, can have consequences not only for the economic system, but also for geopolitical relations. When the hegemonic power of a dominant nation is threatened by a rising power, this can result in tensions and conflicts between the two countries. History provides evidence of many such examples (Allison 2018). This is often referred to as 'Thucydides' Trap' (Thucydides 2009). Thucydides was an Athenian historian who wrote about the war between Sparta and Athens, in which the two powers were battling for hegemony in the classical Greek World. To prevent the further rise of Athens, the Spartans went to war with the Athenians. According to Thucydides, the war between Sparta and Athens was inevitable due to the fact that the dominant power (Sparta) was challenged by the rising power (Athens).

Investments along the New Silk Road have not only been of economic importance to China. China has emerged from the period of "hiding its strength, and

---

[6] https://www.scmp.com/sites/default/files/styles/486w/public/2015/06/30/aiib_initial_subscriptions_countries_with_1_per_cent_or_more_shares_per_cent_of_shares_per_cent_of_votes_chartbuilder_1.png?itok=Kgh5X5pQ.

[7] https://foreignpolicy.com/2015/03/31/the-aiib-is-a-threat-to-global-economic-governance-china/.

biding its time" during Deng Xiaoping's leadership, to becoming more expansionist during Xi Jinping's leadership. This has had consequences for the geo-economic and geopolitical tensions between China and the US.

Changes in the Global Value Chains

Simply put, China's participation in the global value chains, before the launch of the New Silk Road, was like a trade highway between China and the West. Cheap consumer goods were produced in China, while capital initially came from the West, and the profits were also mainly reaped by Western investors (Cohn 2019). This is of course an oversimplified and somewhat distorted description, because Chinese investors were eventually able to invest in Chinese businesses, so that profits could slowly but surely also be accumulated in Chinese hands. Nevertheless, the idea behind the oversimplified description is to point out that the global value chains were radically changed after the launching of the thousands of projects along the New Silk Road. What changed? What mainly led to the changes was that instead of a trade highway between China and the West, where goods went one way, and investments the other way, the picture became more complicated. A network of trade roads was developed, where investments went in many directions, but for the New Silk Road, mainly from China to the various countries, where, primarily, many infrastructure projects were launched. For instance, this involved port development and construction in Pakistan, Sri Lanka, Djibouti, and Athens, amongst others. This is part of China's Maritime Silk Road, expanding the market for Chinese goods. The ports also facilitate the development of other infrastructure, such as the construction of roads and railways. Chinese workers and engineers were involved in the various projects, providing employment opportunities for a growing Chinese population. In Africa alone, between 2009 and 2019, approx. 182,000 Chinese workers were employed on the various projects that were launched along the New Silk Road.[8]

After the launch of the New Silk Road, the Chinese global value chains were greatly changed. As mentioned, this no longer only resembled a trade and investment highway between China and the West. The new global value chains can be viewed as networks of rivers, canals, roads and maritime routes, crossing and interconnecting countries and continents. Cheap goods are still produced in China and shipped to consumers in the West. However, this trade route is becoming increasingly less important for China, although it is important for the many enterprises in China that produce for the Western market. Nevertheless, many of these businesses now also supply the domestic market, and markets in Africa, the Middle East, and large parts of Asia. What began as a trade highway of goods from China to the West has changed into a multitude of trade routes, where China is no longer overly dependent on trade with the West. In addition, China is upgrading its manufacturing and focusing on the production of high-tech products that are sold at a relatively high price (in comparison

[8] https://www.statista.com/statistics/1259279/number-of-chinese-workers-in-africa-by-country/.

with 'cheap goods') in Western markets. Nonetheless, these high-tech goods are still far cheaper and have the same high quality as those produced in the West. For instance, this can concern the production of drones for private consumers and for industrial use, or the production of mobile phones, electric cars and computers. In other words, Chinese high-tech goods are cheaper than the high-tech goods produced in the West. This fact is also contributing to the development of new value chains between China and the West for high-tech goods.

The brief version of the above description is that the three Silk Roads have greatly facilitated China's rise to power. Today, China's trade and economic activity not only encompasses trade with the West (since the 1980s), but now also trade with the various BRI countries, as well as investment in the various BRI projects. Figuratively, China's trade has metamorphized from not only being trade along a highway to the West, but to also becoming 'a flood', fed by 'a river' and all its 'tributaries', connecting China with the BRI countries, involving the transport of goods and services, the investment of capital, and the application of expertise. Thus, although the direction of trade still goes from China to the West, there are now new land and maritime routes, and digital paths, reaching out in other directions, connecting many regions and countries. In other words, the value chains have changed dramatically, from the time when cheap goods went from China to the West, and capital from the West to China. Today, there is a new system of Chinese global value chains, each with its own distinctive feature.

Economic Growth Along the Silk Road

The New Silk Road consists of a system of projects that are distinct but linked. This means that the individual projects stand alone in the various countries in which they are implemented. However, they are linked through various financial institutions led by China, such as the AIIB (Asian Infrastructure Investment Bank). The bank became operational on 25 December 2015, and, as of 2022, has a total of 105 member countries. The UN has stated that this bank can improve economic development in many developing countries around the world, and since its inception, the AIIB has become a potential rival to the World Bank and the International Monetary Fund.

The various BRI projects constitute important economic activities in the countries where they are implemented. One of the BRI projects is the Boten–Vientiane railway, a section of the Laos–China Railway, that runs between the Laos capital Vientiane and the town of Boten on the border with Yunnan, China. The line is directly linked to the Chinese rail system at Mohan in Yunnan. The construction of this railway created a demand for labour, and the various resources needed, such as food, to support the thousands of workers that built the railway. The same kind of economic growth occurs wherever the BRI projects are implemented. The BRI projects have been so successful that President Jo Biden and the G7 leaders initiated an alternative, Build Back Better World (B3W), in order to provide an alternative to China's Belt and Road Initiative (BRI). The B3W further develops, and partly replaces the "Blue

Dot Network" (launched under the Trump administration),[9] which, was also initiated in order to provide an alternative to the BRI. The background for these initiatives implemented by the US is that the BRI has strengthened China's global influence, and its economic and diplomatic ties to other countries, while weakening the US's global position. The United States chose not to cooperate with China on the development of the BRI, but instead, under both the Trump and Biden administrations, views the Initiative as a challenge, and are opposed to its unrestricted further development.

In 2019, the Chinese leader, Xi Jinping, in a speech given to the Communist Party's Central Committee, emphasized the importance of the future development of the BRI, as the country moves towards the Fourth Industrial Revolution, stating that this presents an opportunity that only occurs once every hundred years (Doshi 2021). According to Xi Jinping, China needs to lead future global development, through trade, economic development and not least in the various high-tech fields, such as artificial intelligence, big data, gene editing, intelligent robots, quantum computers, and so on. In this context, the BRI can thus be understood as constituting a security architecture for China. It is part of a global economic and technological transformation, and not just a 'Chinese' economic project (Chay et al. 2020). Against this background, and also taking into consideration the American initiatives to block the further development of the BRI, one can conclude that the BRI is one of the most important inputs in the debate about which countries will play a decisive role at the entrance to the Fourth Industrial Revolution. Although the BRI contributes greatly to China's rise to power, it is not only economic growth that the BRI is securing for China. The BRI constitutes part of the security architecture for China's 'grand strategy', so that it will be able to achieve global domination in the Fourth Industrial Revolution, economically, politically, technologically, and culturally.

Increased Trade Between the Countries Along the Silk Road

Chinese 'infrastructure diplomacy', with its investments, loans, expertise, and political connections, has led to increased trade between China and the Silk Road countries. Between 2013 and 2021, trade between China and the BRI countries reached US$ 10.4 trillion, an unimaginably large sum, which says something about the extent of the trade.[10] One of the reasons for this success is the efficiency of China's e-commerce, where goods are delivered quickly after just a few days.[11] This was before the Covid-19 pandemic. The pandemic, with closures both in the BRI countries and in China, led to a considerable increase in delivery times. The deliveries by rail from China to Nuremberg in Germany can take quite a number of days; to Warsaw in Poland the delivery time is five days. By January 2022, there were 50,000 freight trains that travelled between China and Germany, which clearly indicates the

[9] https://www.nytimes.com/2018/10/14/world/asia/donald-trump-foreign-aid-bill.html.

[10] http://en.qstheory.cn/2021-12/02/c_686845.htm.

[11] http://en.qstheory.cn/2021-12/02/c_686845.htm.

large trade between these two countries, and the rest of Europe.[12] The trade between China and the BRI countries has greatly increased in recent years, benefitting the countries involved. Rail traffic between China and Europe has increased by approx. 55% per year, between 2016 and 2021.[13] It is not only cheap consumer goods that are transported from China to Europe by rail, but also high-tech goods, such as drones, autos, computers, chemical products, excavators, and so on.

An essential prerequisite for the stability of deliveries between China and Europe, both by land and sea, is stable and peaceful conditions along the delivery routes. If this stability is maintained, cooperation and trade will increase, promoting both economic and political interests. It can be said that the 'infrastructure diplomacy' of China along all the delivery routes to the BRI countries has promoted China's rise to power. This does not only apply to economic factors, but also to global strategic factors. In this context, the BRI has become an aspect of China's 'grand strategy' in the innovation economy.

During the Covid-19 pandemic, the close relations between China and Europe were also of great importance. More than 100,000 tonnes of medical equipment was transported from China to Europe.[14] Trade between China and Europe has made China into the EU's most important trading partner in 2021, replacing the US. For China, the EU is the second most important trading partner, surpassed only by the United States.[15]

It is not only Europe and China that benefit from the increased rail trade. Mongolia has also benefited, as most of the freight trains go through this country. Mongolia benefits from the service they provide to the rail traffic, which is paid for in foreign currency, providing a boost for Mongolia's economy, says Amarbayasgalan Altanshagai, the head of freight transport for the Ulan Bator Railway Company.[16]

The importance of the BRI, as a driver of the BRI economies, has been stressed in several speeches given by Xi Jinping. The increased trade between the BRI countries indicates that this is more than just empty rhetoric on the part of the Chinese leader. The shared economic future of China and the BRI countries also leads us into the next section which deals with diplomatic and political relations that have resulted from the launch and further development of the New Silk Road. It can be said that China's 'infrastructure diplomacy' has political overtones, such as is expressed along the rail routes between China and Europe. This 'railway diplomacy' (Lauridsen 2019: 219–249), or 'infrastructure diplomacy', has already had a major impact on the relationships between China and the BRI countries.

---

[12] https://english.news.cn/20220129/cb9889de2b4e48189bc433e3941b5a1c/c.html.

[13] http://en.qstheory.cn/2021-12/02/c_686845.htm.

[14] http://en.qstheory.cn/2021-12/02/c_686845.htm.

[15] Ibid.

[16] http://en.people.cn/n3/2022/0121/c90000-9947990.html.

Diplomatic and Political Relationships

The development of infrastructure connecting China with its bordering countries began under the Chinese President Hu Jintao (2002–2012) (Doshi 2021). However, it was Xi Jinping, in a speech given in Kazakhstan in 2013, who formulated the concept of the Belt and Road Initiative (BRI), also called the New Silk Road (Batzhan et al. 2020). In this context, one can perhaps refer to Henry Kissinger, the American diplomat and former United States secretary of state, who expressed that individuals ("great statesmen") can shape history in important ways, and be a powerful force on the world stage (2020: vii). In other words, it might be said that it was first during Xi Jinping's leadership that China has had the aim of overtaking the United States as the next world power, economically, technologically, and militarily (Macaes 2020: 149–195).

The strategy for achieving this aim can be said to be multifaceted. However, the development of diplomatic and political relations along the New Silk Road is certainly one of the sub-strategies in a larger 'grand strategy' (Hsiung 2015: 291–317). China has established a comprehensive higher education system, unmatched anywhere else in the world (Jain 2021). Over the last thirty years, China's economic development has achieved a much higher rate of GDP growth than other countries; in fact, this is perhaps the most significant economic growth in global terms, since the industrial revolution that started in Britain at the end of the eighteenth century (Allen 2009). Thirty years ago, essentially no one foresaw that China would be able to achieve sustained economic growth, and a radical transformation of its economy. Today, it might be said that the 'Chinese Dream' is to increase people's incomes through collective efforts, and "to make China great again" (Brown 2018). China is well equipped, in terms of competence and economy, to become the leading global nation as we move towards the Fourth Industrial Revolution (Mahbubani 2020). The three Silk Roads are a force that will help China develop its political and diplomatic relations with the BRI countries that will also facilitate China's rise to power (Mahbubani 2018). It is undoubtedly China's intention to become the leading power in Asia first, and later in the world (Bougon 2018: 197–205). It can be expected, that to oppose this intention, regarding Chinese core interests, will be met with consequences (Blecher et al. 2022). In this context, one should be aware of the importance of history to China and its leaders, in particular, the 'Century of Humiliation' (1839–1949), where China suffered at the hands of foreign powers; in other words, the negative impact of colonialism in China in the nineteenth century (including the "Opium Wars") and the early twentieth century. There are many indications that the Chinese leaders, in their relations with the West, still have the 'Century of Humiliation' in mind. In this context, regarding relations with foreign powers, China will not hesitate at 'defending its dignity' in relation to its aim of becoming the leading global economic power (Doshi 2021). In this regard, there are many instances where China has been willing to use powerful means to protect what it deems to be important Chinese interests (Xinyu and Zukosky 2022). For example, when the Chinese dissident, Liu Xiaobo, was awarded the Nobel Peace Prize, by the Norwegian Nobel Committee in 2010, the

Chinese Government responded by freezing diplomatic and economic relations with Norway, and banning the import of Norwegian fish, amongst other things.[17] This was also the case when China responded negatively to Australia's condemnation of human rights violations against the Uyghurs in the Xinjiang Province.[18] Estonia was also subjected to negative Chinese reactions, when the operations of Huawei, regarding the development of 5G, were limited due to issues of national security.[19] In other words, China's diplomatic and political relations are not only limited to positive actions, but can also include negative responses, regarding countries that challenge China's core values.

Analysis of the Three Silk Roads

The "America Competes Act" (January, 2022) gives the US an unfair advantage, and limits China's ability to develop its technologies; in this context, it can be expected that China reacts by attempting to neutralize such legislation, regarding its own interests. US sanctions against China in the form of tariffs and taxes, limiting Chinese companies from competing in the US, have a long history, stretching back to the 1990s, when the US imposed tariffs on various Chinese goods (Kissinger 2012). In this context, the further development of the three Silk Roads can be viewed as a counter move by China, in order to become less dependent on trade with the United States. The WTO has approved the Chinese tariffs on US goods, in retaliation against US tariffs.[20] The trade war against China launched by the Trump administration is being continued by the Biden administration. Moreover, the Biden administration has intertwined its negative economic policy against China, with its foreign policy, accusing China of human rights abuses in the Xinjiang province.

The three Silk Roads are more than just investments in the BRI countries' infrastructures. The Digital Silk Road can also be understood as a social mechanism for the transfer of green technology, so that the BRI countries can gain access to a technology that is future-oriented and less dependent on a carbon-driven economy.[21]

The overall motivation for China's new strategy, through extensive investment along the New Silk Road, is aimed at positioning the country as a major global power (Zhao 2020: 1–2). Through the three Silk Roads, China has gained global position and influence, which is of such a magnitude that the sum of the investments is helping to reinforce China's rise to power. There is no doubt that power positioning and power ambition are expressed in the BRI projects, when we know how they stretch out like octopus arms into the global economy, including countries in Asia,

[17] https://www.nytimes.com/2016/12/19/world/europe/china-norway-nobel-liu-xiaobo.html.

[18] https://www.aph.gov.au/sitecore/content/Home/About_Parliament/Parliamentary_Departments/Parliamentary_Library/Publications_Archive/CIB/CIB9697/97cib23.

[19] https://news.err.ee/1608428282/huawei-legislation-does-not-bar-company-from-estonia.

[20] http://global.chinadaily.com.cn/a/202201/28/WS61f361bca310cdd39bc83e46.html.

[21] http://www.chinadaily.com.cn/a/202112/07/WS61aeb519a310cdd39bc79c08.html.

the Middle East, Europe, Africa, and South America. Nor is it just cheap consumer goods that are exchanged between these countries. There is also an exchange of high-tech expertise and high-tech products. It is the degree of connectivity that, on an analytical level, can be said to increase with the many different projects along the Silk Road. When connectivity increases, the economic, political, diplomatic, social, and cultural ties will also be strengthened, although this may take time. It is this strengthening of connectivity that will be the most important strategic gain for China. Metaphorically, one might say that the Chinese leaders are playing the game of GO in the world economy, while the US are playing chess. In chess, as is well known, the game is won by attacking and checking the opponent's king, so it has no possible move to escape the check, that is, 'check mate'. In GO, the game is won by taking different moves in different areas of the board so that the opponent's mobility is slowly but surely limited. Using such a metaphor, it might be said that China is 'closing down' various areas of the 'global board' through its interests in Africa and Asia, and other regions. China does not necessarily dominate the countries it contains or 'closes down', but hinders the strategic opportunities of other countries, such as the US. This situation seems to have slowly but surely dawned on the leaders in Washington. This awareness has resulted in the introduction of the Blue Dot Network, and the US's establishment of various alliances in Asia, such as AUKUS. However, the American strategy can be said to have chess as its basic metaphor. For instance, this seems to be the case in the build-up of the American military presence in the South China Sea. Although China has responded militarily to the US military build-up, it is unlikely that war will break out in the near future, as both countries have too much to lose. In contrast, China clearly exploits the American 'chess thinking' approach by further 'closing down', like an expert GO player, countries in regions such as South America, for example, Colombia.[22] If one uses the metaphor of China 'playing GO' along the three Silk Roads, while the United States 'plays chess' with the aim of 'winning', then it might be said that the Chinese strategy has a greater degree of requisite variety in its arsenal, and thus many opportunities to react to the American 'chess strategy'. In this context, US blinkered foreign policy has been greatly criticized by the former strategist in Washington, Zbigniew Brzezinski, in his book, *The Grand Chessboard* (2016), where he writes that US foreign policy often results in the opposite of that intended by damaging the reputation of the United States.

The Three Silk Roads as Part of China's 'Grand Strategy'

It seems reasonable to assume that the more power China exerts across Asia and other regions, the more other countries will feel that their security is threatened. This can be understood in relation to Timothy Snyder's idea that history does not repeat itself, but it does instruct (Snyder 2019). During the period of the "Middle Kingdom", the

[22] https://foreignpolicy.com/2022/01/25/colombia-china-latin-america-belt-road-biden/.

countries that bordered China paid tribute, as vassals of the Emperor of China. It may seem that such 'strategic historical instructions' create fear in some countries in the region, now that China is emerging as both a regional and a global power, and challenging the world's strongest power, the United States. China demands 'respect' and to be treated with 'dignity'. Countries which defy Chinese interests are 'punished', as mentioned above in the cases of Norway and Estonia. Such punitive measures against smaller countries set an example, demonstrating to other countries what can happen if they oppose Chinese interests. In short, the 'smaller' countries should know their place in the global hierarchy. This was expressed in 2010 at the ASEAN Ministers Conference by China's foreign minister, Yang, when responding to accusations that China was limiting the freedom of navigation in the South China Sea, when he said, "China is a big country and other countries are small countries, and that's just a fact" (Doshi 2021; Yew 2011). China is currently locked in at least 17 territorial disputes in the Asian region, so it is clear that smaller countries can feel threatened by China's strength.

The Chinese 'grand strategy' has many facets, among them the building of the New Silk Road. China's growing economy and expansion along the New Silk Road was made possible by the progressive development of Chinese expertise in many areas. Following the death of Mao Zedong, the "Four Modernizations" (in the fields of agriculture, industry, defence, and science and technology) were adopted in 1977 (Fewsmith 2008; Goodman 1994). Deng Xiaoping's special focus on one of these areas, science and technology, was perhaps his most important strategic contribution to China's development (Deng 1994). This focus on 'science and technology' facilitated a considerable expansion of the Chinese higher education system. Moreover, by 2021, there were approx. 217,000 Chinese students at American universities, plus the tens of thousands of Chinese students at other foreign universities.[23] This indicates that competence development has been a decisive factor for China's rise to power, from the period of Deng Xiaoping (from 1978) up until today, under the leadership of Xi Jinping. In other words, it is the focus on science and technology, and the expansion of Chinese education, that has made it possible to develop the New Silk Road.

In the tensions and partial conflict that developed between China and the United States from 1989 onwards (Tiananmen Square), and in relation to the negative attitudes of the various US governments towards China's growth, one thing seems clear: China was under no circumstances interested in challenging the US technologically and economically, until the country believed it was strong enough, to mount such a challenge, and emerge victorious from it.[24]

There is little indication that China wishes to build a 'New World Order', at least not until it believes it is economically, technologically, politically, and diplomatically strong enough to realize such a vision. "Hide your strength, bide your time" was for a long time the guiding philosophy of China's foreign policy in the Deng Xiaoping

[23] https://www.statista.com/statistics/372900/number-of-chinese-students-that-study-in-the-us/.

[24] Brown (2019), Bougon (2018), Ferdinand (2016), Hsiung (2015), Yang (2015), and Zhang (2015).

era. However, this strategy began to change during the leadership of Hi Jintao, while, since 2012, Xi Jinping has adopted a more assertive global role.[25]

The tendency that China is more actively showing its strength and taking global leadership should not be confused with the idea that the Chinese leaders actively wish to change the global order, and de-throne the US. Although the Chinese leaders are opposed to unfettered American global hegemonic power, it is improbable that China wishes to replace the US as the leading global power. China has undoubtedly learnt from history and seen what has been the fate in the past of rising powers challenging a dominant power, such as during the Second World War when Germany and Japan tried to challenge the global leaders, Britain, France, and the United States. The Chinese leaders are also undoubtedly aware of what happened in recent decades when the Soviet Union attempted to challenge the United States as the leading superpower. The most likely scenario is that China will continue to develop its economic and technological capabilities, rather than challenging the United States directly. It is such a strategy to become economically strong that we see developing along the three Silk Roads. In other words, its development of technological competence, and its participation in international agreements, such as the RCEP, the world's largest free trade organization.

The three silk roads and participation in the RCEP ensure China's import of many raw materials for its own production, such as the production of electric cars, which has increased sharply in recent years. In 2021 alone, China produced approx. 3.5 million. Seven of the top ten auto brands that produced electric cars in China were at the top of the global sales charts.[26] For this production, China needs imports of many different types of raw materials, such as lithium, cobalt and nickel. To a large extent, China has to import these raw materials from Russia, and African and South American countries, although China also has some lithium reserves in its dried-up salt lakes. In addition, China needs food imports for its growing population. Against such a background, it is crucial for the Chinese leaders that peace and stability exist.

Challenging the US's global leadership directly would not be in China's interest. On the other hand, it will of course be in China's interest to grow economically, technologically and militarily. China's military strength does not need to be a direct competitor to the US military strength. For a long time, China's strategy has been to develop asymmetric military capabilities. In practice, this means that when the US has developed aircraft carriers, China has developed the world's largest submarine fleet, which can intercept the American aircraft carriers and warships if they become a danger to China, such as in the coastal areas around Taiwan, or in the South China Sea (Doshi 2021). The asymmetric military capability that China has developed is based on the question: What are the greatest dangers posed by the various US military capabilities? In other words, the development of their submarine fleet is a response to the possible threat posed by US aircraft carriers; the development of Chinese anti-aircraft capabilities is in response to the US airforce capabilities; and the possible threat posed by the US Army, has resulted in China developing military drones

[25] https://www.ft.com/content/05cd86a6-b552-11e7-a398-73d59db9e399.

[26] http://www.chinadaily.com.cn/a/202205/18/WS6284244ea310fd2b29e5d49b_2.html.

(Doshi 2021). More recently, China has developed its aircraft carrier programme, which aims to support investments along the maritime Silk Road, such as the port of Djibouti (Smith and Bolt 2021). For a long time, the Chinese authorities have been concerned with the security of shipping through the Straits of Malacca, where almost all shipping from China to the West passes through. Against this background, one can also understand China's new interest in developing a more symmetrical build-up of its naval capabilities in relation to the US's capabilities. In order to secure its own interests in relation to national security, but also its security in relation to economic interests, such as food imports, China has implemented dredging operations in the South China Sea to build artificial islands around several reefs that have been transformed into significant military facilities (Hayton 2015; Strangio 2022).

Based on what has been described above, we can say that the three Silk Roads have played a decisive role in China's rise to power. At the same time, one can see tendencies that the maritime Silk Road is being supported and protected by a growing Chinese navy. We know from historical insight that controlling the oceans has always been something great powers and empires have done (Jones 2021). In this historical light, China is sending clear signals about its role as a great power when it builds a navy that can defend its maritime Silk Road.

Theoretical Reflections Related to the Three Silk Roads

It seems reasonable to assume that there are two main factors that will be decisive for the importance of the three Silk Roads for China's rise to power. The first main factor is the degree of economic growth in the countries included in the projects along the New Silk Road. The second main factor is the degree of trade between the countries that have signed up to the Belt and Road Initiative (BRI). The hypothesis here is that the greater the degree of economic growth of the BRI countries, and the more trade increases between the countries, the greater will be the probability that the three Silk Roads will have a major impact on China's rise to power.

There is much to suggest that China's expansion along the three Silk Roads is related to the above hypothesis (Angang 2014; Feng and Liang 2019). There are also many indications that the US reaction to China's expansion strategy has resulted in the US establishing various alliances, and adopting various types of legislation, in order to hinder China's expansion.[27]

China's strategy seems to link geopolitical and geo-economic perspectives. If China were only interested in the geopolitical perspective, then the investments in infrastructure and infostructure along the Silk Road would be of less importance. The geopolitical perspective could have come as a result of the increase in China's military forces, which have grown rapidly in recent years, especially the Chinese Navy.[28]

[27] https://rules.house.gov/sites/democrats.rules.house.gov/files/BILLS-117HR4521RH-RCP117-31.pdf.

[28] https://www.brookings.edu/articles/chinas-hollow-military/.

On the other hand, by strengthening geo-economic relationships, China is able to foster close links with the various countries and organizations that have signed BRI agreements. Amongst other things, the BRI countries economically linked to China are aware of Chinese domestic and foreign policies, and wish to keep in-step with China's global interests, in order to ensure future Chinese investment; for instance, particularly in relation to the Chinese constitutional principle of, "one country, two systems;" this is especially important in relation to Taiwan, where China proposes to apply the principle in the unification it aims for with Taiwan. The same applies to the issue of human rights, and the US claims of genocide against the Uighurs in Xinjiang Province. In other words, the BRI countries are encouraged to adopt the Chinese perspective, rather than the US perspective, on such issues.[29]

If the assumption that a balance between geo-economic and geopolitical interventions will be a strategy that will help promote China as a great power, then it is highly probable that the three Silk Roads will be an important social mechanism in this overall Chinese strategy.

The Chinese policy of increasing the prosperity of people in China can be achieved with a strategy where both economic growth and increased trade along the New Silk Road benefit entrepreneurs and people in China, and the populations along the New Silk Road. A unilateral focus on investments that only benefit China would very likely be counterproductive. This is especially true in the global geopolitical competition that has developed between the United States and China. One might go so far as to say that the countries along the New Silk Road are China's potential allies in alliance-building, while the US creates its alliances in the West. It should be added here that the Digital Silk Road fosters relationships between the BRI countries through competence transfers and joint technology projects. In other words, this should not be underestimated at a time when new technology, especially artificial intelligence, is becoming increasingly important for the creation of new jobs and technological innovations.

The economic foundation of the three Silk Roads is continued Chinese economic growth. Without such growth, the BRI projects would at best have been of a smaller order of magnitude and covered fewer countries. When Chinese economic growth is high, China will have a financial surplus, which can be utilized along the three Silk Roads. The various BRI projects have to a great extent been funded with grants and loans from the Asian Infrastructure Investment Bank (AIIB). The AIIB began operations in Beijing in 2016. This Chinese-led international development bank has the stated goal of improving social and economic conditions throughout Asia. The UN has stated that the bank can improve economic development in many developing countries around the world, and since its inception, the AIIB has become a potential rival to the World Bank and the International Monetary Fund. The capital stock of the bank is $100 billion. To put this amount into perspective, this represents half of the capital stock disposed of by the World Bank, and 2/3 of the capital stock of the Asian Development Bank, headquartered in Manila in the Philippines.

[29] https://foreignpolicy.com/2021/03/31/blinken-uyghur-china-human-rights-report/.

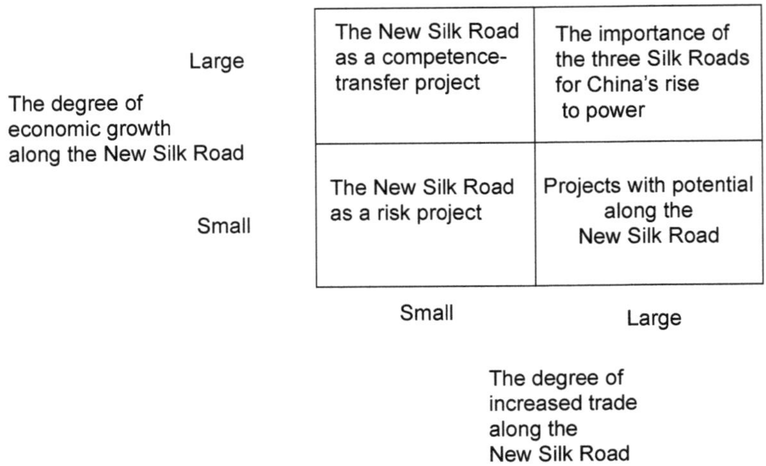

Fig. 2.2 The importance of the three Silk Roads for China's rise to power: a typology

The point of this brief description is to show that the Chinese geo-economic strategy has extremely strong financial resources that will enable it to carry out its strategic projects along the three Silk Roads.

Based on the above narratives, description, analysis, and theoretical reflections, we have developed a typology for the three Silk Roads and their significance for China's rise to power.

In the following, we will briefly review the four elements in Fig. 2.2.

The New Silk Road as a Competence-Transfer Project

When there is a large degree of economic growth along the New Silk Road, but at the same time a small degree of trade between the New Silk Road countries, then in the typology above we have shown this as a situation where a large degree of competence transfer occurs.

In other words, economic growth can occur, even if there is little trade between the countries that are part of the various projects along the New Silk Road. The rationale and explanation is that a transfer of expertise from China to the BRI countries can occur, although there is little trade. This competence transfer can take place in the same way that China developed and is still developing its economy, namely, by developing its education system, especially within higher education and technological studies. In addition, as described above, thousands of Chinese students have travelled from China to study at Western universities, such as in the US. Many of these students gained degrees in fields such as engineering and computer sciences. When these students returned to China, many started businesses that were based on innovative technologies that enabled them to become tech entrepreneurs (Li 2021). A similar development can also occur along the New Silk Road. The various Silk Road countries will be able to develop their education systems, especially in relation to technological studies, by sending students to China. In such a context, China will take the same position as the US did, and still does, for China's competence development. This practice of students from Asian countries studying in China is well under way, and by 2017 there were approximately 70,000 students from ASEAN countries studying in China.[30]

If China assumes this role vis-à-vis the countries along the New Silk Road that are underdeveloped in terms of technological competence, this may have an impact on China's geopolitical and geo-economic position. Such a transfer of expertise will connect these countries more closely to China both diplomatically and politically than would be possible with only increased trade. China, as an emerging economic power, will benefit greatly from developing political and diplomatic relations with many countries in the peripheral zone around China. This could function as both an economic but also a military security zone around China. It is against this background that competence transfer should be considered an extremely important social mechanism for creating stronger links between China and many of the countries along the New Silk Road.

China's education system, especially its higher technological education, is very well developed (Liu 2016: 61–63). We have previously described that Deng Xiaoping emphasized the development of higher education as being crucial for China's development. In other words, Deng, and the leadership of the Communist Party, considered the modernization of higher education, especially in relation to science and technology, to be a crucial prerequisite for China's rise to power (Doshi 2021). Competence transfer can also act as a joint development of culture between countries that exchange students, which Carnoy et al. (2013) have also described.

In this way, economic growth, although not driven by trade, can be an important factor for fostering closer relationships between China and the BRI countries. Having said this, it is beyond doubt that the link between economic growth and increased trade is based on stable conditions and relationships, which we will discuss below in relation to the importance of the three Silk Roads for China's rise to power.

The New Silk Road as a Risk Project

In those cases where there is a small degree of economic growth and a small degree of trade between the countries along the New Silk Road, then the typology indicates that this is a so-called 'risk project'. A good example here is the Hambantota Port, Sri Lanka (opened in 2010), which is Sri Lanka's second largest port, after Colombo, which has been leased to China on a 99-year lease. The port has not resulted in economic growth or increased trade between China and Sri Lanka. When the port

---

[30] https://www.studyinchina.com.my/web/page/china-seeks-students-from-asean/.

became financially unsustainable, it was sold to a Chinese company on a 99-year lease.[31] Although the port is not profitable for China, like the Chinese port, Doraleh, located in Djibouti in the Horn of Africa, at the entrance to the Red Sea, it can be considered part of the Chinese 'security architecture'. For Sri Lanka, on the other hand, the Hambantota Port can turn out to be a risk project for many reasons. As mentioned, the port links the country to China in a 99-year lease agreement. India may develop a negative relationship with Sri Lanka as a result of the port project. A situation may develop where India views Sri Lanka as a type of new 'Cuba' in the Indian Ocean, not that far from its own shores.

Based on what has been written above about risk projects along the New Silk Road, from a Chinese perspective, this can be reformulated; in other words, from a Chinese military-strategic perspective, it can be viewed as positive for China. The large investments that China is making in Africa and several countries in the Middle East have promoted the idea that the military system, such as the Chinese Navy, can be utilized to protect Chinese investments along the maritime Silk Road (Smith and Bolt 2021; Smith and Browne 2019).

China's competition for global resources, and its rise as a geopolitical power, will influence the country's 'grand strategy', and the future development of the three Silk Roads. The point in this context is that what may be considered a risk project from an economic perspective can be considered as a sustainable project from a geopolitical perspective. At first glance, this may seem like a paradox. If, on the other hand, we consider such risk projects in the context of China's 'grand strategy', then certain risk projects can strengthen the overall 'grand strategy'.

Projects with Potential Along the New Silk Road

When trade is large, but there is little economic growth, the typology classifies this as 'projects with potential'. In practice, this means that there may be a time-lag between increased trade and before this impacts the economy. In other words, there is a potential for growth, but which has not yet materialized. It is also conceivable that this occurs because there is not yet sufficient competence in the country to reap the necessary benefits and create ripple effects in the economy. If this is the case, the time-lag will be large, because building up competence in an economy takes a long time. As we have described above, China, under Deng Xiaoping's leadership, from the late 1970s, invested in the development of higher education so as to ensure future economic growth (Deng 1994; Doshi 2021); however, it took around 15–20 years, before the investment began to show results.

In 2019, there were approx. 700,000 Chinese students enrolled at foreign universities.[32] Many of these students gained degrees in fields such as engineering and computer sciences, so that they were able to contribute to China's overall expertise

[31] Ibid.

[32] https://www.statista.com/statistics/227240/number-of-chinese-students-that-study-abroad/.

and innovative technologies, which over time would also promote economic growth. If a country along the New Silk Road has not developed its educational system, especially in relation to science and technology, then it will take a long time before increased trade can result in increased economic growth.

In order to bring about a development where trade is transformed into economic growth, the countries with a low level of expertise and technological development need to balance investment between education and technology, and the military. Too much investment in the military system will mean that it will take much longer before the necessary technological expertise can be developed in order to ensure future economic growth. It is often the case that the military expenditures of developing countries represents too high a percent of their GDP, in relation to investment in higher education and technology development. This is possibly the 'mistake' that both the Soviet Union and today's Russia have made. Military expenditure has been too large in relation to the necessary investment in technology and higher education. This may also partly explain the collapse of the Soviet Union, and Russia's economic position today. Russia's GDP in 2021 was no greater than the combined GDP of the five Nordic countries (despite the fact that the population of Russia is about seven times larger). In other words, Russia is not a global economic superpower. In contrast, Russia spends a large percent of its GDP on its military, and much more than the Nordic countries combined.

The examples above aim to show that if the countries along the New Silk Road are to be able to transform increased trade into economic growth, then it is a crucial prerequisite that the level of expertise needs to be increased, by investing in higher education and the development of technology, while there should also be less military expenditure.

China has probably learned from the mistakes made by the Soviet Union, in trying to compete with the US on military development. On the other hand, it is more doubtful whether all the countries along the New Silk Road have taken this lesson to heart. The key to economic growth in the countries along the New Silk Road lies in investing in skills development. Thereafter, it will be appropriate to focus on investing in the economic system, while spending relatively less on the military.

The Importance of the Three Silk Roads for China's Rise to Power

In order to become competitive with the United States and other Western countries, China invested in modernizing its education system. We have emphasized this throughout this book. However, it cannot be said too many times, because it is possibly the great strides China has made in its technological expertise and development that is the most important reason for China's rise to power. As mentioned above, Deng Xiaoping believed it was crucial to invest in the development of higher education, in order to ensure future economic growth. It may be said that future Chinese growth is dependent on its technological advancement, and development of its technological expertise and skills.

Without this development of skills and expertise, it would have been difficult to effectively launch the three Silk Roads. After the Cultural Revolution (1966–1976), greater focus was given to higher education, especially in the fields of science and technology. The most talented and competent students were selected for technological and natural science studies. These students were educated in both China and abroad (Jain 2021; Thøgersen 1990). This selection process clearly had an integrated social mechanism, resulting in the creation of an 'elite' education in China, largely for the children of 'the elite' (Liu 2021). The exchange of students between China and the US, where it was mainly Chinese students who attended the top American universities, led to the building of relationships on an interpersonal level. This relationship-building was in many ways partly isolated from the growing tensions between the US and China at the political and diplomatic levels (Li 2021). The educated elite also became part of the growing middle class in China. According to Li (2020), this particularly applied to students who had studied abroad.

To a large extent, it is the expertise of middle class workers and entrepreneurs that has facilitated the design, planning and implementation of the various projects along the three Silk Roads. The institutional innovations within China's higher education system also enabled the political control of the development of tech competence in relation to the goals set out by the Communist Party, such as the goal that China aims to become a global leader in the development of artificial intelligence (Ning 2016; Xi 2017, 2020).

There is much evidence that there is a hierarchical division in the development of elite competence in China. This competency hierarchy looks roughly as follows. At the top of the competency hierarchy is science and technology. This is followed by economics education. Closely related to economics education, but more at the business level, comes business management. At the bottom of the hierarchy of 'elite' educations are humanities and language studies (Liu 2021; Ryan 2019).

China's economic growth will inevitably lead to China's expansion abroad. With a population of approx. 1.4 billion, who have a growing expectation of increased economic benefits, China will need to access world markets in the search for raw materials, energy and specialist expertise. In this connection, the three Silk Roads can be viewed as the tentacles of an octopus, which provide the nourishment necessary for survival and growth. The tentacles have rows of suckers. The octopus's suckers are powerful, and once they have grasped something, are very difficult to remove. In other words, once the projects have been established, they are very difficult to deconstruct. These projects can become part of the recipient country's infrastructure, which also promotes the economic development in the country where these projects are realized. At other times, the projects are international, and involve several countries, such as road and rail projects, for example, between China and Western Europe. To plan and ensure the sustainability of these projects, China needs a pool of expertise, which can be found amongst Chinese graduates who have completed higher specialized educations.

China's economic growth has largely been driven by exports of cheap consumer goods to the West which has been possible due to low labour costs. From 2013 onwards, this export-driven growth based on low labour costs has gradually been partially replaced by the export of high-tech goods produced using higher labour costs. Despite the fact that Chinese labour costs have increased in this sector of the economy, the costs are nevertheless lower than high-tech labour costs in the West. In other words, this is resulting in increased competition between China and the West regarding the costs of high-tech expertise.

China may thus end up in a similar position as during the first period of globalization between 1978 and 2013, where the Chinese workers out-competed the American workers in manufacturing and industrial production. In other words, the competition between high-tech workers in China and the West can lead to a relative decrease in wages among high-tech workers in the West. In addition, high-tech labour costs in China are higher than the labour costs during the first period of globalization. In its consequences, this may lead to continued inflation in the West. However, higher labour costs in China will drive economic growth, especially in relation to the implementation of projects along the three Silk Roads. In this way, we can say that the three Silk Roads not only ensure China's rise to power, but also ensure that China can continue to build its strengths on many fronts.

Practical Utility Related to the Three Silk Roads

China's investments along the three Silk Roads are motivated by many goals.

One important goal is economic growth. The infrastructure and infostructure projects are clearly motivated by commercial interests. Investments in roads, bridges, railways and ports promote trade between the BRI countries, often resulting in economic growth for the participating countries. Economic growth also positively impacts people's standard of living, although this is dependent on how the increased wealth (surplus value) is distributed. However, regardless of how the surplus value of economic growth is distributed, those people working on the various BRI projects will benefit. On the other hand, since China is the initiator of the projects, and the principle investor (through the Asian Infrastructure Investment Bank [AIIB]), the economic growth will largely benefit China.

A second goal is linked to China's new foreign policy. On the global stage, Chinese investments in various countries binds these countries closer to China, diplomatically and politically. In the past, countries that China has invested in have proven to be diplomatic allies, such as Greece; for example, this was shown to be the case when Greece blocked EU criticism in the UN of human rights abuses in China.

A third goal concerns strategic competition. The competition between China and the US is increasingly focused on becoming the leader in the development of new technological innovations. In order to escape the US's containment policy regarding technology development, the three Silk Roads can function as arenas where China can test and participate in technological development projects.

A fourth goal is linked to domestic politics. For example, the Silk Road is a means of buttressing the image of Xi Jinping, and the Chinese leaders, as leaders of global eminence amongst the Chinese population. One should be aware of the fact that all the Chinese leaders, since the revolution in 1949, have experienced internal tensions within the Communist Party. Many of these leaders have ended up in political obscurity, only to later be rehabilitated. For instance, this was the case with Deng Xiaoping, who opened up China to foreign investment, making economic growth possible. In other words, the legitimacy of the Chinese government is linked to its ability to deliver economic growth, and provide employment, especially for a growing middle class.

A fifth goal concerns cultural policy. The Chinese government has promoted Chinese culture abroad by establishing Confucius Institutes in many countries. The Confucius Institute program began in 2004 with the aim of supporting Chinese culture, language and history. The Chinese leader, Xi Jinping, has expressed that the institutes have an important role to play in conveying a positive image of Chinese culture.[33] The three New Silk Roads will strengthen links to the countries where investments by the AIIB have been implemented. These strengthened links will probably make it more difficult to criticize or close down the Confucius Institutes, if this should be desired. In the United States, most of the Confucius Institutes have closed their doors. Of the roughly 120 that were open in 2007, only 30 remained in 2021. There are many reasons for this closure of the centres. A clear motivation for the closure of the institutes is the strong criticism of the aims of the institutes, as well as a general souring of the relationship between the US and China.[34]

What seems beyond any doubt is that the three Silk Roads have created geo-economic links between China and the participating countries, such as in Asia, the Middle East, Africa, parts of Europe, and in some countries in South America. This geo-economic strategy also affects the geopolitical conditions (Yu 2020: 3–19). The geo-economic and geopolitical links emerge both from the economic benefits that the individual countries receive from investments, as well as the technological competence transfer that takes place between China and the respective countries. There are thus both financial and competence-related advantages for the countries that participate in the various BRI projects, which also have consequences for the countries' geopolitical connections.

Infrastructure development and technology transfer, which we have described above, concerns more than just increased trade and economic growth. The construction of roads, railways, and ports is also contributing to a global reorientation from the old order, where the US dominated global developments, to a new world order, where the US and China are competing for geopolitical dominance. While the US sends its naval fleet or its military forces to various global regions in an attempt to underline its globally dominant role, China invests in various countries, and encourages the transfer of technological expertise. In this way, the US still dominates globally with its geopolitical superiority, while China has slowly but surely developed its global

[33] Ibid.

[34] https://china.usc.edu/confucius-institutes-united-states.

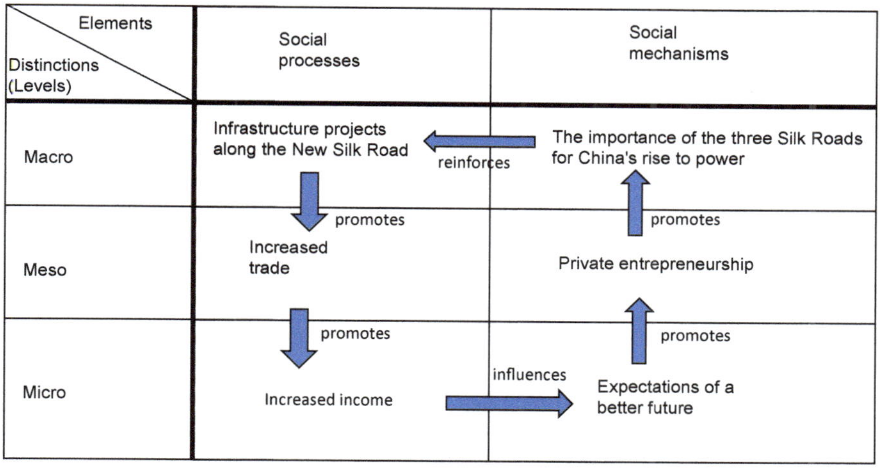

Fig. 2.3 The importance of the three Silk Roads for China's rise to power: A Boudon-Coleman diagram

role geo-economically, through investments in various infrastructure projects along the three Silk Roads. It seems reasonable to assume that China has a strategic intention that geo-economic power will also affect its future geopolitical role. In other words, the country that dominates geo-economically will ultimately also dominate geopolitics.

We have developed a Boudon-Coleman diagram based on the above narratives, description, analysis, theoretical reflections and the review of practical utility.

In the following, we will elaborate on some of the elements in Fig. 2.3.

Infrastructure Projects Along the New Silk Road

The New Silk Road between China and Pakistan, the China–Pakistan Economic Corridor (CPEC), is a 3000 km Chinese infrastructure network project undertaken in Pakistan (launched in 2013). The economic corridor consists of many different projects, developing Pakistan's economy, and also promoting social development. The Economic Corridor also includes the expansion of Gwadar Port in Pakistan which is financed by large Chinese loans. In this context, it is worth noting that there is zero interest on these loans. The Pakistani authorities have stated that the projects that China has developed with Pakistan from 2013 to 2022 have helped develop Pakistan in many ways. This shows several things. Firstly, the infrastructure projects along the New Silk Road have important implications for the countries that China invests in, in this case Pakistan. Secondly, the loan agreement will tie Pakistan to China in areas other than the economic. It is highly probable that the projects and financing of projects, such as the expansion of Gwadar port, will become important for the political and diplomatic relations between China and Pakistan in the future. It also seems reasonable that the CPEC will foster close relations between China and Pakistan, and also have an impact on the security architecture between the countries. If this assumption is correct, and if it can conceivably apply to several countries along the New Silk Road, then in practical policy terms this means that the Belt and Road Initiative (BRI) connects the countries through which the Silk Road passes in many structural ways, economically, politically, diplomatically, socially, culturally and, last but not least, in terms of security.

China is slowly but surely changing from an export-driven growth based on cheap labour, to a more competence-based export, such as the Chinese textile companies that have invested heavily in Pakistani textile companies. The textile industry has become one of Pakistan's most important industries.[35] Against this background, the economic development in Pakistan can be viewed as being historically similar to Chinese development. In other words, Pakistan is attempting to stimulate economic growth by relying on cheap labour. The investments in Chinese growth in the past came largely from the US and the West. The investments in Pakistan today are made largely by China. It seems reasonable to say that in this way China has formed the basis of an economic model, which has been exported to Pakistan.

Pakistan's economy has long suffered from poor transportation conditions, which has restricted Pakistan's economic development. However, today the CPEC construction projects have greatly improved this situation, improving transportation, road communication and other infrastructure along the BRI route. Moreover, between 2015 and 2022, the CPEC has created more than 75,000 jobs in Pakistan.[36]

Of course, China has not invested and developed the BRI projects out of charity. Both economically, politically, diplomatically, and in terms of security, China expects to make gains. The tension that exists between Pakistan and India on the one hand, and the unresolved border disputes between China and India on the other hand, can be resolved to the advantage of both China and Pakistan. In this context, the China-Pakistan Economic Corridor has become an important security dimension for both countries.

The CPEC has definitely contributed to China's rise to power. This is evident economically, and also in relation to political, diplomatic, and cultural relations. The CPEC possibly provides the best example of how the Silk Road has advanced China's position in the region. The CPEC provides Beijing with leverage in Pakistan, and is increasingly becoming a factor for influencing power dynamics in South Asia and globally. In practice, this means that the New Silk Road has created the basis for China's position in the global economy for decades to come. Furthermore, it can be said that China's political leverage extends far beyond the relationship between China and Pakistan, and can be found in the economic relations China has to many countries in Africa, the Middle East, Central Asia and Russia. It is against this background that one can say that China's geo-economic role is progressively increasing its influence in geopolitics in today's world.

---

[35] https://www.globaltimes.cn/page/202202/1251654.shtml.

[36] https://www.globaltimes.cn/page/202202/1251654.shtml.

Increased Incomes in China

According to the Brookings Institute, in 2015 approx. 10% in Asia were living in extreme poverty.[37] By 2021, China had eliminated extreme poverty, due to strong economic growth. In many other countries in Asia, the Brookings Institute expects that extreme poverty will be greatly reduced in a few years. However, in Latin America and Africa, poverty is still a problem. The reduction of extreme poverty in Asia has been spurred by economic growth. In contrast, this development says nothing about how income is distributed, for example, in China.

The economic growth in China has led to greatly increased income inequality. Since the early 1980s, during Deng Xiaoping's leadership (Deng 1994), this has been viewed as necessary, although undesirable, in order to drive economic growth (Vogel 2011). According to Forbes World's Billionaires List (2021), Beijing now has more billionaires than New York.[38]

Well-being and prosperity for the Chinese people is one of the pillars of the 'Chinese Dream' (Brown 2018, 2019). This dream is being pushed forward by the Chinese leaders by giving a growing middle class opportunities to fulfil their increasing expectations (Li 2010, 2021). The Chinese middle class is driving the demand for high-tech and luxury goods. The measures implemented by the Chinese leaders to promote economic growth are also aimed at increasing middle class incomes. In other words, the legitimacy of the Chinese government is linked to its ability to fulfilling the economic expectations of the middle class, in order to avoid social tensions that can arise if such expectations are not met. Against this background, it can be said that income growth in China is a double-edged sword. On the one hand, the Chinese leaders are fulfilling the economic expectations of a growing middle class. On the other hand, these expectations may also function as a social mechanism for future conflicts, because the expectations will constantly increase. In other words, the Chinese leaders need to constantly focus on the expectations of the growing middle class.

The three Silk Roads play a crucial role for the Chinese middle class. Firstly, there are many work assignments precisely for those people in the middle class who have a technological education, because they are drawn into projects along the New Silk road. Secondly, much of the high-tech production in China will be able to be delivered to countries along the New Silk Road. Thus, economic growth in China will be less dependent on the Western countries. The US and the EU are important markets for Chinese exports, both cheap consumer goods, and also high-tech products. The Chinese market is also of great importance to many European countries, such as Germany. The sanctions against Chinese companies imposed by the US and Western countries will to some extent have less of an impact, when China can continue to increase its trade along the New Silk Road. In other words, the Chinese middle class will also be less affected by Western sanctions. On the other hand, US and Western

37 https://www.brookings.edu/research/the-evolution-of-global-poverty-1990-2030/.

38 https://www.forbes.com/billionaires/.

sanctions against China can also negatively affect the German economy more so than the Chinese economy, which may lead to tensions in the Western alliance.

As mentioned above, by 2021, China had eliminated extreme poverty due to economic growth. The Chinese middle class has become an important pillar of the Chinese economy. Despite the large income differences in China, the Chinese leaders declare that Chinese socialism aims to promote "common prosperity".[39] If we take this statement from Xi Jinping as a political goal for the Chinese leaders, then we can expect that the next group to be focused on in future income growth will be the working class. In other words, this is the millions who work in the Chinese factories in manufacturing, such as the textile industry, and in the growing high-tech industrial production. If this assumption is correct, then the future rising wage levels in China will affect the cost structures in China, which will in turn affect the value chain both in China and in the global economy. Such an analysis would indicate a problematic increased inflation in the western countries in the future. It is precisely the expectations of a better future that may become the Achilles' heel that changes global economic relationships.

Expectations of a Better Future

The Chinese leaders and the Chinese people clearly have expectations of a better future, regarding both the economy and national security. For the Chinese, their historical consciousness is greatly influenced by the "Century of Humiliation" from the First Opium War (1839–1842), to the end of the Sino-Japanese War in 1945, and towards the Chinese Revolution (1949). In other words, this is something the Chinese and the Chinese leaders do not want to return to, and which greatly influences future strategic planning in terms of security. Amongst other things, the 'humiliation' is linked to the two opium wars and to the annexation of Hong Kong (Vogel 2011; Doshi 2021). The former Portuguese colony Macau is also part of this 'humiliation'; Macau was first leased to Portugal in 1557, and remained under Portuguese rule until 1999, when it was transferred back to China. Japan's brutal conquest of large parts of China during and prior to the Second World War (1937–1945) is also part of China's historical 'humiliation', and something they seek to avoid in the future at all costs (Kissinger 1995, 2012, 2015, 2020). The brutal conquest included the Nanking Atrocity, comprising mass murder, rape, and looting (1937–1938). Against this background, one can understand China's strategic actions today, and their desire for a better national security architecture. In other words, the aim is to safeguard against similar humiliations in the future, rather than re-create the great power China once was, during the era of the "Middle Kingdom".

"China's peaceful rise", that is, China's peaceful development, is part of the Chinese government's political rhetoric and policy that was first expressed during the leadership of Hu Jintao, in order to assure the international community that China's

[39] https://global.chinadaily.com.cn/a/202108/30/WS612c193aa310efa1bd66be1a.html.

growing power would not pose a threat to international security (Doshi 2021). In other words, the Chinese leaders wish to create a better future for the Chinese people, based on peaceful coexistence. It is this peaceful coexistence that is promoted when there is a greater degree of openness and peaceful cooperation between countries, and a mutual strengthening of relations (Lauridsen 2019). On the other hand, although this may be the aim of the Chinese leaders, much can happen to thwart this aim. In this context, what may be difficult to overcome for most Chinese is precisely what drives their desire for a better future. The point here is that when you have a 'century of humiliation' as part of your 'past baggage', this may have a negative effect on what you are willing to do to achieve your goals. In addition, the Chinese leaders have clearly understood what happened during "the Great Leap Forward", "the Cultural Revolution" and the 1989 Tiananmen Square protests and massacre, and the after-effects of this event on the diplomatic relations with the US, and other countries.

In such a historical context, it is not certain that peaceful coexistence will always be the most effective tool to meet the expectations of a better future for the Chinese people. With such 'past baggage', it is easy to lose your way when you are traversing unknown terrain. This is probably one of the reasons why the Chinese leaders place their policy priority on building internal stability. They are aware of the fact that if this stability is not maintained, much can happen if, for example, the middle class's expectations of a better future are not met. The Chinese leaders also know that if peace does not exist, this will affect the country's ability to promote economic growth. Stability and peace in the world are therefore essential for the Communist Party to be able to fulfil the wishes of hundreds of millions of Chinese in their struggle to create a better future. It is these expectations that influence the actions of the Chinese leaders in the present day.

Global wars and conflicts can negatively affect China's economy. In this context, it seems reasonable to assume that the Chinese leaders will do what is in their power to mitigate the negative consequences of these wars. More specifically, this concerns how the war between Russia and Ukraine can pose problems for China's economy, and what the Chinese leaders are willing to do to avoid the negative effects of the war on the economy. The Chinese leaders know from their own historical experience that there will always be limits to how much governments can utilize nationalism and patriotism as a positive force, especially when this is set against an economic future that will be negatively affected; that is, if China supports one of the conflicting parties, so that the Chinese people will have to pay for the support. Therefore, it may be appropriate to interpret China's 'grand strategy' in relation to international conflicts and wars based on what serves China's interests best.

The Chinese leaders know that they can control information processes, communication, and the media over a certain period of time. However, they also know from historical experience that sooner or later people will come to rely on their 'gut feelings' rather than the 'official news'. It is against this background that the Chinese leaders will do everything that serves China's economic interests, in order to fulfil the expectations of a better future for the Chinese people. It is in this context that the three Silk Roads will play a crucial role in China's future strategy to increase its economic power.

Private Entrepreneurship

Private entrepreneurship based on technological innovations can be understood as the new Chinese growth model. The entrepreneurship path is one of three paths to support and develop the Chinese middle class. According to Li Lulu, a Professor of Sociology at Renmin University in Beijing, the two other paths are competence-based power and network-based power (Li 2021: 70).

However, the Chinese middle class is a complex social group, which includes private entrepreneurs; the entrepreneurs are important regarding their expectations, and the signals they send to the political leadership regarding these expectations. In other words, private entrepreneurship greatly influences the policies of the leadership of the Communist Party regarding their expectations for the future. It may sound paradoxical that private entrepreneurs have such influence in communist China. However, the communist leaders are aware of the fact that their survival depends on delivering results that support the expectations of the middle class. The private entrepreneurs, both small and large, play a vital role in the economic development of China. Many of these entrepreneurs have studied in the US, so they also have a normative influence, apart from their financial strength (Li 2021).

According to Li (2021: 70), the Chinese middle class consists of three clusters, based on their occupation: an economic cluster, political cluster, and cultural and educational cluster. The economic cluster consists of private entrepreneurs, including rich business people in the cities, industrial owners in the regions, rich farmers, and investors who have become rich due to investments and speculation in shares. The political cluster consists of state employees, and members of the Communist party with relatively large incomes. The cultural and educational cluster consists of people in high positions in the fields of education and culture, such as professors at renowned universities; cultural figures; people in the media world, and so on.

Of these three clusters in the middle class, the private entrepreneurs have a normative power, and send signals to the decision-makers at governmental level and also to the decision-makers in the Communist Party (Yu 2020). The private entrepreneurs wish to have less government intervention in the economy (Li 2021: 70). If these signals are heeded by the decision-making authorities, this indicates more liberalization in the Chinese economy in the future. This of course presupposes the assumption that the private entrepreneurs are able to wield influence on the central decision-makers.

Many entrepreneurs have developed their businesses in technology and e-commerce in cities such as Shenzhen and Hangzhou (Li 2021: 142). This development will reinforce the new Chinese growth model.

The expectations of a better future, and the entrepreneurs who develop businesses based on technological innovations, are giving impetus to the three Silk

Roads. Chinese economic growth is a prerequisite for exporting the Chinese model to the many of the countries along the New Silk Road (BRI). If Chinese economic growth does not persist, many of the partner countries will become sceptical of the Chinese model. Against this background, the Chinese economy needs to grow and show its strength. In other words, China's strategy for the BRI countries is simple: China tells the participating countries, "come grow with me". Against this backdrop, private entrepreneurship and the new economic growth model in China are necessary prerequisites for China's rise to power.

Through its economic growth, and its expansion along the New Silk Road, the decisions made in China are affecting countries in the region, and far beyond. The more the various countries along the New Silk Road are integrated into the Chinese economy, the more dependent they will become on the decisions made by the Chinese leaders. Viewed in a negative light, Chinese expansion may be compared to a battle being fought without a single bullet being fired. In other words, China is winning the economic war, without any formal declaration of 'war'. This may be said to be in accordance with the strategic thinking of Sun Tzu's "The Art of War" (written between 475 and 221 B.C.E.). History may not repeat itself, but there has been a trend in China to utilize Sun Tzu's philosophy as expressed in "The Art of War" in conjunction with 'soft power' in order to facilitate China's peaceful development strategy.

Systemic Connections Related to the Three Silk Roads

Since the 1980s up until today, China's strengthened geo-economic position has triggered negative reactions in some quarters. More specifically, the US geo-economic and geopolitical dominance has been threatened by China, and is undermining a US-dominated world order. This has been expressed explicitly by Kissinger (2012). The threat to American hegemony was also expressed in the article, "America's Pacific Century", written by the former Secretary of State, Hillary Clinton (*Foreign Policy*, 2011). The US's geo-economic countermoves came to the surface when President Trump launched a trade war against China. The trade war has been continued by the Biden administration, while the US rhetoric against China has escalated. This became evident in a human rights report where Anthony Blinken, the US Secretary of State, labelled China's actions in Xinjiang as genocide (*Foreign Policy*, March 31, 2021).[40] In other words, China's strengthened geo-economic position, especially along the New Silk Road, is clearly perceived as a threat by the United States. Consequently, the US is doing everything within its means, both economically and rhetorically, to limit China's economic growth.

In the past, when the US government launched trade sanctions against China, American industry has opposed such sanctions; for example, Ford, General Motors and Boeing that had multibillion-dollar contracts in China. However, when Trump

[40] https://foreignpolicy.com/2021/03/31/blinken-uyghur-china-human-rights-report/.

launched a trade war against China, none of the large corporations objected (Mahbubani 2020). An important point in this context is that the US was not only being threatened by China at the political level. It seems that US business interests, which has made billions of dollars and enjoyed super profits in China for almost forty years, have now also understood that China's economic strength may be a threat to their own existence in the near future. This is a flashback to the 1980s when the increased sales of Japanese autos in the US were viewed as a threat to the US auto industry. To prevent a collapse in the American auto industry at the time, President Ronald Reagan, known for his support of free trade, intervened to limit the unrestricted import of Japanese cars to the US, as it was believed that this could harm the American auto industry and negatively affect American jobs. In other words, Reagan implemented various measures to restrict the sale of Japanese autos in the US in order to save the American auto industry. Mahbubani (2020) says that if Reagan had not intervened, then it is very probable the American auto industry would have collapsed. Regarding the US trade war against China, Trump railed against China for allegedly stealing American jobs. There were few voices, if any, that countered this rhetoric; in other words, not among the Democrats nor the Republicans, nor among the industry leaders. However, the truth is often more complicated. Trump's accusation that China stole American jobs is right and wrong at the same time. The trigger for the loss of jobs was American investment in Chinese industry, because labour costs were low, and it was cheaper to produce goods. In other words, China didn't 'steal' US jobs, US businesses and investors outsourced jobs to China because of low labour costs and higher profits. Another point regarding US jobs is that without the Chinese market, many of the US jobs in the auto and aerospace industries would have disappeared. Mahbubani (2020) explains that Ford Motors and General Motors had billion-dollar contracts in China, not because US autos were cheaper or better than the Japanese and German autos, but because a political decision was made by the Communist Party that they would not be dependent on only a few suppliers to the Chinese auto market. In other words, many thousands of jobs in the American auto industry were saved due to this development. The same goes for the aerospace industry, where Boeing had billion-dollar orders in China, at a time when the industry would otherwise have had particularly large problems competing with the European Airbus.

The American government's policy of trade sanctions against China, as well as the political rhetoric regarding the accusation that China has committed genocide in Xinjiang, is an attempt to hinder China's economic expansion, among other things, along the New Silk Road. However, it appears that this American strategy towards China has backfired, leading to the opposite of what was intended. China's economic relations with the countries along the New Silk Road have only increased in scope, depth, and strength (Zhao 2020).

Based on the above narratives, description, analysis, theoretical reflections, practical utility, and the systemic connections, we have developed a loop diagram (Fig. 2.4).

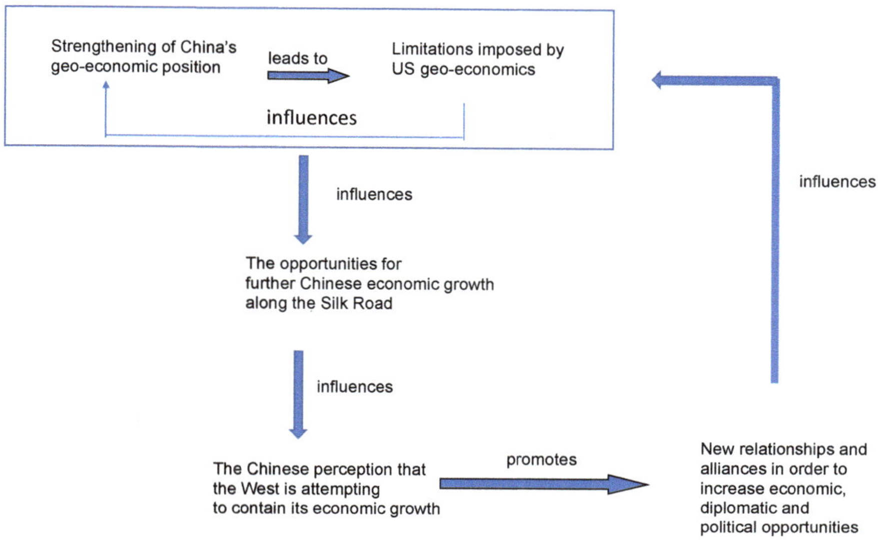

Fig. 2.4 The importance of the three Silk Roads for China's rise to power: A loop diagram

The Strengthening of China's Geo-Economic Position

Edward Luttwak was one of the first economists to suggest that after the Cold War, economic factors would play an increasingly important role in geopolitical competition. It is against this background that one can say that geo-economic realities influence geopolitical positioning, and vice versa.

There are three levels of geo-economic analysis that have been pointed out. These three levels are:

1. International Political Economy

   This level of analysis is a sub-discipline of international relations, and is concerned with global economic interactions between political actors, systems and institutions. Globalization and international trade are central units of analysis in this context. The New Silk Road is a good case for studying international political economy from the perspective of relations between China and international political actors.
2. Economic Geography

   Economic geography studies economic activities from a geographical perspective. It examines, among other things, the localization of industries, raw materials, and productivity development in different geographical and technological contexts, often referred to as "the economies of agglomeration". Also in relation to economic geography, the New Silk Road can serve as a case example regarding various economic factors.
3. Industrial Organization

Industrial organization is a field that examines the structure of relations between businesses and markets. For instance, it is concerned with costs, information, and competition. The various ways in which businesses and institutions operate along the New Silk Road, and how they are interconnected via organizational infrastructures can provide an object of study at this level.

Financial operations provide an analytical level that functions as a social mechanism for transactions between these levels. The financial operations are institutionalized through, among other things, the International Monetary Fund (IMF), and the World Bank.

Using this as the theoretical background for the study of China's geo-economic progress, the three Silk Roads constitute an exemplary case to show how China has taken control at the geo-economic level, and at the same time influenced the geopolitical level. The best indication of this is the fact that the US perceives China to be a strategic enemy. However, this is not a situation that will necessarily lead to war, which Allison (2018) suggests, in his discussion of "Thucydides' Trap".

It is conceivable that China's strengthened geo-economic position will trigger economic and political competition, where the US will lead an alliance against China. This alliance will in some contexts cooperate with China, because it will be able to benefit from large trade transactions; in other contexts, the US-led alliance will compete with China, for example, in the field of new technology, such as information technology, artificial intelligence and robotics. This assumption is based on the idea that the nation that controls the new technology will be able to establish a strong position geo-economically and geopolitically.

China's geo-economic position has developed along at least three paths. The first path is the export-driven growth from the 1980s up until 2013, when the New Silk Road was launched. The second path towards geo-economic progress is the New Silk Road, or what we call here the three Silk Roads, the land-based, the maritime and the digital silk roads. The Digital Silk Road is still in its infancy, but there are many indications that the Digital Silk Road will be decisive for China's geo-economic positioning in the future. This positioning is, among other things, linked to the third path, China's entry into the world's largest free trade organization, the RCEP (1 January 2022).

There are many indications that China will strengthen its global position by taking over economic control of various areas. This is also in line with Marxist economics thinking, which the Chinese Communist Party has as its basic ideology. This is expressed in the Marxist principle that the economic base dictates the political superstructure.[41]

[41] Marx (1976, 1978, 1991), Marx and Engels (1976), and Mandel (1972, 1977, 1990, 1991).

Geopolitical Sanctions: The US's Technological Containment of China

During the Cold War, the US pursued a policy of containment towards the Soviet Union to prevent the expansion of communism.[42] This strategy can also partly explain why the US established diplomatic and economic relations with China in the 1970s (Doshi 2021). The policy of containment towards the Soviet Union was part of the US's effective 'grand strategy',[43] and is often associated with George Frost Kennan, the American diplomat and historian. It is against this background that many analysts in the United States advocate a containment strategy against the rising China.[44]

China is now the leading economic power in Asia, and the second largest economy in the world, trailing only the United States. Moreover, China has announced its goal of leadership in artificial intelligence by 2030. In this context, the United States feels threatened by China's rapid technological development (Frey 2019, 2020).

The policy of containment towards China has the goal of securing the economic, diplomatic and security interests of the US. However, there is a large difference between the Soviet Union in the Cold War period, and China of today. For instance, China has a stronger economic and competence foundation than was the case with the Soviet Union. The United States is of course aware of this fact, which possibly explains why a further containment of China will follow a different pattern than against the Soviet Union. It is conceivable the United States will adopt the following strategies.

The US is waging a "values war" with China related to human rights, such as the accusations of human rights abuses against the Uighurs in Xinjiang. In this context, the United States is attempting to form a broad alliance against China related to the condemnation and opposition to China's human rights abuses. On this basis, the idea is that when China oppresses its own citizens, it will most probably also oppress the citizens of other countries, especially when it is gaining more global influence, such as along the New Silk Road. When it has been established 'in the eyes of the world' that the Chinese system of government undermines human values and rights, then other strategies can also be used to contain China.

One of the strategies employed by the US administration has been to link the emerging Chinese information technology to issues of national security. The US has managed to achieve this in its campaign against the Chinese telecom giant Huawei, barring the company from operating in its 5G networks. These networks are essential for the integration of the economy in the innovation economy. In addition, we have seen an increasing strategic focus on a trade war with China, where Chinese goods have been subjected to tariffs and taxes.

---

[42] https://www.foreignaffairs.com/articles/china/1963-04-01/threat-and-opportunity-communist-schism.

[43] https://foreignpolicy.com/2021/01/15/containment-russia-china-kennan-today/.

[44] https://foreignpolicy.com/2021/01/15/containment-russia-china-kennan-today/.

It seems reasonable to assume that restrictions will also be placed on the trade of high-tech products between the US and China, such as all the technological products related to artificial intelligence and robotics.

At the same time as the US is pursuing an economic containment strategy of China, it is also strengthening its intelligence alliances in the South China Sea, such as “the Five Eyes” intelligence alliance, which involves joint cooperation in signals intelligence between Australia, Canada, New Zealand, the UK, and the United States. This alliance is intended to monitor Chinese military operations in the South China Sea. There is also another alliance developing among 14 nations, known as “14 Eyes”, which, from a Chinese perspective, is probably viewed as an ‘intelligence encirclement’ of China.

New military alliances against China include AUKUS. Based on the above description, the development of the US’s economic and military containment of China will represent a different containment strategy than the one launched against the Soviet Union during the Cold War.

Regarding the US’s containment strategy, the three Silk Roads will play a decisive role for China. There are approx. 130 countries involved in various projects along the New Silk Roads. In other words, China is economically, diplomatically and politically involved in many regions and countries around the world. In practice, this means that if the US is to contain China, it cannot merely raise the spectre of communism, as it did with the Soviet Union during the Cold War. However, as described above, the US has attempted to establish an alliance against China on the basis of opposition to China’s human rights abuses. If this strategy is successful, then it will also be possible to form alliances against China in relation to economic issues, diplomacy and politics.

It is against this background, where the US is trying to create an alliance against China, that we can also understand China’s further development of the New Silk Roads, as well as China’s alliance with Russia. The sanctions against Russia after the country’s annexation of Crimea in 2014, and especially after Russia’s invasion of Ukraine on 24 February 2022, seem to have strengthened relations between China and Russia. Both countries are being subjected to US sanctions and containment policies. Against this backdrop, it is conceivable that one of the results of the new containment policy towards China will only lead to the creation of alliances that the US could have preferably done without.

It is precisely China’s economic expansion via the three Silk Roads that will make the US’s possible containment strategy difficult to implement. There is a difference between containing the Soviet Union with clear borders in Eastern Europe, and China, which does not have equally visible borders for its interests along the New Silk Road.

According to Lee Kuan Yew (2021: 8), the US system is more innovative than the Chinese system. If this assumption is correct, then this could slow down Chinese economic growth in the future. On the other hand, even if the assumption is correct, it may not severely negatively affect Chinese economic growth, when we take into account the relations China has developed along the Silk Road. The Silk Road provides China with a lever to promote continued growth, even though the US is more innovative, and more advanced in its development of technological innovations. As long as the US allows Chinese students to complete technological studies in the US, it is unlikely that the US will have the ability to keep its technological innovations a secret for long. The three Silk Roads stimulate economic growth, because trade and projects increase the demand for goods, services and expertise from China. The Chinese students who return home from their studies in the US are able to transfer much of the knowledge they have gained in the development of technological innovations. Many of these Chinese graduates become entrepreneurs and start up new technology companies in China (Li 2021).

Against this background, there is much evidence that suggests China will surpass the US to become the number one economic power. There is also much to suggest that the US's innovative capacity, as pointed out by Yew, will not have a major negative impact on China, because of the country's openness to the outside world.

Although Yew claims that China, with its 1.4 billion people, is not as innovative as the US, there are at least two factors that go against this argument.

One factor concerns the law of large numbers. With a population of 1.4 billion people, and with an increasing proportion completing higher education, it is likely that this will stimulate the development of technological innovations. China may be lagging behind the US, but when so many people participate in the development of technological innovations, then sooner or later this will show results.

The second factor is China's openness to the outside world. When China has so many students abroad, in the US, England, France, etc., these students will return to China with a competence that will be decisive for developing technological innovations. It is possible that China will copy Western technologies. We have seen this development previously in both China and, before that, Japan. The point in this context is that both of these countries further developed, improved and promoted a continuous quality improvement of the technological innovations that originally came from the US and the West.

Further Economic Growth Along the New Silk Road

The numerous projects that are implemented along the three Silk Roads will benefit China and result in economic growth as long as the centre remains stable. In this context, the centre refers to China. China will be able to maintain economic and political stability, as long as it does not get involved in major international issues and conflicts. In other words, China's foreign policy needs to keep a low profile, especially with regard to the crisis over Taiwan and US-China relations.

On the other hand, if the centre is weakened, the periphery will also be negatively affected. In this situation, the three Silk Roads would most probably be unable to compensate for the weakened centre. In this context, China's foreign policy needs to keep a low profile, and prioritize economic growth that benefits the population at large, and especially the middle class that constitutes around 700 million people. If the Chinese government can meet the expectations of the middle class, then this will contribute to stability and economic progress, and China will benefit from most of the projects along the New Silk Road.

It may be interesting to consider a Danish saying about entrepreneurship in the context of the rise of entrepreneurship in China. In Denmark, there's a popular saying that everyone in North Jutland is a 'king'. What this means in practice is there is a particularly strong entrepreneurial culture in this part of Denmark. Everyone in North Jutland wants to try their hand at being the next leading entrepreneur. At the same time as wanting to be 'king', everyone in North Jutland knows that the Denmark's actual ruler is far away in Copenhagen (even though Denmark is a small country), and so as 'king', they can basically do what they want. If we transfer this idea to China, we can imagine that if everyone had the opportunity to earn vast sums through entrepreneurship, then everyone would create their own rules and norms to do so. As a result, the central government authorities would have less influence on decision-making in outlying regions. The point of this small digression is to highlight that if the centre is weak, then outlying regions will experience the emergence of self-anointed petty 'kings', who will fight for their own interests. That is why we say that if the centre is strong, then China as a whole will benefit from the trends emerging on its periphery, including in the many projects along the New Silk Road.

In the above description, we have expressed the view that the New Silk Road will benefit China economically, diplomatically and politically, as long as the Chinese government is able to maintain a stable and strong leadership. The many different interests of the Chinese population represent a challenge for the Chinese leaders. It is not the case, which some people in the West believe, that the Communist Party is homogeneous, and that power flows along a direct line from the top down through the ranks, where everyone bows to the decisions made in Beijing (Brown 2019). In reality, the situation is much more complicated. China is a multifaceted country, with decision-making processes that go in many different directions (Fang and Fu 2020). Therefore, the leaders of the Communist Party are constantly dependent on making alliances and being able to meet the expectations of a growing middle class. If discontent were to arise in the population due to an outlying international conflict that negatively affected economic and social development, then this would present a challenge for the communist leadership. The upheavals in Eastern Europe in 1989 are a good example of this phenomenon. The Chinese leaders are obviously anxious to avoid similar developments in China (Vogel 2011). This may provide a partial explanation of the Tiananmen Square protests and massacre in 1989.

The Chinese leaders cannot predict when new student-led demonstrations, similar to those in 1989, may occur. What they do know, however, is that as long as they can meet the expectations of the middle class and the growing numbers of entrepreneurs, then their position in power is secure. It is against this background that we can understand the government's commitment to invest in the three Silk Roads. The Chinese leadership knows that as long as skilled and unskilled workers are able to find relatively well-paid jobs in the projects along the New Silk Road, then their expectations will be fulfilled. Stability in the centre and dynamism in the periphery seems to be a formula for Chinese economic growth going into the future. In particular, this applies to the Belt and Road Initiative which constitutes the dynamic economic element in the outer periphery. The inner periphery is the regions of China. These regions will also be able to benefit from a strong and stable centre and the projects being developed in the outer periphery. In particular, this applies to all the infrastructure projects that are essential for connecting China's regions, and at the same time linking China with the outside world.

Sub-conclusion

We have examined the following question: How have the three New Silk Roads influenced China's role in the development of AI?

The short answer is that the three Silk Roads have been crucial to China's economic, political and diplomatic progress. In particular, this became apparent when the US initiated a sanctions policy against China, while escalating its negative rhetoric, with the aim of reducing China's global influence.

References

Allen RC (2009) The British industrial revolution in global perspective. Cambridge University Press, Cambridge

Allison G (2018) Destined for war: Can America and China escape Thucydides trap? Scribe, London

Angang H (2014) Silk road economic belt: strategic considerations, positioning and implementation routes. J Xinjiang Norm Univ 2:1–10

Batzhan A, Alpysbayeva S, Kapsalyamova Z (2020) The Belt and Road Initiative: Case of Kazakhstan. In: Chay YW, Menkhoff T, Low L (eds) Chinas Belt and Road Initiative: understanding the dynamics of a global transformation. World Scientific, London, pp 71–97

Berlie JA, Hung S (2020) The greater Bay area and the role of Hong Kong and Macau SARs in the Belt and Road Initiative. In: Berlie JA (ed) China's globalization and the Belt and Road Initiative. Palgrave, London, pp 77–100

Blecher M, Goodman DSG, Guo Y, Rocca J-L, Tang B (2022) Class and the communist part of China, 1978–2021: reform and market socialism. Routledge, London

Bougon F (2018) Inside the mind of Xi Jinping. Hurst, London

Brown K (2018) China's dream. Polity, London

Brown K (2019) The world according to Xi. I. B. Tauris, London

Brzezinski Z (2016) The grand chessboard: American primacy and its geostrategic imperatives. Basic Books, New York

Carnoy M, Loyalka P, Dobryakova M, Dossani R, Froumin I, Kuhns K (2013) Constructing world culture. Stanford University Press, Stanford

Chay YW, Menkhoff T, Low L (2020) China's Belt and Road Initiative: understanding the dynamics of a global transformation. World Scientific, London

Clinton H (2011) America's Pacific century. Foreign Policy 189, 11 October

Cohn SM (2019) Competing economic paradigm in China. Routledge, London

Deng X (1994) Selected works of Deng Xiaoping, Vol III (1982–1992). Foreign Language Press, Beijing

Doshi R (2021) The long game: China's Grand Strategy to displace American order. Oxford University Press, Oxford

Fang N, Fu Y (2020) China's political system. Springer, London
Feng DH, Liang HM (2019) Belt and Road Initiative: Chinese version of Marshall Plan. World Scientific, London
Ferdinand P (2016) The China dream and one belt one road: Chinese foreign policy under Xi Jinping. Int Aff 92(4):941–957
Fewsmith J (2008) China since Tiananmen, from Deng Xiaoping to Hu Jintao. Cambridge University Press, Cambridge
Frey CB (2019) The technology trap: capital, labor, and power in the age of automation. Princeton University Press, Princeton
Frey CB (2020) Attitudes towards technology: part II. In: Skidelsky R, Craig N (eds) Work in the future: the automation revolution. Palgrave, London, pp 89–97
Goodman DSG (1994) Deng Xiaoping and the Chinese revolution: a political biography. Routledge, London
Hayton B (2015) The South China Sea: the struggle for power in Asia. Yale University Press, New Haven
Hillman JE (2021) The digital silk road: China's quest to wire the world and win the future. Profile Books, New York
Hsiung JC (2015) The Xi Jinping era: his comprehensive strategy toward the China dream. CN Times Books, New York
Jain R (2021) China's soft power and higher education in South Asia. Routledge, London
Johannessen J-A (2021) China's innovation economy: Artificial Intelligence and the New Silk Road. Routledge, London
Jones BD (2021) How control of the world's oceans shapes the fate of the superpowers: to rule the waves. Scribner, New York
Kissinger H (1995) Diplomacy. Simon & Schuster, New York
Kissinger H (2012) On China. Penguin, New York
Kissinger H (2015) World order. Penguin, New York
Kissinger H (2020) Foreword. In: Allison G, Blackwell RD, Wyne A (eds) Lee Kuan Yew: the grand masters insights on China, the United States, and the world. The MIT Press, Boston, pp vii–ix
Lauridsen LS (2019) Changing regional order and railway diplomacy in South East Asia with a case study of Thailand. In: Xing L (ed) Mapping China's One Belt One Road initiative. Palgrave, London
Li C (2010) China's emerging middle class beyond economic transformation. Brookings Institution Press, Washington
Li C (2021) Middle class Shanghai: reshaping U.S.-China engagement. Brookings Institution Press, Washington, DC
Liu S (2021) Neoliberalism, globalization and "Elite" education in China, becoming international. Routledge, London
Liu Y (2016) Higher education, meritocracy and inequality in China. Springer, London
Macaes B (2020) Belt and road: a Chinese world order. C. Hurst &, London
Mahbubani K (2018) Has the west lost. Allen Lane, New York
Mahbubani K (2020) Has China won? PublicAffairs, London
Mandel E (1972) Introduction. In: Marx K, Capital, vol II. Penguin Books, pp 11–80
Mandel E (1977) Marxist economic theory. Merlin Press, London
Mandel E (1990). Introduction. In: Marx K, Capital, vol I. Penguin Books, pp 11–87
Mandel E (1991) Introduction. In: Marx K, Capital, vol III. Penguin Books, pp 9–91
Marx K (1976) Capital, vol I. Penguin Classics, London
Marx K (1978) Capital, vol II. Penguin Classics, London
Marx K (1991) Capital, vol III. Penguin Classics, London
Marx K, Engels F (1976) The Communist Manifesto. In: Marx and Engels collected works, vol 6. International Publishers, New York

Ning K (2016) Institutional innovation in higher education resource allocation in China's transitional economy. McGraw Hill, New York
Ryan J (2019) Education in China: philosophy, politics and culture. Polity, London
Smith JM, Bolt PJ (2021) China's strategic arsenal, worldview, doctrines and systems. Georgetown University Press, New York
Smith B, Browne CA (2019) Tools and weapon. Penguin, New York
Snyder T (2019) The road to unfreedom, Russia, Europe, America. Crown, New York
Strangio S (2022) In the dragons shadow: South East Asia in the Chinese century. Yale University Press, New Haven
Thøgersen S (1990) Secondary education in China after Mao: reform and social conflict. Aarhus University Press, Aarhus
Thucydides (2009) The Peloponnesian war. Oxford University Press, Oxford
Vangeli A (2018) Normative foundation of the Belt and Road Initiative. In: Wenhua S, Nuotio K, Zhang K (eds) Normative readings of the Belt and Road Initiative. Springer, London, pp 59–83
Vogel EF (2011) Deng Xiaoping and the transformation of China. Harvard University Press, Cambridge, MA
Xi J (2017) The governance of China, book II. Foreign Language Press, Beijing
Xi J (2020) The governance of China, book III. Foreign Language Press, Beijing
Xing L (2019) Understanding the multiple facets of China's "One Belt One Road" initiative. In: Xing L (ed) Mapping China's One Belt One Road initiative. Palgrave Macmillan, London, pp 29–56
Xinyu L, Zukosky M (2022) The future of China: three critiques of Neoliberalism. Palgrave, London
Yang J (2015) China's new diplomacy under the Xi Jinping administration. China Q Int Strat Stud 1(1):1–17
Yew LK (2011) Hard truths to keep Singapore going. Straits Times Press, Singapore
Yu H (2020) Motivation behind China's One Belt, One Road initiative and establishment of the Asian Infrastructure Investment Bank. In: Zhao S (ed) China's new global strategy. Routledge, London, pp 3–19
Yuan F (2019) The One Belt One Road initiative and Chinas multi-layered multilateralism. In: Xing L (ed) Mapping China's one belt one road initiative. Palgrave, London, pp 91–116
Yuzhu W (2020) New regional cooperation and integration strategy and the 21st-Century Maritime Silk Road initiative. In Jianglin (ed) 21st-Century Maritime Silk Road initiative, aims and objectives, implementation strategies and policy recommendations. World Scientific, London, pp 211–225
Zhang J (2015) China's new foreign policy under Xi Jinping: towards peaceful rise 2.0? Glob Chang Peace Secur 27(1):5–19
Zhao S (2020) Introduction. In: Zhao S (ed) China's new global strategy. Routledge, London, pp 1–2
Zou L (2018) The political economy of China's Belt and Road Initiative. World Scientific, Singapore

Chapter 3
The Rise of the Middle Class in China

Core Idea
"It's what you are good at that will be your downfall".

Key Points

- China's economic leverage is the 700 million members of its middle class.
- If the Chinese middle class were for some reason to change their spending patterns to the disadvantage of goods produced in France, for example, then this change could have huge socioeconomic consequences for people in rural France.
- The Chinese middle class has a national and international political power that is equal to, or even exceeds, the significance of the three New Silk Roads.
- In any foreign policy event that China is involved in, stability is the crucial factor for understanding China's strategy.
- The Communist Party and the middle class have become Siamese twins that are mutually dependent.
- We have summarized 33 principles that have guided the policies of the Chinese Communist Party since 2022 (the 20th Party Congress).
- China has a clear lead in the development of artificial intelligence. The Chinese middle class is being strengthened by this development.

Introduction

In this chapter, we will examine the following question: What has been the role of China's middle class in the development of AI?

The original version of the chapter has been revised. A correction to this chapter can be found at https://doi.org/10.1007/978-3-032-10138-9_6

J. Johannessen, *The AI Battleground Between the USA and China*, Global Power Shift, https://doi.org/10.1007/978-3-032-10138-9_3

The growth of the middle class in China results from a combination of three factors: education; increasing job complexity; and industrialization that has caused mass migration from rural to urban areas. The same thing happened in the West when industrialization took off in the mid-eighteenth century (Bowden 1965). In China, industrialization happened more than 200 years later than in Europe.

One of the consequences of the growth of the Chinese middle class is economic inequality. Similarly, there was an increase in economic inequality as industrialization gathered pace in England and elsewhere in Europe (Allen 2009; Mantoux 1961). In China, economic inequality is intergenerational, because it is mainly younger people who are getting the higher educational qualifications that are in demand in urban areas. There is also increasing economic inequality between cities and the countryside, because middle-class people, along with all their income, are concentrated in urban areas. A second consequence of the growth of the middle class in China is that higher education and higher incomes are leading people to adopt new values, ideas and expectations. A third consequence is that this burgeoning new class has become a lever for China's rise to power. This is because demand from 700 million people for consumer goods has major implications for economic growth. China's leaders consider this development to be positive. In their view, the existence of the middle class maintains a kind of dynamic stability that prevents China from slipping back into disorder and chaos (as happened previously under Mao Zedong). Mao's "Great Leap Forward" and "Cultural Revolution" are examples of policies that were socially devastating and brought about economic decline.

Narratives Related to the Rise of the Middle Class

Case Letter 4: The "Dual Circulation Development Paradigm"

China's economy is undergoing very large changes, which is due to many factors. One of these factors concerns the growing number of students in China completing their higher education; many of these students also study abroad at universities in England, France, the US, Australia, and other countries. It is also interesting to note that the majority of Chinese students return to their homeland after finishing their education abroad—more than 80%.[1] This increase in the number of graduates is also linked to an overall increase in China's high-tech competence. In addition, China's economic strategy has been undergoing change, which was evident when the country launched the "Dual Circulation Development Paradigm".

The Chinese economy is undergoing a gradual transformation—from being the main supplier of cheap consumer goods to Western consumers, to focusing more on domestic demand, as a result of the growing middle class. In other words, there is now a focus on the production of consumer goods for the middle class in China. The

[1] http://en.people.cn/n3/2022/0930/c90000-10153971.html.

fact that the Chinese middle class comprises approx. 700 million people means that there is a huge market for the sale of products and services, such as mobile phones, video games, cars, restaurant visits, branded clothes.

The economic transformation of China is also being facilitated by the development of the Belt and Road Initiative (BRI) (also called the New Silk Road), which was launched in 2013. This Initiative includes the involvement of 130 countries that have signed up to participate in numerous projects (2022). In addition, the Initiative also involves the participation of many organizations and institutions. The numerous projects, and cooperation with other countries, is transforming China's economy, as well as its diplomatic relations. In other words, the BRI is making a significant geo-economic and geopolitical impact.

The "Dual Circulation Development Paradigm", the New Silk Road and China's membership of the world's largest free trade area, the RCEP, are all contributing to the economic transformation of China. This transformation does not involve China closing the country to the outside world, but rather the opposite. In the transformation process, the Chinese middle class is being used as an economic lever to facilitate the transformation. The RCEP and the New Silk Road can be viewed as social mechanisms that are reinforcing the transformation, and opening up China to the outside world.

The transformation can be understood in at least two ways. Firstly, it can be seen as a reaction to the US's increasing sanctions policy. Secondly, it can be understood as a natural evolutionary development linked to economic theory, where a country's cheap labour over time becomes no longer a comparative advantage, and where the country in question moves up the value chain, in order to sustain growth and remain competitive. However, it can also be said that China's rapid transformation has been accelerated and reinforced by the US's sanctions policy, and the US's rhetorical war against China, involving human rights abuses, lack of democratic freedoms, accusations of committing genocide, and so on.

When a country faces such accusations without clear evidence, other than inexplicit 'stories', this can negatively affect the political climate, and the relations with the country making the accusations, in this case, the accusations made by the US against China. In addition, the Chinese leaders are no doubt aware of the human rights violations committed by the US throughout its history, as well as its numerous war crimes, atrocities and abuses. This list is a long one: the genocide of native Americans in the US; the large-scale CIA program involving the torture of prisoners in Guantanamo without trial over more than two decades (2001–2021); covert US involvement in the overthrow of democratically elected leaders in other countries, such as the CIA-backed coup in Chile on 11 September 1973, which removed the democratically elected president Salvador Allende; and the 1953 Iranian coup d'état, which was instigated by the US and the UK, and involved the overthrow of the democratically elected Prime Minister Mohammad Mosaddegh; the United States war against Vietnam over a period of almost 20 years (1956 to 1973), and involved the US military's use of napalm against civilians (and other abuses), and the many thousands of civilian deaths resulting from US bombing; the invasion of Iraq, on the basis of evidence that proved to be false, namely that Iraq had weapons of mass destruction. In January 2003, the UN's appointed weapons inspector, the Swede Hans Blix, said that Iraq had cooperated in all areas, but that his team had not found any indications that Iraq possessed any weapons of mass destruction. Nevertheless, the US launched its invasion of Iraq. Considering the above list of US war crimes, atrocities and abuses of power, and the US's accusation of China committing genocide against the Uighurs in Xinjiang province, it might be appropriate to say that: "it takes one to know one".

The escalation of the US military presence in the South China Sea, as well as the new military alliance AUKUS, reinforces China's need for a complete restructuring of its economy, diplomatic relations and a greater degree of focus on South East Asia through the RCEP agreement. A clear consequence is a change in the global value chains. Such a change in the global value chains could be an unintended consequence of the US strategy towards China. Kissinger (2012) was perhaps correct when he said that the US has no coherent long-term strategy towards China. If this is correct, the US operates more on the basis of pragmatically responding to the signals that emerge from the various international situations. In such a context, there is much to suggest that the US, even if it is militarily superior, will end up being outmanoeuvred, both psychologically and politically. One of the explanations for this assumption is the New Silk Road towards Europe and Africa, as well as the BRI projects in South America, and not least, the new support China is showing towards the ASEAN countries through its membership in the RCEP.

Case Letter 5: The Expectations of the Chinese Middle Class

Europe exports many types of goods to China to satisfy the demands of the Chinese middle class. For instance, both Denmark and France have large exports of pork to the Chinese market, while Germany has considerable exports of autos and machinery. In 2021, China became the largest export market for Germany, with the US in second place. In other words, the Chinese middle class have clear expectations that their kitchens are stocked with quality foods, while their garages are filled with 'luxury' cars. It is these expectations that form the basis for the import agreements between China and European countries.

In December 2021, a major agreement was signed between France and China on the import of pork to China. It is at this concrete level that the farmers in France and the middle class in China have common interests. For the French farmers, the certainty of the future sales of pork at a relatively fixed price is crucial for the economic success of their farms, and expectations concerning their own future sustainability. The Chinese have eaten pork for generations, so the Chinese middle class have a clear expectation that they will be able to continue this culinary tradition in the future. In other words, the relations between China and Europe regarding trade can often be reduced to a simple understanding. The agreement between China and France regarding the import of French pork is expected to be followed by similar agreements between

China and other European countries.[2] The deliveries of pork from Europe can now be transported by train along the New Silk Road, via countries in Central Asia and then into China; the transport takes approx. 5 days.[3] In this way, it is not difficult to understand that specific products, such as pork, can lead to trade agreements between China and the EU.

In other words, the trade between China and Europe is crucial for many reasons, and the New Silk Road plays an important role in facilitating the smooth and effective transport of goods exported by European farmers, and supplied to the Chinese middle class, so that they are able to maintain and improve their standard of living.

If we disregard the EU's tough rhetoric towards China, and the efforts of 'spoilers' including Lithuania, the overall situation of China-EU trade is relatively good. For Germany, the trade with China is absolutely crucial. In 2020, China became the largest trading partner for Germany in terms of exports of machinery.[4] The growing middle class in China represents a massive consumer market for German automakers, such as Volkswagen, Mercedes, and BMW. For instance, BMW are producing X5 luxury SUVs in China. In other words, the growth of the middle class in China is driving Chinese economic growth, and also driving economic growth in Germany, or more specifically, the growth of the German auto industry.

When we are attempting to understand and interpret the US sanctions policy and possible containment of China, we should keep in mind the picture we have drawn in this case letter. Put simply, the French, Danish, Italian, and Spanish pig farmers will have little interest in allowing diplomatic conflicts to negatively affect their important market in China. It is beyond any doubt that German industrial policy makers will shy away from being lured into implementing major sanctions against China, given that China is Germany's largest export market for autos. It is at this concrete and geo-economic level that one should orient oneself if one is to understand the limitations of the geopolitical situation that is developing between the US and China.

In 2021, Taiwan opened the "Taiwanese Representative Office in Lithuania", which was heavily opposed by China, which doesn't recognize Taiwan sovereignty. In other words, this was interpreted as a challenge to China's core interests. For a while, this negatively affected China-EU relations, because the Chinese Taiwan policy has been made clear to the West, at least since Kissinger's and Nixon's opening of China in the beginning of the 1970s. However, this was only 'a scratch in the paint', regarding the relationship between China and the EU, which was easily smoothed over, due to the fact that the trade in Danish pork and German autos is far more important than such a diplomatic 'hiccup', caused by the actions of the small EU state, Lithuania.

The same perspective can also be applied to Chinese human rights abuses, or, more specifically, the accusations made by Anthony Blinken, the US Secretary of State, that China has committed genocide against the Uighurs, in the Xinjiang province. However, this accusation made by the US is deemed far more serious than the dispute

---

[2] https://www.globaltimes.cn/page/202112/1241488.shtml.

[3] https://english.news.cn/20220129/cb9889de2b4e48189bc433e3941b5a1c/c.html.

[4] https://www.globaltimes.cn/page/202112/1241488.shtml.

between Lithuania and China following the diplomatic row over Taiwan; among other things, this is because Germany, and many of the EU countries, have a history of genocide. Nevertheless, we are of the opinion that in the context discussed here, geo-economic factors will influence geopolitical conditions more than the other way around. Put bluntly, for the EU negotiators, trade in French pork and German autos is more important than human rights abuses.

Case Letter 6: The Political Force of the Chinese Middle Class: Patriotic Mobilization

When 700 million middle class Chinese purchase goods that are produced domestically and abroad, it goes without saying that this will have very large economic consequences. The huge middle class Chinese consumer market has consequences for all the countries that export goods and services to China. In addition, the Chinese middle class represent a considerable political force in China. China is being transformed from "the world's factory" to becoming the largest trading partner for many countries. At the same time, China has moved up the value creation hierarchy. In plain language, this means it is now able to also produce high-tech goods and services.

The New Silk Road has had a major impact on the development of middle-class skills and income opportunities, as well as being a physical and digital safety valve for China's relationship with the United States, a country that feels threatened by the 'newcomer' on the economic, political and diplomatic scene. However, the growing Chinese middle class has also more indirect consequences for the United States and the West. The Chinese middle class represents the world's biggest multiplier effect for production, distribution and consumption. For instance, if the Chinese middle class were for some reason, such as patriotic reasons, to change their spending patterns to the disadvantage of goods produced in France, for example, then this change could have huge socioeconomic consequences for people in rural France. Put simply, if 700 million consumers demand certain products, or if they change their purchasing behaviour, this will have direct consequences for economic and political conditions far beyond China's borders. From this perspective, the Chinese middle class has a national and international political power that is equal to, or even exceeds, the significance of the three New Silk Roads.

In 2001, joined the World Trade Organization (WTO). In the more than twenty years since China has become a member of this organization, China's trade with the outside world has increChinaased considerably. It is also during this period that the Chinese middle class has increased towards 700 million.[5] If we imagine that the Chinese middle class increases its income and thus its demand, then it can well be imagined that both the global supply chain and the domestic value chain built up during the last 50–70 years will be changed and transformed. More precisely, if the demand from the Chinese middle class increases considerably, then the transport of

[5] https://www.globaltimes.cn/page/202111/1238203.shtml.

goods and services will to a greater extent go from west to east, and not vice versa, as was the case as long as China was 'the world's factory'. In this transformation, the value chain will change, so that the production of goods for the Chinese middle class will to a greater extent take place closer to the Chinese market; we have described such a development above, regarding the production of BMW X5 SUVs in China. It may be envisioned that there will be a similar transformation with regard to other types of goods that are produced today in countries such as Germany, France, Denmark, and the Netherlands. If such a development takes place, not only will the supply chain change its character, but also the value chain. For the Chinese middle class and many Chinese workers, this will have enormous significance. This will create new jobs in new factories in China, and Chinese workers, with increased skills, will be able to earn higher incomes.

There are many indications that this will become a real scenario, based on historical facts about industrial development in Europe; namely, one country becomes the supplier, while the other country becomes the market. This development changed for the various European nations throughout the history of industrialization. From a global perspective, it can also be imagined a similar development will occur in the relationship between Europe, the US and China. If the Chinese middle class increasingly impacts global production and distribution in a geo-economic context, then this will greatly increase their political power, to say the least. If the middle-class demand can be controlled by social mechanisms introduced by the Chinese government, then a situation would occur where the geo-economic factors affect the geopolitical realities.

The point in this context is that the Chinese middle class is turning into a 'one-headed troll'. This one-headed troll can decide on a 'grand strategy' in order to position itself in the best possible way in a geo-economic context. Important in this context is that the Chinese system, in contrast to the political systems in countries such as the US and the UK, and countries in the EU, can to a great extent determine the actions of the 'one-headed troll' in the global market. Of course, the Chinese middle class is not a homogenous unit that can consciously make decisions. On the other hand, the Communist Party leaders can motivate the Chinese middle class to behave in certain ways. The Chinese middle class, like many other social systems, can be motivated and mobilized by a so-called patriotic mobilization. We have seen this countless times throughout history. Patriotic sentiments that drive nationalist efforts in one direction or another. In other words a country's population can be motivated to defend a nation's values and interests.

Against this background, we can state with a great degree of certainty that the Chinese middle class has had, and will continue to have, a very large importance for China's rise to power..

A Brief Description of the Rise of the Middle Class

In China, there is a clear and proven relationship between education and the level of income (Knight et al. 2013: 142), which has been shown in many studies.[6] Correspondingly, there is also a relationship between income and middle class identification. Education and income also drive strong mobility. For instance, young Chinese people who complete their higher education often move to urban areas. They first move to urban areas during the course of their studies, and then later, they move there permanently when they have completed their studies. This development also sharpens the contrast between rural and urban areas, and between the generations. Today, more young people in China take higher education than in the past. However, it is not only the young people who complete their higher education who move from rural to urban areas, but also young people with a lower level of education who find jobs in factories, as well as people in other age groups who look for jobs in the cities.

The young people who find jobs in the factories in urban areas are not that well paid, and the working conditions are poor (Saich and Hu 2016; Rocca 2018). On the other hand, many of the young people who complete their higher education are able to find knowledge-based jobs in the cities; these are often high-tech jobs and jobs in innovation, where the work complexity is relatively high. Therefore, these jobs demand workers with a high level of education. These are middle-class workers, who expect a good salary. In recent years, the Chinese middle class has greatly increased in numbers, and today comprises approx. 700 million.[7]

While there is no standard definition of "middle class", it is common to define the middle class by income range. For instance, the Chinese government defines incomes ranging from $7250 to $62,500 (RMB 60,000 to 500,000) per year as middle class.[8]

The growth of the Chinese middle class has led to an increase in income inequality. This disparity is evident if we consider the income differences between those people with a high level of education and those with a lower level of education. Moreover, income inequality is evident between the older and younger generations (Knight et al. 2013: 142–197). In addition, there is also income inequality within the middle class.

The growth of the Chinese middle class has also resulted in an increase in the demand for goods and services. To meet this demand, the Chinese government has implemented a new economic strategy, the "Dual Circulation Development Paradigm", which has a special focus on domestic demand, as well as international

---

[6] https://www.researchgate.net/publication/340179911_The_relationship_between_education_income_economic_freedom_and_happiness.
https://blogs.worldbank.org/education/strong-link-between-education-and-earnings.
https://www.jstor.org/stable/1167162.

[7] https://www.globaltimes.cn/page/202111/1238203.shtml.
https://www.businessinsider.com/china-middle-class-starting-to-look-like-americas-2021-12?r=US&IR=T.
https://www.cnbc.com/2019/09/30/chinas-giant-middle-class-is-still-growing-and-companies-want-in.html.

[8] https://chinapower.csis.org/china-middle-class/.

trade. Amongst other things, this new economic strategy aims to reduce the dependence of the Chinese economy on export-driven growth, and thus reduce its dependence on the US and European markets. With its new values, ideas and expectations, the middle class therefore ensures a dynamic stability in the Chinese economy.

Roughly speaking, the historical development of education in China, and the growth of the middle class, can be described as a 'seven-stage rocket':

1. The first stage was the goal of abolishing illiteracy. This can be dated to the period from 1949 to 1952. During this period, there was an increase from 24 to 50 million children enrolled in primary schools (Hannum 1999: 193–211).
2. The second stage was linked to the first five-year plan (1953–1957). The aim was rapid industrialization; consequently, there was an increased focus on training and educating industrial workers for specific industrial skills (Løfstedt 1980).
3. The third stage, "The Great Leap Forward" was in reality a giant step backward, which instead of stimulating the country's economy, resulted in mass starvation and famine. In addition, education suffered greatly (Løfstedt 1980: 102).
4. The fourth stage, "the Cultural Revolution" (1966–1976), was, if anything, even worse than the third stage. It was during this period that "the Gang of Four" came to prominence. During the Cultural Revolution, intellectuals came under strict government control, and many were sent out into the countryside to do hard agricultural work, while many schools and universities were closed, resulting in a loss of expertise and competence amongst the general population (Thøgersen 1990).
5. The fifth stage started in 1986 when the Law on Nine-Year Compulsory Education took effect, which established requirements for universal education and guaranteed school-age children the right to receive at least nine years of education (Hannum et al. 2008: 215–249).
6. The sixth stage started around the mid-1990s. Private foreign investors were now allowed to invest in education in China. This led to many Chinese students receiving parts of their education at departments of western universities located in China, and parts of their education in countries such as England and the United States. Hundreds of thousands of Chinese students from this time onward studied abroad, and returned to China with new values, ideas and expectations. Many of these graduates also became entrepreneurs in China (Li 2021).
7. The seventh stage is an extension of the sixth stage, but is included here as a separate stage, because from the 2000s onward there was a stronger emphasis on the need for high-tech education in order to be able to compete with the US and promote the development of technological innovations (Johannessen 2021a). The Chinese authorities also increased subsidies for education in the rural parts of China during this period (Hannum et al. 2008).

Based on the above narratives and description, we have developed a conceptual model for the rise of the Chinese middle class (Fig 3.1).

In the following, we will elaborate on the five elements in the above model.

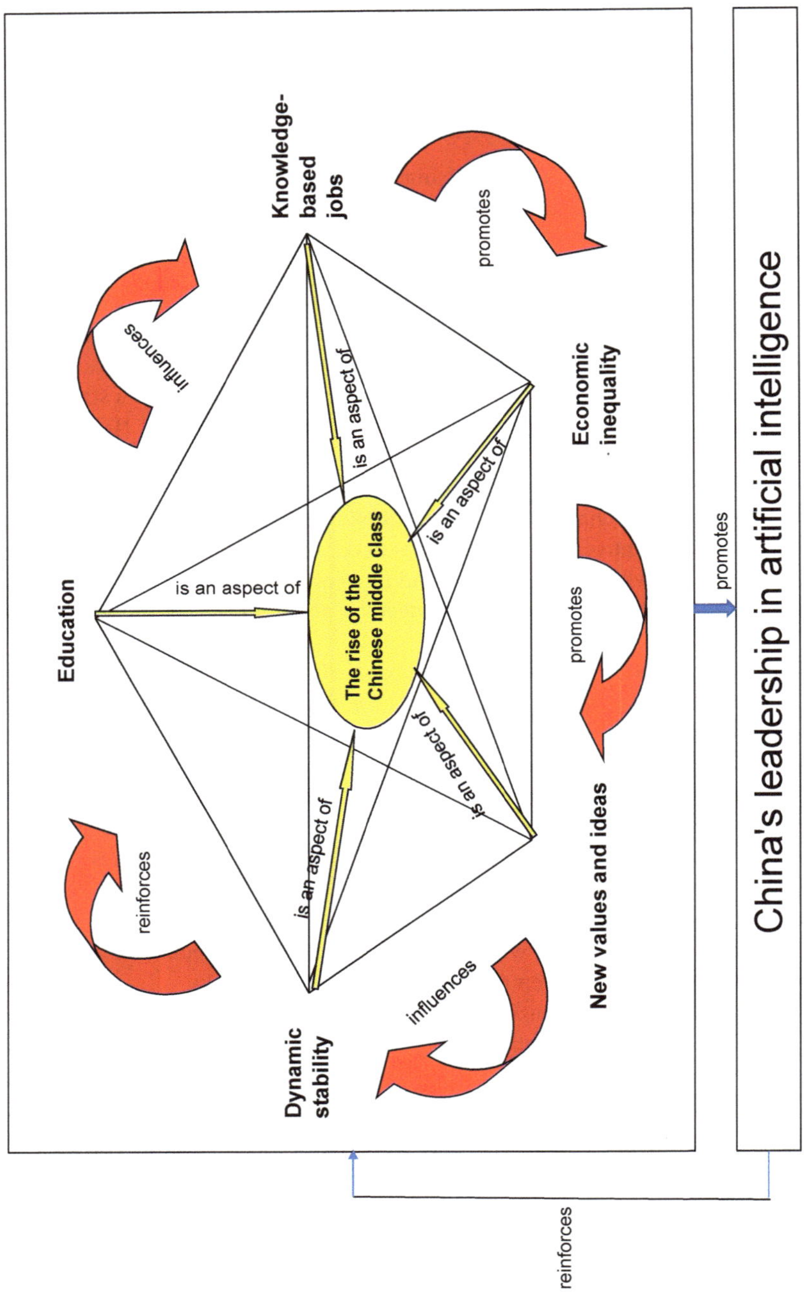

Fig. 3.1 The rise of the Chinese middle class: a conceptual model

Education

The growth of the Chinese middle class is directly related to China's 'education explosion'. In 2022, 11.93 million students took China's college entrance exam, also known as "gaokao".[9] In 2021, more than ten million took this exam. Of these, it can be assumed that approx. four million will complete a master's degree.[10] One can of course debate whether it is necessary that so many students should have a master's degree. However, a college education in China, as in many other countries, has the potential to promote social mobility, especially up into the middle class. In the United States, the middle class has begun to show a different trend, as it is breaking into upper and lower sub-categories, where the latter sub-category isn't doing so well, while the former sub-category is thriving (Reves 2018). This trend is not yet evident in China (Li 2021; Miao 2019), where there is still a clear relationship between college education and upward social mobility. This relationship has to some extent broken down in the West (Ainley 2014, 2016).

Apart from the large increase in the number of college graduates, Chinese universities are also achieving their highest ever global rankings.[11] In the 2022 edition of the 'Times Higher Education World University Rankings', Tsinghua University and Peking University jointly achieved the Chinese mainland's highest-ever ranking position, tying for 16th place. Oxford University in England retained top spot for the sixth consecutive year. A record number of 10 universities from the Chinese mainland were in the top 200.[12] In addition to this development, Chinese researchers are submitting more international articles than researchers in other countries, including the US. If there is a connection between the number of research articles published and the number of patents registered, then this development suggests that China's time as a 'copycat' is over, and that, in the near future, China will be able to lead the way in the development of innovation and new patents. This development will very probably strengthen the growth and prosperity of the Chinese middle class.

There is a close relationship between higher education, innovativeness and economic growth (Frey 2019, 2020; Ford 2016, 2021). In order for China to continue to increase its economic growth, increase its investments in the many Belt and Road projects, export more high-tech goods, and strengthen its domestic demand, then continued growth of the Chinese middle class is crucial.

Investment in human capital is necessary if China is to increase its economic growth.[13] It is especially the investment in the development of science, technology, engineering and mathematics (STEM) competences that will facilitate this growth, and enable China to achieve its economic goals. It is against this background that the increase in the number of Chinese graduates, and the increase in the quality of

---

[9] https://english.news.cn/20220531/df1fbb5dafc04684bae92f01793dd50c/c.html.

[10] https://global.chinadaily.com.cn/a/202012/26/WS5fe68b11a31024ad0ba9eab5_1.html.

[11] https://www.chinadaily.com.cn/a/202109/02/WS6130250fa310efa1bd66cc1d.html.

[12] Ibid.

[13] https://learningportal.iiep.unesco.org/en/library/exploring-stem-competences-for-the-21st-century.

Chinese higher education, is of relevance. On the one hand, the investment in human capital will lead to the continued growth of the Chinese middle class. On the other hand, it will also lead to China being in a completely different position regarding its competitiveness vis-à-vis the United States. It can be assumed that the investments China has made, and is still making, within the educational sector, will have a positive impact on the global competition with the US. Xi Jinping, the leader of the Chinese Communist Party, has clearly stated that "talent is a strategic resource to achieve national revitalization and win the initiative in international competition".[14]

The above description has shown that the development of education and human capital is decisive for the development of the Chinese middle class and its rise to power. On the other hand, the growth of the Chinese middle class also has a potential Achilles heel, regarding the resulting economic inequality in China. Relevant in this context is how the Chinese leaders will address this issue in the future. We will focus on this theme in the next section.

Economic Inequality

With the shift to the open-door policy, Deng Xiaoping indicated that it was acceptable for some people and regions to become wealthy before others (Vogel 2011). In today's China, this has become a reality. Firstly, there is a wealth gap between rural and urban areas, where urban workers have higher earnings than rural workers (Hong 2021). Secondly, there is a wealth gap between those with higher education and those with only primary and secondary education (Jain 2021). Thirdly, many entrepreneurs have become rich in China by starting up successful companies (Li 2021). Fourthly, China has eradicated extreme poverty around 2019, according to *The Economist*.[15] One of the final places declared poverty-free is Ziyun, a county in the south-western province of Guizhou. The eradication of poverty has been possible due to economic growth.

In order to get rid of extreme poverty in rural areas, in addition to stimulating rural economic growth, several political programs have been initiated. One of these programs is the "New Socialist Countryside" (Chuliang and Sicular 2013: 197). According to Chuliang and Sicular (2013), the role of the authorities in the fight against poverty has been investment in infrastructure, minimum wage policy for farm workers, reduction of taxes on farmers' production, a medical cooperative system for the countryside, as well as compulsory nine-year education. In addition, the authorities have eased restrictions on geographical mobility and improved working and living conditions for rural immigrants to urban areas.

In 2021, the United Nations Secretary-General Antonio Guterres congratulated China on its success in eliminating extreme poverty in rural areas. In a letter to President Xi Jinping, he wrote that "It shows the importance of political commitment

---

[14] https://www.csis.org/analysis/how-chinas-human-capital-impacts-its-national-competitiveness.

[15] https://www.economist.com/china/2021/01/02/extreme-poverty-is-history-in-china-officials-say.

at all levels of government and policy stability to improve the conditions of the poorest and most vulnerable. It also underscores the opportunity of development models that are innovation-driven, green, open and which work to deliver for all".[16]

If we examine the development of Chinese industrialization, we can observe a historical process or historical regularity, which can also be observed in the industrial development of other countries throughout economic history. More specifically, when a country is transformed from an agrarian into an industrial society, this results in economic growth and an increase in prosperity, but also an increase in economic inequality. As mentioned above, in order to achieve economic growth in China, it was viewed as being necessary for some classes of people and regions to become wealthy before others. Furthermore, industrialization in China and in the Northern European countries has shown that government intervention is necessary in order to secure the part of the population that has been "left behind" in the industrialization process, in order to lessen the development of greater economic equality.

Despite government interventions to reduce economic inequality, there are still many underlying tensions that exist between urban and rural areas (Hong 2021). Many of these tensions and possible conflicts are the result of the rapid speed of urbanization and industrialization (Smith 2021). This rapid industrialization has not been a win–win situation for both the cities and the countryside, which is often claimed by the Chinese leaders (Smith 2021: 3). It is often the case that young people go from rural to urban areas in the quest of work, and in order to complete their studies within higher education. These young people almost never return to the village they grew up in. This has resulted in an ageing population in rural areas compared to urban areas. Those who remain in the countryside are also economically "left behind", even though the state has implemented various programs in rural areas to reduce the largest negative effects of rapid industrialization and urbanization.

New Values and Ideas

The development of new values and ideas in China can largely be related to the growth of the middle class in general, and the entrepreneurial spirit in particular. In other words, this concerns creativity, which can unleash the potential for idea generation, and the development of innovations. During the first period of economic growth in China, the Chinese government largely ignored workers' rights and climate issues. During the same period, the Chinese government largely neglected the growing economic inequality, as it was believed economic growth was more important, so that the government would be able to be in a position to tackle the various social, economic and environmental challenges. As economic growth took off, and reached double digits, Chinese self-confidence also grew. Sustainability, climate, environment, labour rights, and economic inequality became increasingly important to the Chinese leaders (Shi et al. 2013; Fan et al. 2009).

[16] https://global.chinadaily.com.cn/a/202103/10/WS6048011ca31024ad0baae0bd.html.

The values that accompany Chinese entrepreneurship, both in relation to private entrepreneurs and the entrepreneurial state, from the end of the 1970s until today, can be listed as follows:

1. Willingness to take risks in order to increase future rewards
2. Focus on innovation
3. Emphasis on rapid growth
4. Emphasis on technology, as a mechanism for economic expansion
5. Networking that facilitates financial support
6. Thinking big, working small
7. A new socialist rhetoric
8. Focusing on winning industries, rather than 'winners' within these industries
9. Increased focus on the importance of financial capital and the banks' new role in entrepreneurial development
10. A focus on state funding, and the state as a guarantor of profit in designated areas of technology.

In order to create economic growth and change the values, ideas and expectations that had been shaped and created by Mao Zedong's ideological communism, and the Gang of Four's "Cultural Revolution", the new leaders after Mao Zedong needed to prioritize the growth of a 'new' social class that could understand the benefits of economic growth, that is, the middle class. In this context, the Chinese government had to promote the idea that it was acceptable for some people, social classes and regions to become wealthy before others. The Chinese leaders also needed to promote the idea that developing new businesses was something that would benefit society as a whole. In other words, in order to promote these ideas, develop new businesses, and promote economic growth, the Chinese leaders needed to prioritize the interests of the growing middle class.

The values and expectations of the middle class coincided with the Chinese leaders' desire to strengthen China's global position, which would act as a safeguard for avoiding the humiliations of the past, or more specifically, "the Century of Humiliation", when China was defeated, occupied and oppressed by numerous foreign powers. The period began with the First Opium War (1839–1842), and ended in 1949 with the victory of the People's Republic of China in the Chinese Civil War. Amongst other things, 12 to 14 million lost their lives during the Second Sino-Japanese War (1937–1945).[17] In other words, the "Century of Humiliation" is something the Chinese leaders do not want to return to in the future, and which they will seek to avoid at all costs.

As mentioned above, in order to create economic growth, the Chinese leaders had to create new values that would motivate people. It was against this background that the middle class became an important instrument for the new political leaders in Beijing. In order for this class to be motivated to make the extra effort needed to promote the Chinese economy, the Chinese leadership needed to promote completely new values, expectations and norms, which we have listed in the above ten points.

---

[17] https://www.history.com/news/china-role-world-war-ii-allies.

In retrospect, the rapid sustained expansion of China's economic growth, since the end of the 1970s, can be characterized as a huge economic success. However, this growth has also created new challenges and problems, such as the growing economic inequality. Nevertheless, the economic growth has also resulted in an eradication of extreme poverty. Without the growth of the middle class, it is difficult to imagine how China could have managed to become the world's second largest economy.

An Analysis of the Rise of the Chinese Middle Class

China's transition from a planned economy to a market economy has taken roughly forty years. However, the Chinese market economy is regulated by the state that sets the conditions for the freedom of investment of capital. Amongst other things, this regulation of the economy has been characterized by the creation of specialized economic zones (SEZs) in the 1980s; the SEZs granted free market-oriented economic policies. This economic strategy allowed the government to experiment with various economic policies, as it was shown that the SEZs made significant contributions to China's economic growth in terms of GDP. Today, it might be said that the government is focusing on realizing "the Chinese Dream", that is, to increase general prosperity by raising everyone in China up to a middle-class income through collective effort (Brown 2018, 2019).

The Chinese Communist Party established the creation of the SEZs in December 1978. This successful economic strategy contributed to the growth of the middle class which today numbers approx. 700 million, measured by Chinese standards.[18] Incomes for the middle class vary widely, which is also the case regarding the middle class in the West.[19] As mentioned above, the extreme economic growth from the 1980s up until the 2020s, not only brought prosperity to a growing middle class, but also resulted in increased economic inequality (Shi et al. 2013: 1; Xinyu and Zukosky 2022).

The economic inequality can be expressed along three axes:

1. The first axis is centre-periphery: The incomes are higher in urban areas than in rural areas (Saich and Hu 2016).
2. The second axis is education: There is a wealth gap between those with higher education, especially those with a high-tech education, and those with only primary and secondary education.
3. The third axis is expressed by the relationship between the young and old generations (Hong 2021): There is a wealth gap between the old and young generations, especially in relation to those young people that have been able to complete a college education in China or abroad. In most cases, these young graduates can expect to earn higher incomes than their parents.

[18] https://www.statista.com/statistics/875874/middle-class-population-in-china/.

[19] https://factsanddetails.com/china/cat11/sub70/item156.html.

The three axes can be generalized as follows: the middle class is largely constituted by young people with higher education who live in urban areas (although there are also economic inequalities in the urban areas). On the other hand, the migration of young people from the rural to the urban areas has resulted in an ageing population in the rural areas; many within this ageing population have low incomes, although extreme poverty was eradicated in China by 2020, according to a World Bank report.[20]

As mentioned above, the economic growth in China has led to the growth of the middle class, and an eradication of extreme poverty. In order to meet the consumer demand of the growing middle class, the Chinese government implemented a new economic strategy in 2021, the "Dual Circulation Development Paradigm", which aims to reorient the country's economy by focusing more on domestic consumption, as well as on international trade. The markets for China's trade in the past have largely been the US and Europe. However, when the US and European countries began to impose sanctions on Chinese technology companies, and prevent Chinese companies from competing fairly in the US and European markets, China has begun to access other markets (Mahbubani 2020; Brown 2019). In particular, this concerns markets along the New Silk Road, and markets within the RCEP, the world's largest free trade area. In addition, China has strengthened and expanded its relations with countries in Central Asia, as well as strengthened its relations within the SCO (Shanghai Cooperation Organization). The emphasis on relations with the Central Asian countries in the SCO was shown by the fact that the first two countries Xi Jinping visited after the Covid-19 pandemic were Kazakhstan and Uzbekistan.

One of the consequences of the economic growth in China is that the Chinese middle class functions as an economic lever, boosting domestic consumption, and thus also driving domestic production and distribution of goods and services. Another consequence is that the US and European markets are now given less focus, while there is an increased focus on other markets in relation to the SCO and RCEP.

The Economic Lever: A Bipolar World Is Developing

China has participated in two waves of globalization. The first wave transformed the country into an export-driven economic locomotive that was propelled by cheap labour and low taxes on invested capital. During this period, China laid the foundation for an educational revolution, especially higher education, which later formed the basis for the development and growth of the middle class.

During the second wave of globalization, China was able to reap the benefits of its education revolution that was launched during the first wave. In addition, the Chinese government implemented the Belt and Road Initiative (BRI) in 2013, also called the New Silk Road. This enabled China to boost its economy by utilizing high-skilled low-cost labour. The New Silk Road strengthened China's economic and diplomatic relations with around 130 BRI countries. It was also during the second wave of

[20] https://global.chinadaily.com.cn/a/202104/12/WS60738cc0a31024ad0bab4c0c.html.

globalization that China's export industry began to focus on high-tech production, and not only on the export of cheap consumer goods to the West. In other words, during this period, although China was still the main supplier of cheap consumer goods to Western consumers, it was also producing high-tech goods that were far cheaper than similar goods produced in Western countries. The high-tech exports, and the stated intentions of the Chinese leaders that China aimed to become the world leader in artificial intelligence, heightened the tensions between China and the United States.

It might be said that the world today is moving towards a period of de-globalization and decoupling, with weakened interdependence between countries, such as the weakened economic ties between the US and China. It may also be said that this trend has been under development as far back as 2011, when Hillary Clinton, the former Secretary of State, published the article, "America's Pacific Century" in *Foreign Policy*. In other words, the Obama administration thus laid the ideological foundation for an assertive US foreign policy, which later materialized into specific actions, when President Trump launched a trade war against China. The decoupling with China was also evident during the Biden administration which continued the trade war, in addition to the US government's rhetoric against China, regarding human rights abuses in the Xinjiang province. In other words, de-globalization and decoupling are increasingly leading to a new bipolar world order, in which the two poles are the US and China. In the bipolar world one can use the term distinct but linked. During the Cold War there were political and military tensions between two blocs of nations. Although the bipolar world is something different from the Cold War, we can also see two blocs or alliances emerging in the bipolar world. One alliance is being led by the United States, while the other alliance is being led by China.

If might be said that a shift to de-globalization began in 2022, when Russia invaded Ukraine. What then followed was a development in the West that no one could have predicted. The EU implemented sanctions against Russia. Although NATO did not become actively involved on the ground, most NATO countries supplied Ukraine with weapons for defence against the Russian invasion. China remained passive and did not participate actively by shipping arms, but chose to abstain rather than vote in the United Nations Security Council, concerning a resolution condemning Russia's actions in Ukraine. However, at the SCO Council in September 2022, China and India expressed their concern over the Russia-Ukraine war.[21]

Regardless of which perspective one adopts, it seems that it was Russia's invasion of Ukraine that marked the end of globalization. A new era is developing, characterized by de-globalization, de-coupling and a development towards a bipolar world. Although this development may be traced back many years, a historical demarcation line can possibly be set to February, 2022, when Russia invaded Ukraine.

---

[21] https://www.fmprc.gov.cn/eng/zxxx_662805/202209/t20220916_10767162.html.

The "Dual Circulation Development Paradigm"

The "Dual Circulation Development Paradigm", the New Silk Road, the RCEP free trade area, the SCO (parts of Central Asia, Iran and Russia), as well as a growing Chinese middle class (700 million) provide the Chinese government with great flexibility regarding economic strategies.

The "Dual Circulation Development Paradigm" is a flexible economic strategy that enables China to expand domestic demand, focus on the domestic market, reduce dependence on foreign markets, while at the same time remaining open to the outside world. In practice, this new economic strategy can be implemented due to the growth of the Chinese middle class which provides a large domestic market that is able in part to replace the decline in exports to the US and Europe. More specifically, the US barred the Chinese telecom giant, Huawei, from operating in its 5G networks. The argument given by the US was that Huawei has strong relations with the Chinese military system, the People's Liberation Army (PLA), and could therefore pose a security risk. It is difficult to counter such an argument, because Huawei was originally closely related to the PLA, as it was a former deputy director of the PLA who founded Huawei. It is also true that the Central Military Commission (CMC) is chaired by the General Secretary of the Chinese Communist Party. However, similar arguments could be made regarding the American technology companies, even if there are no direct links between the companies and the US government. The American president can at any time, especially during a national crisis, issue an order that the technology companies must primarily serve the interests of the United States. The point in this context is that the US, through it sanctions against Huawei and other Chinese telecommunications companies, blocked the companies from tendering for contracts in the US, as well as in several European countries. However, Huawei and other Chinese companies compensated for the loss of these markets by using two paths of investment. One path focuses on further investment in the countries along the New Silk Road. The other path of investment focuses on the domestic market and the growing consumer demand fuelled by a growing middle class.

This example is just one of many where Chinese domestic demand outweighs the loss of foreign markets. The "Dual Circulation Development Paradigm" focuses specifically on this re-orientation of the economy towards the domestic market from 2021 onward.[22] Concretely, this increased domestic demand is evident in Haikou, the capital of Hainan province in southern China. In Haikou, efforts are being made to increase domestic demand in several areas, such as public services, particularly in education, health and elderly care.[23] It is emphasized by several regional authorities in China that it is the demand for goods and services that is China's biggest economic challenge going forward. This is why the Chinese leaders are re-orienting the economy more towards the domestic market, where they have control over both supply and demand, which is not the case with export-driven economic growth.

---

[22] https://global.chinadaily.com.cn/a/202012/28/WS5fe90e99a31024ad0ba9ec90.html.

[23] Ibid.

We can suggest the following proposition based on this global economic development: The greater the degree of sanctions and containment that China is subjected to, the more emphasis will be placed on increasing domestic middle-class demand.

In this way, the Chinese middle class plays an increasing role in China's rise to power. The relationship that exists between sanctions and perceived containment on the one hand, and the development of the middle class and its importance for the Chinese economy on the other hand, is of interest. The following assumption may be worth noting. The Chinese middle class, which also has strong ties to the Chinese Communist Party, is objectively interested in a policy from the US and the West, where sanctions and containment are further accelerated. The rationale is that the middle class will then receive increased attention and focus. This will improve their own economic and political position. In its consequences, this assumption can lead to the fact that it is not only the United States that is interested in heightened tensions between China and the United States. The Chinese middle class may also be interested in growing tensions and possible conflict with the United States. If this argument is correct, then we will see a Chinese middle class arguing for a tension-increasing relationship with the United States.

The Younger Generation, the Middle Class, and Expectations

In China, the young adults who complete their higher education have expectations of finding well-paid jobs, so they can establish themselves in the middle class. Many Chinese students study abroad in countries such as the US, England, France, Germany, Japan, and so on. When these students return to China they often have expectations regarding prosperous future economic prospects. It has been shown that it is largely the students who have studied abroad that use their skills and competences to create new businesses in China (Li 2021; Miao 2019).

The Chinese Communist Party is using the middle class as an economic lever to tackle the US sanctions policy, and to boost domestic demand. Moreover, many of the leaders in the Chinese Communist Party come from middle-class families. Historically, social democracy in Europe was well-grounded in the working class. On the other hand, it was the peasants who played a leading role in the Chinese Revolution, while later the middle class became important for social stability and economic progress. The deindustrialization in Europe, and the fall in the numbers of industrial workers, led to a decline of the socialist parties, while the middle class strengthened its political position. In China, on the other hand, the Communist Party has utilized the growing middle class to consolidate its position of power. In this way, the middle class has become the backbone of the Chinese Communist Party, and it is the middle class who will set the course for most policy decisions in the future.

Wealth in China has not been created by the middle class, but it is the middle class that have mainly consumed the wealth of the export-driven growth that has been dependent on the production of the Chinese working class. However, automation processes in the global economy, and also in China, has led to job losses for industrial workers in certain sectors, such as manufacturing. Consequently, the traditional working class has been reduced, while the middle class has grown in numbers. In the future, it is the expectations of the middle class that the Chinese Communist Party will aim to fulfil. As long as the middle class has its expectations met, it will be very probable that the Chinese Communist Party will be secure. On the other hand, if an economic downturn were to negatively affect the expectations, wishes and dreams of the middle class, then the seven hundred million of the middle class could create political insecurity and threaten the stability of the entire political system. This is of course something the leaders of the Communist Party are aware of. Therefore, at all costs, the Communist Party will aim to ensure that the expectations of the middle class are met, especially the economic expectations. The overall economic strategy of the Chinese leaders for this to happen is to ensure stability in all areas, and at all levels, of society.

It is this stabilization factor that can be used to understand most of the foreign policy decisions of the Chinese leadership. If we take the example of Russia's war against Ukraine, we saw that the Chinese leaders tried to balance their relationship to the various countries in order to avoid coming into conflict with Europe, and especially the EU, so that its trade relations would not be negatively affected. In the same way, China also tried to balance its relationship with Russia, in order to secure supplies of oil and gas that the European countries had cut themselves off from with their sanctions policies. In any foreign policy event that China is involved in, stability is the crucial factor for understanding China's strategy. Thus, the Chinese leaders will not allow China's power and growing economic and military strength to jeopardize the overall principle of stability. It is possible that a situation may arise in the future where stability is no longer the overall strategy for the Chinese leaders. The point, however, is that if and when this time comes, it will be a reaction to the fact that the political situation in China has radically changed. In such a situation where stability is no longer the overall strategy, the Chinese political system will differ from today's political system. As long as the Chinese Communist Party is dominant within the political system, and the Chinese middle class is a decisive factor when the country's leaders determine policy, stability at the economic level will also form the backdrop for any domestic and foreign policies. On this basis, we can say that the middle class not only maintains China's rise to power, but is also crucial for maintaining the political system in China. Paradoxically, the Communist Party and the middle class have become Siamese twins that are mutually dependent. The Communist Party of China and the Chinese middle class have developed into an economic-political ecosystem where they interact together, and nourish each other.

Paradoxically, communist ideology perceives the bourgeoisie (the middle class) as the enemy of the proletariat. However, historical developments in China have turned this adversarial relationship into one of mutual dependence, where the survival of one appears to strengthen and depend on the survival of the other. What used to be ideological competitors have, through distinctive historical developments, become interdependent in an ecosystem.

Theoretical Reflections on the Rise of the Middle Class

There are two main factors that seem to be driving the growth of the Chinese middle class. One factor is the level of education. This applies both to the general education of the population, but also to the level and structure of education. The second factor is the degree of knowledge-based jobs that are being created. These two factors do not have a linear relationship to each other, but a systemic one. This means in practice that the more education increases in breadth and depth, the more knowledge-based jobs will become available. On the other hand, an increasing number of well-paid and meaningful knowledge-based jobs will lead to more people taking a higher education.[24] Against this background, the greater the degree of breadth and depth in China's education system, and the more knowledge-based jobs that are available, the greater the likelihood of the rise of the middle class.

Those students who complete their higher education will thus be able to look forward to finding well-paid jobs in the urban areas. On the other hand, those people without higher education will remain in a worse economic position in both rural and urban areas. In the recent past, there has been a mass migration in China from rural to urban areas, where there have been more and better job opportunities in factories; this rural–urban migration will most probably continue into the future. The growth of the middle class has been a creative development, where new jobs have been created, but also a destructive development where many jobs have been eliminated. The destructive development can be related to the migration to urban areas, because many villages in the rural areas have become so-called 'ghost villages', where only the old, and those who did not make the transition to jobs in the cities, remain (Knight et al. 2013; Hong 2021). On the other hand, from a slightly longer perspective, the development of industry in the urban areas has promoted productivity and economic growth in China, which benefits the entire population. For instance, according to a report from the World Bank in 2020, extreme poverty has been eradicated in China.

Based on what has been described above, it can be said that the growth of the Chinese middle class has in it both destructive and creative elements. This is not unlike Schumpeter's 'creative destruction', where innovations in manufacturing increase productivity, while destroying old methods of production.[25]

Throughout European and American history, the middle class has supported the economic policies that have been pursued, and at the same time shared in the increasing prosperity that productivity growth has led to. However, around the 1980s, this development was reversed for the middle class in the West, especially in the US (Reves 2018). In China's case, it is still the middle class that the political leaders focus on in order to promote both dynamism in the economy, and social stability. The

---

[24] Saich and Hu (2016), Rocca (2018), Miao (2019), Hong (2021), Li (2021), Hannum (1999), Hannum et al. (2008), Jain (2021), Knight et al. (2013), Liu (2016, 2021), Løfstedt (1980), Ning (2016), Ryan (2019), and Thøgersen (1990).

[25] Andersen (2009), Schumpeter (1951, 1954, 1989, 2010), Elliott (1980), McGraw (2007), Rahim (2009), Reinert and Reinert (2010), and Rosenberg (2000).

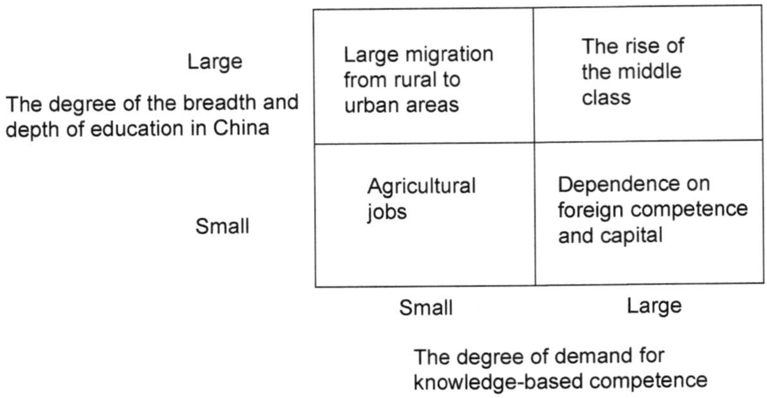

Fig. 3.2 The rise of the Chinese middle class: A typology

middle class is utilized as a social mechanism for maintaining this dynamic stability that political leaders in China use to promote economic growth.

Chinese middle-class consumers are demanding an increasingly larger share of Chinese production. This is reflected in the production of Chinese autos. These autos are bought by Chinese consumers, but also exported to the West, such as Europe. In the past, China's production focused on cheap goods produced by low-cost labour. However, today, the Chinese auto industry produces and exports high-tech autos that can compete with high-tech autos in the West. In other words, China is not only producing high-tech mobile phones, such as Huawei, but is now also producing high-tech products in other sectors.

It can be said that the well-being and prosperity of the middle class is largely what influences the policies of the Chinese leaders, including foreign policy. If the 700 million middle class Chinese discover that their expectations are not met, then this could quickly negatively affect the Chinese Communist Party, and its current leaders. It therefore seems reasonable to assume that Chinese foreign policy in the future will be related to the expectations of the middle class.

Based on the above narratives, description, and theoretical reflections, we have developed a typology that shows the important drivers for the rise of the Chinese middle class (Fig. 3.2).

In the following, we will elaborate on each of the four cells in the typology.

Migration

With regard to migration, we can extract the following proposition from the above typology: The greater the breadth and depth of the Chinese education system, and the fewer jobs there are for knowledge workers in the rural areas, the greater the likelihood that there will be a large migration from rural to urban areas. This proposition is also supported by, Hong (2021), Smith (2021), and Saich and Hu (2016). Moreover, the migration from rural to urban areas is also fuelled by the increased demand for factory workers, and the fall in demand for agricultural workers.

During the historical period of industrialization in the West, migration from rural to urban areas radically impacted family structures. Similarly, the rural–urban migration in China, in recent decades, has also radically changed family structures, according to Hong (2021: 177–207). Hong writes about the way in which extended families in rural areas are torn apart by the seismic changes in Chinese society, brought about by the changing tectonic plates in the Chinese economy. She writes about the rural village she grew up in, in the Henan Province. What she found was a village hollowed-out by emigration and social and cultural neglect. Henan, a central province in inland China, has an essentially agricultural economy. The word 'henan' literally means 'south of the (Yellow) River'. For a long time, Henan was the most populous province in China. Due to the large migrations from the interior to the industrial areas in the coastal regions, Henan became a less populous province around the 2000s. Hong's social-anthropological account is of particular interest, because her description of her own family and the village she grew up in, and the changes that had taken place, mirrors the lives of many other people in other regions in China, regarding how the great rural-to-urban migration has twisted the structures of families. As in the West, historically speaking, the rural–urban migration was mainly due to the demand for labour in the factories in the urban areas. Around the 2000s, higher education in China was greatly expanded. Many of the children of the first great wave of immigration to urban areas were able to complete higher education, which enabled them to find jobs in the new 'knowledge factories'. It is this gradual transition from an industrial to a knowledge-based society which has also occurred in the West. Of course, the difference here is the time perspective. The first period of industrialization which occurred in Britain started around 1750. Other northern European countries and the United States also went through a process of industrialization in the following decades. On the other hand, the period of major economic growth in China, associated with industrialization, began around 1980. In other words, this represents roughly a 150–200-year gap between the industrialization of the West and the industrialization of China. This time gap is of great importance if we are to understand and explain the industrialization of China and the internal migration. When China started to industrialize, technology in the West had already been developed, and capital had been accumulated. On the other hand, when industrialization in the West took off, technology was still being developed, and capital had not been accumulated to the same extent. The technology and capital available in the West meant that China could rapidly develop its economy if it opened up to foreign investment, which occurred around the end of the 1970s. However, up until 1976, there was great resistance in China to the influx of capital from the West. In summary, rapid Chinese industrialization, and the large migration from rural to urban areas, began around the 1980s, and continued into the 2000s.

In the same way as the Industrial Revolution that began in Great Britain in the 1750s, the industrialization of China was fuelled by the migration of workers from rural to urban areas. These workers were able to find jobs in the newly-built factories.

These factories were characterized by harsh conditions and there was little protection of workers' rights, especially as independent unions were illegal. The Chinese leaders argued that there was no need for independent unions as the Communist Party represented the workers, so any organization of the workers was tightly controlled by the government, and aligned with the Communist Party. However, 'only the wearer knows where the shoe pinches'; in other words, the representatives of the government did not understand the struggles or suffering of the workers, and were unable to provide the necessary help to improve the working conditions in the factories. Workers who for one reason or another lost their jobs also lost the right to live in the city. This overhanging threat also meant that there was little opposition to the state-run trade unions. Those workers who opposed the unions were often fired and then sent home in shame to the village they came from, or they had to hide in the big cities and become part of the reserve army of labour, working in jobs that were even more poorly paid than farm jobs.

The workers who toiled under poor working conditions in the factories had expectations that their children would have a better life than what they had had. This development also has its parallel in the history of industrialization in the West, where expectations of a better life eventually materialized for future generations. In China, this process of expectations of a better life for one's children can be observed in the transition from industrial factories to 'knowledge factories'. It is also the knowledge factories that are strengthening the Chinese middle class.

Agricultural Jobs

With regard to agricultural jobs, we can extract the following proposition from the above typology: the less depth and breadth there is in the Chinese education system, and the fewer knowledge-based jobs that are available, the greater will be the probability that many jobs will be within the agricultural sector.

Before the reforms of 1978, China was predominantly a rural society (Smith 2021: 3–5). The Chinese Communist Party held clear ideas that industrialization and urbanization in China, as elsewhere in the world, would follow objective social processes, almost approximating social laws (Marx and Engels 2020; Smith 2021: 3). It is in this context that we can understand Deng Xiaoping's belief that it was acceptable for some people and regions to become wealthy before others (Vogel 2011). Deng believed this was a 'social law' and in accordance with Marxist ideology. In other words, economic growth was dependent on industrialization and urbanization, which would inevitably create differences in wealth in the industrialization process. Therefore, economic inequalities were not viewed as a 'moral' problem by the communist leaders. Consequently, this was considered to be a 'social law' that one had to accept in a rapid industrialization process. This 'social law' also applied to the economic inequalities between rural and urban areas. The rural areas were based on the production of agricultural goods, while the urban areas were based on industrial production. In the same way as the Communist Party accepted it as a 'social fact' that economic inequalities must exist between people in urban areas during a period of growth, they also accepted that greater economic inequalities between town and country were inevitable. This way of thinking was applied both during the first period of industrialization in China, and still exists today. This is evident if we consider the fact that according to 'Forbes World's Billionaires List', Beijing now has more billionaires than New York.[26] On the basis of the above, it is clear that Chinese communism, like Soviet Union communism, is not based on the principle of economic equality. The Communist Party is focused on economic growth, and not economic equality. On the other hand, it can be said that the principle of economic growth is related to the 'Chinese Dream', which is to raise everyone in China up to a middle-class income through collective effort (Brown 2018). In other words, this can be achieved by developing and strengthening the collective economic and social efforts, and not through the motivation of the individual. This is in contrast to the individualist 'American Dream' which asserts that you can become whatever you want, as long as you work hard enough.

It has never been a principle of Marxism to think in terms of individual solutions or individual consequences, but in collective solutions and collective consequences (Mandel 1972, 1977, 1990, 1991). In contrast, the Marxists will claim that there is a circular relationship between the collective and the individual; that is, when the prosperity of the collective is raised, this will positively affect the individuals working in the collective, i.e. the villages and the factories. This insight forms the basis of Deng Xiaoping's idea that some people need to become wealthy if others are also to become more prosperous. First the collective, then the individuals that are part of the collective, forms the basis of Deng's view.

The early stages of Chinese urbanization were driven by agricultural workers migrating to urban areas. This also occurred during the first period of industrialization in Great Britain, and other countries in the West, two hundred years earlier. However, the difference between Western industrialization and Chinese industrialization lies precisely in the distinction between the collective and the individual. In China, the focus is on the collective; in other words, improving the living standards of the collective will positively affect individuals, and facilitate a development whereby people can be raised up to middle-class prosperity.[27] This focus or view has not been evident in Western societies, or proposed by politicians as a principle driving industrialization, urbanization and migration processes. In China, to a great extent, we can say that the agricultural workers became industrial workers, whose children became part of a growing middle class.

[26] https://www.forbes.com/billionaires/.

[27] Vogel (2011), Deng (1994), Beeson and Li (2016), Blecher et al. (2022), and Brown (2018).

Dependence on Foreign Capital and Competence

With regard to dependence on foreign capital and competence, we can extract the following proposition from the above typology: the less breadth and depth there is in the Chinese education system, while at the same time there is a high demand for knowledge-based competence, the greater will be the probability that China will become dependent on foreign capital and competence.

During the first period of globalization, from the end of the 1970s until approx. 2013, when the New Silk Road was launched, China was dependent on both foreign capital and foreign competence. During the second period of globalization, from 2013 onward, China had the necessary capital and expertise to develop the thousands of projects along the New Silk Road, or more specifically, the three silk roads, the land-based, maritime and digital silk roads.

In other words, between the late 1970s and roughly 2013, Chinese industrialization and economic growth was dependent on foreign capital and competence. The year 2013 is set to make a distinction between the first and second periods of globalization. This distinction can also function as a demarcation for the US's growing negative attitude towards China. This change in US foreign policy was perhaps first expressed in the article, "America's Pacific Century", written by the former Secretary of State, Hillary Clinton (*Foreign Policy* 2011), in which she implicitly indicated that China was a threat to American hegemony in the Asia–Pacific region. From 2011 onward, the US devoted a good deal of its political rhetoric to emphasize that China posed a threat to democracy and democratic rights and freedoms. This political rhetoric has focused on several issues, such as accusing China of human rights abuses against the Uighurs in the Xinjiang Province; the issue regarding the sovereignty of Taiwan; and so on. In this context, it should be pointed out that, prior to 2011, the West's criticism of China regarding the lack of democratic freedoms and human rights abuses was more or less conspicuous by its absence. For instance, "The Great Leap Forward" (1958–1962) resulted in mass starvation and famine in China; during the "Cultural Revolution" (1966–1976), the Communist Party established "re-education" camps, where millions of Chinese were confined. During these historical atrocities and abuses, committed by the Chinese government against its own people, governments in the West seldom mounted their 'moral high horse', criticizing China. The massacre in Tiananmen Square in China in 1989, the student protest, calling for democratic rights, was brutally put down by the People's Liberation Army. This event may have shocked the US and the rest of the world, but it did not disrupt the West's trade and investment in China. The point being made here is that it was first during the second period of globalization, from 2013 onward, when China became more independent in terms of capital and competence, that the US and the West altered its stance towards China, expressed in the negative political rhetoric, and later by specific sanctions and policies.

In particular, our assumption here is that when China had begun to develop its level of competence around 2011, when Clinton wrote her article mentioned above, the US perceived this as a threat to its hegemony. In other words, China's level of competence, and its accumulation of capital, led to growing tensions between the US and China. The Chinese leadership is also aware of what may be at stake in the near future. If the US feels threatened, the US may strengthen its policy of containment and introduce further sanctions against China, in an attempt to hinder China's technological and economic development.

The Chinese government led by Xi Jinping, launched the Belt and Road Initiative (BRI) in 2013. This economic strategy provided China with an opportunity to become less dependent on the US, economically, technologically, and diplomatically. Subsequently, the development of the BRI has meant that US policies aimed at China have been to a great extent impotent, especially taking into account that China is no longer dependent on foreign capital and competence. In addition, the BRI (the New Silk Road) has proven to be absolutely crucial for the growth and development of the Chinese middle class.

The dependence on foreign capital and expertise occurred when China opened up to the West at the end of the 1970s. This policy was driven forward by Deng Xiaoping, although Mao was involved in the actual opening up of China, where Nixon and Kissinger also participated. However, there is much evidence to suggest that Mao promoted China's relationship with the US during this period, in order to counteract the Soviet Union's dominance, which was perceived as a threat at this time (Vogel 2011). Deng Xiaoping's aim to open up China to foreign capital was motivated by other factors. Deng believed foreign capital and expertise were vital if China was to develop its economy (Vogel 2011; Deng 1994). Amongst other things, Deng's growth policy was characterized by the establishment of special economic zones (SEZs) in China. Without opening up China to Western capital and expertise, it is difficult to imagine how China could have managed to become the world's second largest economy.

The Rise of the Middle Class

With regard to the rise of the middle class, we can extract the following proposition from the above typology: The greater the breadth and depth there is in the Chinese education system, while at the same time there is a high demand for knowledge-based competence, the greater will be the probability that we will witness the rise of the middle class in China.

The investment in higher education in China has been a continuous process since the end of the Cultural Revolution in 1976. This investment is directly related to the 'Chinese Dream', which is to raise everyone in China up to a middle-class income through collective effort (Brown 2018). Education, 'the Chinese Dream' and the growth of the middle class are systemically linked and mutually dependent on each other.

The education revolution in China began when China increased its export-driven economic growth that was fuelled by cheap labour. As mentioned above, many Chinese students study abroad in countries such as the US, England, France,

Germany, Japan, and so on. It has been shown that it is largely the students who have studied abroad that use their skills and competences to create new businesses in China. However, this development took a long time, roughly from the 1990s to the beginning of the 2000s (Li 2021). The growth of the Chinese economy also impacted the economies of other countries, resulting in China becoming an increasingly important global player. On the domestic front, the middle class grew strongly, while extreme poverty was slowly but surely eradicated.

The growth of the middle class (approx. 700 million) had an ever-increasing political impact. The Communist Party could not ignore this social class's growing expectations regarding its economic future.

During the Cultural Revolution, the expectations of the middle class meant very little. There was more of a negative attitude towards members of the middle class that expressed ideas about their own futures. Those who raised objections to the Gang of Four's policies soon found themselves sent to the rural districts, where many so-called re-education projects had been established. This applied regardless of what position an individual had previously held in the Communist Party. Even Deng Xiaoping ended up in exile. Moreover, Deng Pufang, his son, was injured by the Red Guards, becoming a paraplegic.

The point of this look back into history is to show that the period in which the middle class grew in size and importance has been very short. Another point is that the chaotic events of the Cultural Revolution have resulted in a very strong focus on some central principles being developed in the Chinese Communist Party today. These principles have been developed so that China will not end up in such a chaotic era again. However, it must be emphasized that the principles are not laid down as a unified governing policy of the Communist Party, but rather as rules and norms that the Communist Party has been governed by from 1978 up until today.

These rules and norms can be summarized as 33 principles in the following statements and/or propositions[28]:

1. The Chinese leaders wish to build a society that develops a strong nation, where unity is essential.
2. The development of the Chinese military (PLA) will be decisive for China's internal and external stability.
3. Chinese democracy is important to the Communist Party, but it is distinctly different from Western parliamentary democracy.
4. The Chinese Communist Party has opened up membership for people with a completely different background than previously. People from the middle class have gradually become a central part of the Communist Party.
5. The Chinese nation will be developed through strengthening the quality of the country's expertise. In this context, the quality of the education system will be important.

---

[28] Berlie and Hung (2020), Brown (2018: 132–137), Cao (2004), Chay et al. (2020), Croll (2006), Drach et al. (2019), Jain (2021), Johannessen (2021a, b), Kroeber (2020), Li (2021), Ma (2016), Vangeli (2019), Xing (2019), and Yu (2020).

6. The Chinese development towards prosperity will be facilitated through harmonious balance. This is where the Communist Party focuses on China's historical, cultural and philosophical development, especially Confucius philosophy.
7. Liberty for the Chinese is not, as it is in the West, related to liberal democracy and personal freedom. Liberty for the Chinese is freedom from foreign coercion in order to accomplish the goals that have been set for the nation. Freedom in China is also related to raising everyone's prosperity through collective effort, and to be free from poverty.
8. The "Century of Humiliation" constitutes a backdrop for modern Chinese political consciousness.

   The Century of Humiliation was characterised by:

   a. The Opium Wars,
   b. The colonial period when, among other things, the British occupied Hong Kong, and the Japanese occupied Taiwan,
   c. American, French and British gunboat diplomacy forced China to sign unequal treaties of trade.

9. Economic equality. Over time, ideas concerning what constitutes economic equality have been expressed in different ways by the leaders of the Communist Party. Ideologically, during both the Great Leap Forward and the Cultural Revolution, economic equality was a central tenet. However, negative developments during these historical eras resulted in new ideas emerging. In other words, economic equality did not make much social sense if everyone were equally poor, as this would lead to poverty and a lack of opportunities. It is against this background that Deng Xiaoping expressed the view that to stimulate economic growth that would benefit everybody, then it was acceptable for some people and regions to become wealthy before others (Vogel 2011).
10. In China, the new understanding of economic equality is to raise everyone to a middle-class income through collective effort.
11. The Chinese government has implemented several measures to promote the growth of the Chinese middle class.
12. The Communist Party has taken many steps to eradicate extreme poverty.
13. Economic equality in China has a distinctive Chinese characteristic, in the same way that democracy and freedom also have distinctive characteristics.
14. An unequal distribution of value creation. This is only a means to promote economic growth, not a goal.
15. The goal of the Chinese Communist Party is to ensure that wealth creation eventually benefits everyone. This is the 'Chinese Dream', as expressed by Brown (2018).
16. Laws and rules are the basis of governance of China. However, this principle is something that emerged after Mao's death in 1976, and has been operational since Deng Xiaoping led the Chinese government from 1978. During the Mao era, governance was based on the idea that he was the leader and he was the Law. In other words, he was a strong and authoritarian leader who ruled China from 1949 to 1978. Some commentators may express the view that the structure of

the Communist Party has not changed since the Mao era. This is largely correct (Brown 2019), but the point is that the structure is now subject to completely different framework conditions than during the Mao era. Even although Xi Jinping has been awarded a third five-year term as the nation's president (rather than the maximum of two terms, as stipulated by law), the laws and rules still apply to whoever is elected by the party congress.

17. Patriotic conservatism. This concept relates to the fact that the Chinese Communist Party has looked back into the history of the various Chinese dynasties and to the various Chinese philosophies, in order to develop trends and mechanisms towards a common future for the Chinese people.
18. Unity and stability have become a main principle for the Chinese Communist Party since 1978. However, it should also be emphasized that the revolutionary, chaotic and dictatorial era under Mao Zedong has also been highlighted as something that should be understood within a historical context. In other words, none of the Chinese leaders or institutions have criticized Mao or his leadership.
19. Patriotic conservatism is also used by the Communist Party as an organizing principle to create unity and stability, so that the goal of prosperity for most people can be achieved.
20. Anti-corruption. Corruption in China has existed over many years. Xi Jinping was himself involved in tracking down corruption early in his career in the Communist Party (Brown 2018: 56). It was especially during the period after the opening of the Chinese economy that corruption became a serious problem for China. Premier Wen Jiabao stated that corruption was the greatest threat to the Chinese Communist Party (Wedeman 2012). Xi's political control of the Communist Party has been a continuous battle against corruption among party members and other actors in China. At the 19th Party Congress in 2017, Xi stated that corruption was still a problem in China, but that this would be cracked down on.
21. A zero-tolerance program for corruption has been developed in China. Those engaged in corruption will be given severe penalties.[29]
22. The anti-corruption program that Xi led started in 2012. It is considered crucial for the Communist Party's survival and legitimacy that all forms of corruption are cracked down on. According to a survey, 40.7% of the interviewees expressed the view that the results of the Communist Party's anti-corruption campaign have been positive.[30]
23. If the Communist Party fails to control corruption in China, then this could be the nail in the coffin for the current political system.
24. Enthusiasm and dedication. One problem of the strong economic growth in China is that the middle class, which comprises approx. 700 million, may become indolent and satisfied with the state of things. In this way, one may risk that they enter into a mode of indifference. Such psychological and social

[29] https://www.globaltimes.cn/page/202201/1246320.shtml.

[30] https://www.globaltimes.cn/page/202201/1246320.shtml.

lethargy would pose a threat to the Communist Party and the pursuit of the 'Chinese Dream'.

25. If the middle class becomes no longer interested in the fact that some people are being "left behind" amid economic growth, then this may quickly change the way of thinking amongst the financial elite and the middle class.
26. The indifference of the middle class can quickly lead to a type of thinking where it is believed that it does not matter who rules in China, as long as the needs, wishes, dreams and expectations of the middle class are fulfilled. It is this type of thinking that may pose a real danger for the Communist Party, along with the acceptance of a mild form of corruption.
27. If it is believed that a mild form of corruption is important to lubricate the system, then an idea may easily develop within the middle class that the Communist Party does not serve its interests when the Party clamps down on corruption, thus taking away a source of 'extra income'. Enthusiasm for realizing the 'Chinese Dream' may thus be diminished, and the middle class may ally itself with the financial elite, which may result in political changes in China. This is why commitment and dedication are important to the Communist Party.
28. The struggle to influence people's psychology and behaviour is important to the Communist Party. In other words, people need to be motivated beyond just satisfying their own individual needs, and the needs of their families. It might be said that the Communist Party is engaging in an 'educational project' in order to create motivation amongst people that Chinese communism serves everyone in China, and not just those who, as expressed by Deng Xiaoping, have become wealthy before others. If these people are not motivated by a moral and ideological responsibility beyond their own economic progress, then this could lead to the decline of the Communist Party.
29. Continuous support for communism with Chinese characteristics. It is this particular form of communism that Xi has formulated, but which also shows itself historically in Mao's struggle and distrust of Soviet communism, as well as Deng Xiaoping's distrust of communism in Vietnam. Confidence in the Chinese form of communism will be decisive for the survival of the Communist Party. However, many people in the West, and especially in the United States, would like to see the end of communism in China, and the adoption of a Western style liberal democracy.
30. To prevent communism with Chinese characteristics from being transformed and degenerating into something else, in the way Soviet communism was transformed and degenerated into something that was unsustainable, it is necessary to develop trust. In other words, there needs to be trust between the people and the Communist Party. Therefore, support for the Chinese Communist Party is crucial for the party's continued existence. Trust can be ensured by continuing the anti-corruption campaigns. Trust can also be ensured by increasing the number of members in the Communist Party, and by changing the composition of the Communist Party, by allowing membership of people from varied backgrounds. For example, by gradually allowing membership of people without a working class background. In other words, people with higher education, and

entrepreneurs with high incomes. In this way, these people can help set the political course for China.[31] During the past decade, more than 900,000 members have been expelled from the Party for violating ethical and financial norms.[32]

31. Multilateralism. For the Chinese Communist Party, this term means inclusive cooperation based on an understanding that all parties in a political relationship, or an economic project, should be based on a form of reciprocity, where win–win is always the basis of the relationship. Multilateralism contrasts with unilateralism where the right of the strongest applies. Against this background, multilateralism is important for small nations, and gives small powers a voice and influence that they could not otherwise exercise. The alternative to multilateralism can be described by the popular adage that "the big countries do what they like and the small ones have to obey and behave".
32. For Xi Jinping, the objective of multilateralism is to construct a "community of a shared future for mankind".[33] Preserving multilateralism and promoting global cooperation on public health crises, the climate crisis, economic inequalities, war and conflicts in many regions, and poverty, are all likely to top China's diplomatic agenda this year.
33. Non-interference in the domestic affairs of sovereign states. This principle was historically enshrined in the Peace of Westfallen in 1648. This peace ended the Thirty Years' War from 1618–1648, and the Eighty Years' War from 1568–1648. In these two European wars, approx. eight million people died. Many scholars of international relations have identified the Peace of Westphalia as the origin of principles crucial to modern international relations, including the non-interference in the domestic affairs of sovereign states, because it is believed that it was this that triggered, and was the probable cause, of the two wars mentioned above. In other words, China opposes the interference in China's internal affairs in the name of human rights, democratic freedoms and issues of sovereignty, such as the issues of democratic development in Hong Kong, the handling of the conflicts in Xinjiang, and the Taiwan issue. Against this background, in 2021, 65 countries opposed interference in China's internal affairs in a joint statement issued by the United Nations Human Rights Council.

Practical Utility Related to the Rise of the Middle Class

A distinctive feature of the Chinese economy is what can be termed 'dynamic stability'. This is evident if we consider China's new economic strategy, the "Dual Circular Development Paradigm". This strategy focuses on the simultaneous existence of change and continuity. We also find such thinking in early Chinese philosophy as represented by Yin and Yang. These two dimensions are not so much opposites, but are dependent on, and presuppose, each other, just as night and day form

[31] https://daily.jstor.org/communist-party-of-china/.

[32] https://www.globaltimes.cn/page/202201/1246320.shtml.

[33] https://global.chinadaily.com.cn/a/202103/05/WS6041716ba31024ad0baacdc2.html.

a unit. The philosophy of the simultaneous existence of change and continuity is perhaps best expressed in the writings of the Chinese philosopher Confucius. Change and stability can be demonstrated metaphorically by the tightrope walker who has to constantly change the position of his/her arms and legs to remain 'stable' on the tightrope.

In our context, high-tech competence acts as a social change mechanism, which brings the economy into disequilibrium. The development of high-tech skills is facilitated through education. On this basis, it should be noted that China has had an explosive growth in education since the 1980s, especially in relation to high-tech education. High-tech skills are necessary in order to drive innovation. In turn, high-tech innovations drive entrepreneurial processes, and facilitate the growth of new entrepreneurial companies in China. High-tech innovations, and the innovative entrepreneurs who promote these innovations, create gaps in the market, resulting in an imbalance in the economy. Other entrepreneurs then fill the gaps in the market with new start-up businesses. Some of these businesses are created precisely on the basis of the technological innovations. The entrepreneurial actions bring the market back into balance. It is precisely this process which we can term dynamic stability.

When innovative entrepreneurship makes use of technological innovations, the demand for knowledge-based competence increases. Academic institutions, such as both Chinese and foreign universities, supply personnel with competence to the Chinese high-tech companies, which enables these companies to compete in the global market. Moreover, the new economic strategy, the "Dual Circulation Development Paradigm", also focuses on domestic demand. It is primarily the Chinese middle class that boosts the demand for high-tech consumer goods, which are increasingly produced in China. This increasing domestic demand will eventually result in an increase in the wages of the Chinese workers. One of the consequences for Western consumers is that the goods they could previously buy cheaply will increase in price, because wages in China are rising.

The synthesis of the development described above is that the middle class in China, as well as the trade with the RCEP countries, are setting the tone for the future of Chinese production. This development is a deliberate and stated policy of the Chinese leaders. This is expressed in the various economic strategies, such as the "Dual Circulation Development Paradigm" mentioned above, and also in the strategic plans, "Made in China 2025" and "China Standards 2035".

In practice, the Chinese universities will increase their supply of personnel with high-tech competence to the Chinese manufacturing, distribution, digital and consumer industries. Many of these tech workers will aspire to be middle-class, which will also result in an increase in the demand for Chinese high-tech consumer goods.

Many in the West are interested in seeing the Chinese economic 'bubble' burst, that is, in reducing Chinese economic growth (Orlik 2020). However, as long as workers with high-tech competence are increasingly supplied to high-tech entrepreneurial companies, then there is nothing to suggest that the economic bubble will burst in the immediate future. A scenario can also be envisaged where the increase in high-tech workers will increase the numbers of the middle class, and thus also increase

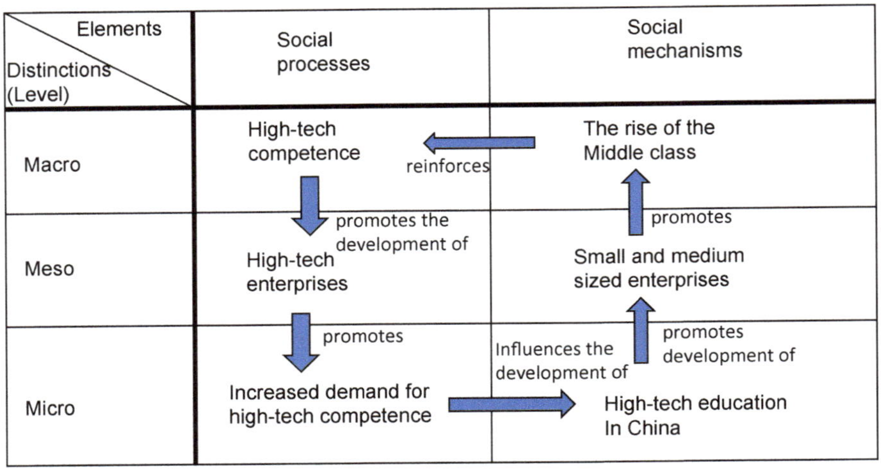

Fig. 3.3 The rise of the Chinese middle class: A Boudon-Coleman diagram

demand and economic growth. When the tightrope walker becomes too old, and is no longer able to balance on the tightrope, he/she will be replaced by a younger tightrope walker. This is also how we can imagine the Chinese economy. Of course, the Chinese economy cannot continue its unrestricted growth in the same way as before, but it can continue its growth by changing continuously. The 'bubble' does not need to burst, because it is not one single bubble, but thousands of bubbles that grow and change continuously. Some of these bubbles, such as the 'housing bubble', will probably burst, in the sense that it has grown too large. However, this does not mean that the thousands of other bubbles will burst, because the bubbles are not systemically linked, but distinct even if they seem linked.

Based on the above narratives, description, analysis, theoretical reflections, and the review of the practical utility, we have developed a Boudon-Coleman diagram for the rise of the Chinese middle class (Fig. 3.3).

High-Tech Competence

The results of the PISA 2012 assessment showed that China was the top performer in mathematics, science, and reading (Zhao 2014: 119). On the other hand, critical questions have been raised by several commentators regarding the creativity of Chinese educational institutions.[34] Creativity is a prerequisite for innovation (Hamel 2002, 2012). Can it be imagined that the assumption that the Chinese education system does not promote creativity may be somewhat distorted, and does not tell the whole

[34] https://www.caixinglobal.com/2020-08-05/qian-yinyi-where-does-creativity-come-from-101589143.html.

truth about the Chinese form of creativity. In this context, we will refer to the ideas of the American psychologist Carol Dweck, of Stanford University, to argue for a slightly different understanding of creativity.

Carol Dweck wrote the book "Mindset: The New Psychology of Success". Dweck points out in her book that there are four different mindsets that characterize creative and successful people. I will present four examples of the different mindsets in the following.

The first mindset is to apply theories to understand, explain and change phenomena and solve problems. This can be termed 'Einstein's mental model' for investigating problems and phenomena. Einstein's point in this context was that if one could not explain phenomena or solutions to a problem in a simple way, then one has not understood the problem.

It is in this context that we believe the Chinese education system, contrary to several assumptions, has the ability to educate creative students. The reason is the strong emphasis given to science and mathematics. It is the theories from these fields that can enable Chinese students to understand and solve problems in a simple and innovative way.

The second mindset is about thinking differently. The example here is Steve Jobs of Apple. IBM dominated the personal computer market, and became the industry standard. However, Apple established its own operating system and platform. Jobs developed the brand by challenging IBM and by 'thinking differently', and by encouraging consumers to "Think Different".

The Chinese education system certainly promotes the learning of theories and concepts in the fields of science and mathematics. The Chinese education system develops within the Chinese culture, which is intrinsically different from the culture of the capitalist West. In this context, a necessary condition for survival in the global market is not to imitate the Western production and way of thinking, but to think in new ways. Admittedly, like Japan in the past, China 'copies' Western products. However, more recently, Chinese tech-companies have become more innovative, such as in the case of Huawei.

The third mindset is the counter-intuitive thought model. The example that is often referred to in this context is Elon Musk and his company Tesla. He developed this company based on an approach that seemed counter-intuitive, that is, producing autos powered by non-fossil fuels. At the beginning of production, this seemed counter-intuitive, because there were few charging stations for electric cars, or workshops that could repair the cars. Yet, Tesla turned out to be a success. The Chinese education system promotes a type of innovative thinking that anyone who wishes to establish an entrepreneurial enterprise needs to create their own niche that does not exist in China. For instance, we can mention Alibaba, which was seemingly created out of nothing, an idea to develop online shopping, which did not exist in China at the time the idea was conceived.

The fourth mindset is what can be described as the "reverse thinking model". With reference to Peter Thiel, this involves thinking along other paths, than those paths used by others, in order to solve a problem. More specifically, this refers to his creation of PayPal. When others were thinking in technical terms, his approach was to think in terms of business models, and then leave it to the engineers to solve the technical problems. The Chinese entrepreneurs often encounter a business global environment that is increasingly sceptical of the Chinese social model and the Communist Party's intentions. In order to succeed in the global competition, they will have to do precisely what Peter Thiel did. That is, they will need to think along other paths than the well-trodden traditional ones. The best example here is perhaps the New Silk Road, which has created economic conditions for the prosperous activities of Chinese and foreign businessmen, with regard to participation in the numerous New Silk Road projects.

Although the Chinese education system, from a Western perspective, does not encourage creativity, many innovations have been the result of precisely this education system. The explanations can be many. We have attempted to understand Chinese creativity and innovativeness by looking at education in a more holistic system, where the Chinese context and culture play decisive roles. It is precisely when the Chinese education system meets the Chinese challenges that innovations emerge. Even if the Chinese education system is different from the Western one, it is conceivable that the degree of innovation in China will be just as great as in the West. The creative talents are the result of the education system. However, this system can be different from the Western one, but still produce the best innovative results. Education linked to the practical context is the prerequisite for creativity and innovation, not necessarily the education system as such. It is knowledge that is related to practical problems that creates innovations, not the education system alone.

High-Tech Enterprises

It is not only the large and medium-sized technology companies that dominate the business environment in China, such as Huawei, Tencent, Alibaba Group, DIDI global, Meituan, Net Ease, ByteDance, MiHoYo, Lilith, Fun-Plus, Baidu, and so on. In a report published by a US-based mobile analytics company, China has overtaken the United States for the first time to dominate a new list of the Top 52 app publishers for smart phones around the globe. Seventeen small and medium-sized enterprises were at the forefront of this development.[35] One of the explanations for this development of technology competence in China is what we have emphasized above, namely, that the Chinese education system is able to supply creative and innovative graduates to Chinese businesses. This is despite the fact that many critics in the West believe that there is a lack of focus on creativity and innovation within the Chinese education system.

Another complementary explanation is that China has become the world's largest market for smart phones. It is the demand from this customer group that has driven the development of the Chinese app market.

Against this background, it is the demand-driven technological development in the Chinese domestic market that provides the conditions for the development of

[35] https://global.chinadaily.com.cn/a/202204/13/WS62562500a310fd2b29e56a00.html.

technology companies in China. These IT technology companies first develop applications for the Chinese market. This market functions as a mechanism for quality improvements and new innovations to meet the needs of consumers. In the next stage, some of these tech companies launch their products on the global market after they have thoroughly tested and improved the products in the domestic market. The trial and testing in the Chinese market results in the products being more competitive when they enter the global market. This development is exemplified by Huawei, which became technologically at the forefront, while being cost-effective. In its consequences, this led to American technology companies feeling threatened by the technological and market progress of Huawei. The Chinese company was consequently barred from operating in US 5G networks (as well as in other countries allied to the US). The US authorities stated that Huawei represented a threat to national security. However, there were perhaps other factors than national security at play here; the American companies were finding it difficult to compete with Chinese technology on price and quality. In this context, one might quote the Norwegian philosopher Zapffe that "It's what you are good at that will be your downfall".[36] In other words, Huawei were too good in relation to quality and cost, which led to its downfall, at least in the context of US and Western markets.

China's leaders have stated that China aims to become a world leader in artificial intelligence. Within the artificial intelligence sector, China's social media operator, Tencent, and China's gaming outfit, NetEase, have retained the top two spots in data.ai's 2022 "Top 52 Publishers list" for the fifth consecutive year.[37] The US-based gaming company Activision Blizzard came third on the list. Other Chinese companies that also featured on the list were: ByteDance, MiHoYo, Lilith, Fun-Plus, Alibaba Group, and Baidu. What is also interesting is that 63.5% of the companies on the list have their headquarters in Asia. This indicates new developments in technological innovations, where the focus on artificial intelligence within several industries is changing many of the economic and technological frameworks.

The US-based mobile analytics company, data.ai.[38] also has other lists which show that the Chinese company ByteDance topped the list of AI companies with the largest revenue in overseas markets. According to data.ai, Chinese developers have nearly doubled their market share in global app downloads over the past 10 years, from 8% in 2011 to 14% by the first half of 2021. This development will very likely create great opportunities for Chinese entrepreneurs and small and medium-sized Chinese technology companies.

It is mainly Chinese middle-class workers, the graduates of Chinese and foreign universities, who are driving this technological development forward. At the same time, this technological development is boosting the growth and strength of the middle class.

[36] https://philosophynow.org/issues/45/The_Last_Messiah.

[37] https://global.chinadaily.com.cn/a/202204/13/WS62562500a310fd2b29e56a00.html.

[38] https://www.data.ai/en/.

Knowledge-Based Competence

International researchers agree on the view that the Chinese development of knowledge, via national and international universities, has strengthened China's competitiveness.[39] Human capital is defined by the World Bank as the skills, knowledge, and experience possessed by an individual or population, viewed in terms of their value or cost to an organization or country.[40] It is this human capital that is the most important driver of economic growth in the innovation economy (Johannessen 2022b; Johannessen and Sætersdal 2020). It is through exploiting human capital that China has been able to develop a knowledge-based competence, which provides the fundament for the creation of technological innovations, which then forms the basis for the development of new tech enterprises. In this way, China is able to secure a better competitive position in the global innovation economy. It is precisely this knowledge-based competence that has made it possible for China to transform the country's production and production methods, and to expand globally. The transformation has been made from an export-driven growth based on cheap consumer goods exported to the West, to high-tech production. The driver of the global innovation economy is scientific discoveries, and their application in a practical context, according to Professor Georg Langelett.[41]

China's new 'grand strategy' in the global economy is to develop Chinese talent through the education system. In this context, China's highly educated graduates are becoming China's new economic crowbar in the global economy. It might be said that the real competition between the US and China is the battle to develop highly-skilled talent. This strategy has been explicitly stated by Xi Jinping on several occasions (Brown 2019; Zhang 2015). For example, when speaking at a conference on talent-related work in 2021, he stressed the need to implement a strategy on developing a quality workforce, to enable China to become a major global centre of professional talent and innovation.[42] This focus on investment in higher education will boost the strength and growth of the middle class. In other words, the Chinese leaders thus have a clear strategy, which is to utilize the Chinese middle class as an economic lever, in order to enable the Chinese economy to become a world leader. It is therefore not the Chinese working class, but the middle class that is the driver behind economic growth, transforming China's economic system from a low-cost producer to a country that exports high-tech products to the global market.

When China's 1.4 billion people are able to receive an education, and the education system focuses on training in high-tech studies in science, technology, engineering, and mathematics (STEM competences) (Johannessen 2020a, b), then it is very probable that a completely new global competition between China and the US will emerge. This competition will to a great extent be determined by the Law of

[39] https://www.csis.org/analysis/how-chinas-human-capital-impacts-its-national-competitiveness.

[40] https://www.worldbank.org/en/publication/human-capital/brief/the-human-capital-project-frequently-asked-questions#HCP2.

[41] https://www.jstor.org/stable/40704155.

[42] Http:// www.gov.cn/xinwen/2021-09/28/content_5639868.htm.

Large Numbers. In other words, China has a population of 1.4 billion compared to the US's 330 million; that is, approx. a difference between the two countries of one billion people. Although the US education system is in many respects ahead of the Chinese education system, China is catching up in most areas (Liu 2016, 2021).

However, there is a great deal of uncertainty regarding the Chinese economic system related to demographic development. This concerns the one-child policy that was implemented between 1979 and 2015 to curb the country's population growth. In the longer perspective, this will have a negative social and economic impact due to a rapidly ageing population. In a study by Stein Emil Vollset published in the journal *Lancet*,[43] he suggests there will be a sharp decline in the Chinese population heading towards 2050, with a possible decrease of fifty percent. If this were to prove true, then many of the knowledge-based industries and public services in China will have limited access to highly-educated workers towards 2050. This challenge can be solved in at least three ways by the Chinese authorities.

1. The quantitative strategy. This strategy is to ensure that there are more high-tech graduates in the future. Thus, the relative proportion of the Chinese population entering the middle class will also increase sharply.
2. Innovation strategy. The second strategy is related to innovation theory. This theory proposes that innovations will emerge in the following areas (Johannessen, 2020a, b, c; 2021b; 2022a):
   a. where relative productivity is falling,
   b. where the relative costs are increasing,
   c. where knowledge can most quickly be converted into technology and
   d. where innovations spread the fastest.
3. Focus on artificial intelligence. The third strategy is to focus on the development of artificial intelligence, so that automation processes can overcome the challenges a declining population can pose to the Chinese economy.

Small and Medium-Sized Enterprises (SME)

There has been a strong increase in SMEs in China. This development started in the late 1970s, when China was opened up to Western investment (Vogel 2011). Some of these businesses also carry out research and development aimed at using artificial intelligence in the areas in which the business specializes. One such example is Shanghai Westwell-Lab Technology Company, which utilizes artificial intelligence for automating operations at the Abu Dhabi Terminal and Khalifa Port in the United Arab Emirates.[44]

---

[43] *The Lancet* 396, no. 10258 (2020): 1285–1306, 10.1016/S0140-6736(20)30677-2.

[44] https://www.zawya.com/en/business/projects-abu-dhabi-implements-middle-easts-first-autonomous-port-truck-system-ifie85oj.

Hubei Kofon is another Chinese SME, which specializes in the research and development, and production, of reduction gear. The company invests 15% of its annual sales revenue in R&D, and 80% of its annual profit on technological upgrading.[45] Through its specialization and research in artificial intelligence, the company has managed to break the monopolies that international companies have had in this type of specialized production. The demand for the company's products is so great that it now manufactures large quantities. "All of the raw materials and components used by the company are produced in China", says CEO Wu Junfeng.[46] Hubei Kofon is a typical example of a Chinese SME. They conduct advanced research, and thus use the knowledge-based expertise developed at Chinese and foreign universities. In this way, Chinese companies, such as Hubei Kofon, are able to develop and strengthen the Chinese middle class. These companies are unique in the sense that they are highly innovative, and focus on utilizing artificial intelligence in production.

The strong commitment in China to high-tech development facilitates the supply of high-tech workers to such companies. We should not ignore the fact that these companies, which focus on the development and utilization of artificial intelligence in their specialized operations, will be able to help to mitigate the challenges to the Chinese economy in the future, due to a possible decline in the population, mentioned above. Our point here is that artificial intelligence can be used to automate many work processes, thereby reducing the challenges of a negative population growth. A population decline coupled with a strong increase in the automation of work processes can, on the other hand, be to China's advantage. This advantage is related to the social challenges of a growing population, as well as problems related to food production and the import of food for an ever-growing population. It is precisely the development and utilization of artificial intelligence and robotics, the increase in automation processes, and development of specialized SMEs, that can help secure the Chinese economy in the future, despite a possible decline in the population.

At the 2021 Central Economic Work Conference, the Chinese Communist Party adopted the policy of investing heavily in SMEs, especially companies that specialize in the development and applications of artificial intelligence.[47] The heavy investment in AI companies will give China an advantage in relation to international competitors. In addition, the aforementioned conference emphasized the importance of making Chinese companies competitive with foreign companies.

The rapid development of specialized SMEs in China is evident within many different industries. We have mentioned two examples above. Another example of a specialized SME is Jiangsu Yingyou Textile Machinery Co., Ltd., which has been recognized as a "little giant" enterprise in China. "Little giants" are highly innovative smaller companies that focus on the production of special products and know-how in strategic sectors. These "little giants" have on average around 50 international patents

---

[45] https://www.kofon-motion.com.

[46] http://en.people.cn/n3/2022/0127/c90000-9950086.html.

[47] https://thediplomat.com/2021/12/china-states-economic-priorities-for-2022-emphasizing-stability/.

within their niche related to high-tech production.[48] These companies will probably be of great importance to the development of the Chinese innovation economy. The researchers and management of these companies are highly qualified, often with university educations. In this way, they strengthen the development of the middle class, and the middle class becomes increasingly important for the development of Chinese economic growth.

Systemic Connections Related to the Rise of the Middle Class

Creating stability during a time of change seems to be a feature of Chinese culture, which can also be related to the teachings of Confucius (Schuman 2015). This type of thinking is non-linear, but interactive and circular. This is not unlike the part-whole perspective in systemic thinking (Kwan 2021). In our context, such interactive and circular thinking is manifested in the following way. When the Chinese government invests in higher education, this indirectly promotes the growth of the middle class, and is circuitously related to realizing the "Chinese Dream", which is to raise everyone up to a middle-class income through collective effort (Brown 2018). The political leaders also know that when resources are allocated to boosting the development of the large middle class, this will negatively affect the rural districts, due to the migration of rural workers to urban areas (Brown 2019).

The governmental authorities are aware that in the short term this could lead to tensions and conflicts between rural and urban areas (Mahbubani 2020). However, from a longer perspective, this development will result in economic growth that will benefit everyone (Ma 2016, 2021).

The point being made in the above discussion is that dynamic stability is firmly rooted in Chinese culture and Confucian philosophy, and is not a product of the ideology of the Chinese Communist Party (Jacques 2012). As follows, the success of the middle class will not necessarily create conflicts with the agricultural workers, because Chinese thinking is holistic and interactive. In practice, this means that the agricultural workers who migrate to urban areas are in search of better paid work, and a better future, although the economic inequalities will increase in the short term due to this economic dynamism. Chinese thinking is characterized by the interrelationship between economic dynamism and economic stability (Brown 2019). In this context, the Chinese leaders adopt policies that aim to counteract social and economic chaos at all costs (Mantzopoulos and Shen 2011). Consequently, chaos is viewed as an undesirable element in Chinese thinking; paradoxically, 'chaotic' systems and measures are implemented to prevent chaos. This was evident in Mao Zedong's Great Leap Forward, and in the Cultural Revolution. The chaotic student protests in Tiananmen Square in 1989 grew larger and eventually resulted in a chaotic military suppression, the "Tiananmen Square Massacre". Order and stability are so intertwined in Chinese thinking that, paradoxically, chaotic measures are used to

[48] Ibid.

promote stability and order. The Chinese handling of the Covid-19 pandemic can also be interpreted in the context of the fight against chaos. Stability is so important that every imaginable method is used to oppose anything that may have the potential of promoting chaos.

In this context, the Chinese middle class functions as a social lever to facilitate stability and order. The rationale is that a growing middle class has an expectation of increased prosperity. This prevents opposition to any policy that might reduce the prosperity of the middle class. If the leaders of the Communist Party cannot deliver on the expectations of the middle class, then the middle class may demand political changes. This can quickly lead to tensions and conflicts within China, which the Chinese leaders want to avoid at all costs. Any leader in the Communist Party will go to great lengths to prevent such a development from evolving. The reasoning is related to the fact that throughout Chinese history, various rebellions have occurred resulting in the attempted overthrow of rulers and governments. For example, the Taiping Rebellion (1851–1864), the Boxer Rebellion (1898–1899), and the protests in Tiananmen Square (1989). The Chinese authorities know that a growing and satisfied middle class will create dynamic stability in China (Batzhan et al. 2020; Pan 2020).

It is against this background that one can understand the major investment in the New Silk Road. The Chinese leaders know that if the West, and especially the United States, attempt to decouple economic relations with China, then this can be harmful to economic growth. Therefore, China has implemented a new strategy for economic growth, the "Dual Circulation Development Paradigm", which aims to increase domestic demand, while also focusing on markets along the New Silk Road and in the RCEP countries.

Based on the above narratives, description, analysis, theoretical reflections, and the review of practical utility, as well as the description of the systemic relations, we have developed a loop diagram for the development of the Chinese middle class (Fig. 3.4).

Middle-Class Success

There seems to be a relationship between China's current integration into the global value chain and the growth of the Chinese middle class. China was a country that previously based its exports on low production costs, but it has now moved up the value chain through a transition from quantity to quality in all stages of its production processes. In practice, this means that China exports more high-tech products than before. This production demands a more highly skilled workforce, which also boosts the growth of the middle class. However, relative to Western countries, wages are still lower in China, both for the unskilled and highly-skilled workers. In other words, although China has moved up the value chain with its high-tech products, these products can be produced and distributed at a lower price than the same products in

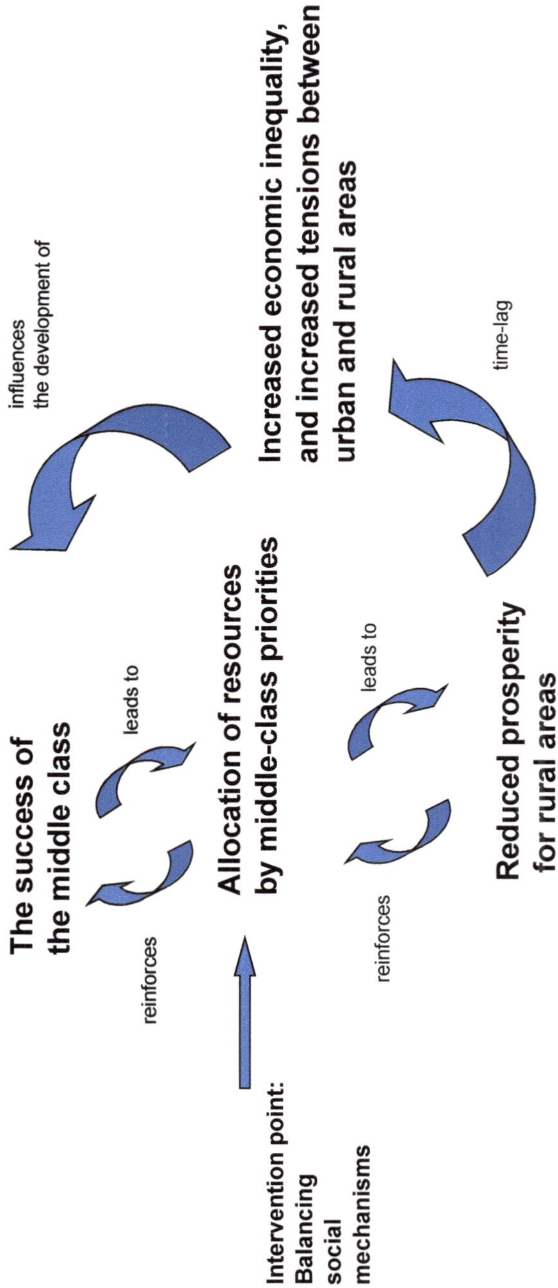

Fig. 3.4 The development of the Chinese middle class: a loop diagram

the West. Thus, this has weakened the competitive position of countries in the West, such as the US, regarding high-tech products.

As long as China manages to keep its export markets open for its high-tech products, there is much to suggest that China's products will be more competitive than similar Western products in the global market, due to lower prices. It is against this background that we can understand the US policy of barring Huawei from operating in US 5G networks, due to issues about 'national security'. This can be said to be part of the US containment policy aimed at China, or more specifically, a technological containment policy.

According to a report released by the Asian Infrastructure Investment Bank (AIIB) in 2021, China's GVC (global value chain) exports increased from 37.9% to 44.6%. This relates to high-tech products that require a highly-skilled workforce in production processes.[49] In other words, this indicates that China has become a producer of high-tech products and services for the global markets, and not only a producer of cheap consumer goods. In this context, one might refer to Allison's 'Thucydides' Trap' (2018), which proposes that a conflict can develop when a rising great (economic) power (e.g. China) challenges the dominant great (economic) power (e.g. the US). More specifically, the US will attempt to contain China's technological development as mentioned above, especially in high-tech fields such as artificial intelligence.

The question that can be asked is how China has managed to move up the global value chain (GVC) so quickly. There can be many answers to this question, but some points stand out more than others. Firstly, there has been large-scale investment in the education system in China, as far back as the late 1970s, when Deng Xiaoping was leader (Vogel 2011). Another important point is the investment in high-tech education. In recent years, China has focused on becoming a leader in artificial intelligence, which is a decisive factor for continuous progress up the global value chain. A third point is the opening of foreign direct investment (FDI) in China from 2000.[50] These capital injections in China have made it possible to increase the degree of innovation and entrepreneurial ability of Chinese businesses.[51]

There are many indications that this technological progress for Chinese businesses has become a competitive counterforce to the United States and many other Western countries. Sanctions and protectionist policies aimed at China have increased tensions between the US and China. The rationale behind such policies is not difficult to grasp. Historically, it has been shown that the nation that leads technology is also the most dominant power globally. This was true of the three previous industrial revolutions from 1750 onward. It is also probable that this will apply to the Fourth Industrial

[49] https://www.globaltimes.cn/page/202112/1241590.shtml.

[50] https://blogs.worldbank.org/developmenttalk/how-has-china-moved-global-value-chains.

[51] https://hal.archives-ouvertes.fr/hal-03373508/document.

Revolution. The most important technology of the future will most probably be artificial intelligence.[52] It is in this context that China threatens the United States, that is, in relation to becoming the nation that will emerge as the leader in this technological competition. It seems reasonable to assume that it is against this background that the US reacts so strongly to the Chinese businesses that have moved up the global value chain; this can be viewed as a development towards a new US 'grand strategy' of technological containment of China.

In the context we are discussing here, it is the Chinese middle class that has made this development possible. It is the middle class that largely drives this rise along the global value chain.

This development indicates that a new form of international division of labour is emerging. In the past, China has produced cheap consumer goods, while high-tech products have been produced by the US and other Western countries. This division of labour seems to be now changing markedly.

China's trading and business activities along the New Silk Road, which involves more than 130 countries, provides an opportunity for China to counteract Western sanctions, tariffs and other restrictions placed on Chinese goods. If the US and its allies increase the sanctions against China, China may focus more of its attention on the New Silk Road, as well as increase its trading activities with the RCEP countries. In addition, China has introduced new economic strategies to offset the fall in exports due to sanctions, such as the "Dual Circulation Development Paradigm" which aims to increase domestic demand which is being fuelled by a growing middle class of 700 million. In this context, it might be said that the Chinese middle class has become an economic lever that is facilitating the transformation of the Chinese economy from a focus on quantity to a focus on quality.

Allocation of Resources by Middle-Class Priorities

The development of the middle class came as a result of the investment in education, especially higher education. This raised the level of skills and expertise that enabled China to move up the global value chain. As China became a competitive threat to the US, sanctions against China were slowly introduced. For instance, the Trump trade war against China concerned a series of tariffs, and included the import of various goods and raw materials, such as washing machines, steel and aluminium. The sanctions were justified on the grounds of reducing the United States trade deficit with China. Later measures against China, under the Biden administration, barred Chinese companies from American markets on the basis of national security. These measures were adopted against a background of a political rhetoric launched against China, accusing China of abusing human rights, amongst other things. In sum, these

[52] There are many other technologies that will dominate the Fourth Industrial Revolution, such as Block Chain, Big Data, Gen-editing, etc., but it is artificial intelligence that will in all probability have the greatest ability to transform social systems.

sanctions and measures emerged as a new containment policy, or more specifically a new technological containment policy. As a counterweight to this development, which can be viewed as having its starting point in 2011, with the article, "America's Pacific Century", written by the former Secretary of State, Hillary Clinton (*Foreign Policy* 2011), which stressed the importance of the US maintaining its hegemony in the Asia–Pacific region. To counteract these developments, China introduced various strategies, such as the "Dual Circulation Development Paradigm", which aimed to increase domestic consumption, especially the consumption of the Chinese middle class. In short, this strategy involved increasing the domestic consumption of Chinese-made goods, such as electric cars, mobile phones, and other high-tech products, which would make China less dependent on exporting its goods to US and Western markets.

This strategy targets high-value products as well as high-tech products, in order to maintain demand, production and employment. One such high-value product is gold jewellery. According to an industry report, jewellery retailers have stated that in 2021 the consumption of gold jewellery, by mainly young middle class consumers, overtook the levels in 2019. A survey has indicated that 13% of young female consumers buy precious jewellery as a way of 'rewarding themselves'.[53]

The increased focus on domestic demand has, among other things, led to an increased demand for goods in so-called brick-and-mortar stores, where businesses showcase their products, so that customers can visit the stores, browse items, try on or test products. In other words, consumers are provided with diversified shopping experiences. One shopper at Chengdu IFS mall, typical of many others, said the following, "Even if I didn't want to buy anything, it would still be fun to look around in the mall".[54]

The increased interest in off-line shopping at physical locations is changing the purchasing behaviour of many middle-class Chinese. For example, this applies to the increased demand in shopping malls that offer catering, leisure, entertainment and fitness, with the types of stores ranging from bookstores to musical instruments, tea houses, flower shops, beauty salons, and fitness centres. Many of the new well-off consumers are young middle-class people. The shopping malls often have food courts and cafes, which are particularly popular among young people, because they can satisfy their needs for eating together, or just drinking coffee and meeting friends. In addition, health products and health services have become an increasing part of middle-class demand. In other words, the brick-and-mortar stores in China have been able to win back consumers through transformation, by making their supply structure more flexible and adaptable to new changes in consumer demand. In addition, several of these shopping malls offer products and entertainment for children and young people, such as 3D screens, where various forms of virtual games can be hired or bought. Some of these centres also have virtual reality equipment, intelligent robots, hologram projectors and virtual livestreaming studios. Innovation is the direct driving force for the transformation of the brick-and-mortar stores in China. Compared to

[53] http://en.people.cn/n3/2022/0130/c90000-9951795.html.

[54] http://en.people.cn/n3/2022/0128/c90000-9950638.html.

online shopping, these stores make it possible to come into contact with other people, and try out completely new technological products. In other words, these newly transformed brick-and-mortar stores have become a place where friends meet and new relationships are created, as well as increasing the domestic demand for goods and services.[55]

The Chinese leadership has purposely opened up for increased domestic demand in order to secure the economy at a time of sanctions and the exclusion of Chinese goods in Western markets, especially in relation to the US technological containment policy, and the containment policies of several countries in Europe. In this context, the Chinese middle class has become an economic lever to tackle the western sanctions and containment policy.

Increased Economic Inequality Between Urban and Rural Areas

Economic inequality in China can be expressed along three axes. The first axis is related to education and competence. The second axis is related to urban and rural areas. The third axis is a geographical one, and related to the inland and coastal areas. We have discussed the competence axis several places in this book. Those people with a high-tech education, who use their expertise to start businesses, are the people who, as a general rule, come out best on the income statistics (Li 2021; Liu 2016). Regarding the first axis, competence, those people with little education will often have low incomes. Regarding the second axis of rural and urban areas, those who live in urban areas will have higher incomes than rural workers. Regarding the third axis, people along the coastal regions have, on the whole, higher incomes than people in inland regions. If we unite the three axes into a proposition, it can be said that those people with high-tech educations, that live in the cities in the coastal regions, will most probably have high incomes, and be part of the middle or upper-middle class.

The development we have described above concerns the period from the 1980s up until today. Moreover, the figures show that there is a greater difference in income between urban and rural areas than between inland and coastal areas (Kanbur and Zhang 2009: 16–31).

In addition to the geographical and competence-related drivers of inequality, there are three historical events that have driven economic inequality from 1949 up until the present day.

1. The first historical event concerns the Great Leap Forward from 1958 to 1962. In this Maoist experiment, millions of people died from famine in China, with estimates ranging from 15 to 55 million, making the famine one of the largest in human history.

---

[55] http://en.people.cn/n3/2022/0128/c90000-9950638.html.

2. The second historical event concerns the Cultural Revolution from 1966 to 1976, the year of Mao's death. Estimates of the death toll during the Cultural Revolution vary widely, ranging from 500,000 to 2,000,000. In relation to economic inequality, the consequences of the experiment for the Chinese economy were very large. Red Guards and other groups were sent around the country to retrain and imprison people they believed had converted to a capitalist mindset. Many of the managers in Chinese businesses and officials in the state apparatus were subjected to mockery, humiliation, dismissals and relocations from the cities to the countryside. This also extended to leading figures in the Communist Party, such as Deng Xiaoping (Vogel 2011). The Cultural Revolution was characterized by violence and chaos across Chinese society. This period saw numerous atrocities and massacres, including a massacre in Guangxi, which was perhaps the worst. There were also incidents in Inner Mongolia, Guangdong, Yunnan, and Hunan. The Red Guards destroyed historical artefacts, and ransacked cultural and religious sites, which they believed represented old values associated with capitalism.
3. The third historical event was the opening of China to foreign capital, especially capital from the West. This facilitated China's economic growth, and lay the foundation for developing an economy that was eventually able to compete with the United States. Initially, it was the farmers and the Chinese working class who created the conditions for strong economic growth. However, from around 2012, it was the Chinese middle class that ensured stable economic growth. In this context, China's GDP per capita grew from 6300 dollars in 2012 to more than 12,000 dollars in 2021, i.e. a doubling.[56] It was during this period that the US began to regard China as a competitor on the global stage.

The 20th National Congress of the Chinese Communist Party, held in Beijing from 16 to 22 October 2022, emphasized that Chinese production needs to focus more on quality than quantity. In other words, high-tech production will constitute the fundamental economic principle for further economic growth. Previously, the Chinese authorities had laid the foundations for a new dynamic economic stability by implementing two central measures. The first was the launching of the Belt and Road Initiative (BRI), colloquially known as the New Silk Road. This measure ensured that China became an international partner that all countries in the global economy had to take into account when making their own strategic choices. The second measure was China's response to the US's sanctions policy and technological containment of China. The US's more assertive stance on its relations with China can be said to have started as far back as 2011 (Clinton 2011) during the Obama administration. This tougher stance towards China was continued during the Trump administration with the launch of a trade war directed at China. This assertive stance was reinforced by President Biden's sanctions policy, banning Chinese high-tech products from American markets, and the US's interference in China's domestic affairs in the Xinjiang province, and also related to the Taiwan issue.

[56] https://www.globaltimes.cn/page/202206/1269277.shtml.

China's response to the US measures can be said to be based on textbook Keynesian economics, that is, to increase domestic demand in order to drive supply and stimulate economic growth. In other words, China began to focus more on domestic demand, especially the consumption of its growing middle class. This concerns consumer goods, and high-tech and high-quality goods, such as cars, refrigerators, and smart phones. Domestic demand was also increased by various financial operations, so that it became easier for innovative entrepreneurs to invest in high-tech production.[57] In addition, China's membership of the world's largest free trade agreement, the RCEP (1 Jan. 2022), functions as an important driver of economic growth.

Sub-conclusion Regarding the Rise of the Chinese Middle Class

We have examined the following question: What has been the role of China's middle class in the development of AI?

The brief answer is that the middle class in China has been an important factor in China's development of artificial intelligence. This began to be evident when economic growth took off around 2012. After this point in time, the new leadership in China used the middle class as an economic lever to boost economic growth and prosperity.

References

Ainley P (2014) Follow your dreams and attend to universities if possible. Latitude, 21

Ainley P (2016) Betraying a generation: how education is failing young people. Policy Press, Bristol

Allen RC (2009) The British industrial revolution in global perspective. Cambridge University Press, Cambridge

Allison G (2018) Destined for war: can America and China escape Thucydides trap? Scribe, London

Andersen ES (2009) Schumpeter's evolutionary economics. Anthem Press, London

Batzhan A, Alpysbayeva S, Kapsalyamova Z (2020) The belt and road initiative: case of Kazakhstan. In: Chay YW, Menkhoff T, Low L (eds) Chinas belt and road initiative: understanding the dynamics of a global transformation. World Scientific, London, pp 71–97

Beeson M, Li F (2016) China's place in regional and global governance: a new world comes into view. Global Pol 7(4):491–499

Berlie JA, Hung S (2020) The greater Bay area and the role of Hong Kong and Macau SARs in the Belt and Road initiative. In: Berlie JA (ed) China's globalization and the belt and road initiative. Palgrave, London, pp 77–100

Blecher M, Goodman DSG, Guo Y, Rocca J-L, Tang B (2022) Class and the communist part of China, 1978–2021: reform and market socialism. Routledge, London

Bowden W (1965) Industrial society in England. Routledge, London

[57] https://english.www.gov.cn/premier/news/202206/16/content_WS62aa64d7c6d02e533532c34b.html.

Brown K (2018) China's dream. Polity, London
Brown, K. (2019). The world according to Xi. I. B. Tauris, London
Cao C (2004) Zhongguancun and China's high-tech parks in transition: growing pains or premature senility. Asian Surv 44(5):647–668
Chay YW, Menkhoff T, Low L (2020) China's belt and road initiative: understanding the dynamics of a global transformation. World Scientific, London
Chuliang L, Sicular T (2013) Inequality and poverty in rural China. In: Sji L, Sato H, Sicular T (eds) Rising inequality in China: challenges to a harmonious society. Cambridge University Press, Cambridge, pp 197–229
Clinton H (2011) America's pacific century. Foreign Pol 189
Croll E (2006) China's new consumers: social development and domestic demand. Routledge, London
Deng X (1994) Selected works of Deng Xiaoping, vol III (1982–1992). Foreign Language Press, Beijing
Drache D, Kingsmith AT, Qi D (2019) One road many dreams: China's bold plan to remake the global economy. Bloomsbury, New York
Elliott JE (1980) Marx and Schumpeter. Q J Econ 95(1):45–68
Fan S, Kanbur R, Zhang X (2009) Regional inequality in China: an overview. In: Fan S, Kanbur R, Zhang X (eds) Regional inequality in China. Routledge, London, pp. 1–13
Ford M (2016) The rise of the robots. Oneworld, London
Ford M (2021) Rule of the robots. Basic Books, New York
Frey CB (2019) The technology trap: capital, labour, and power in the age of automation. Princeton University Press, Princeton
Frey CB (2020) Attitudes towards technology: part II. In: Skidelsky R, Craig N (eds) Work in the future: the automation revolution. Palgrave, London, pp 89–97
Hamel G (2002) Leading the revolution: how to thrive in turbulent times by making innovation a way of life. Harvard Business School Press, Boston
Hamel G (2012) What matters now: how to win in a world of relentless change, ferocious competition, and unstoppable innovation. John Wiley & Sons, New York
Hannum EJ (1999) Political change and the urban-rural gap in basic education in China, 1949–1990. Comp Educ Rev 43(2):193–211
Hannum EJ, Behrman M, Wang M, Liu J (2008) Education in the reform era. In: Brandt L, Rawski TG (eds) China's great economic transformation. Cambridge University Press, Cambridge, pp 215–249
Hong L (2021) China in one village: the history of one town and the future of the world. Verso, London
Jacques M (2012) When China rules the world. Penguin Books, London
Jain R (2021) China's soft power and higher education in South Asia. Routledge, London
Johannessen J-A (2020a) Automation, innovation and economic crises: survival in the fourth industrial revolution. Routledge, London
Johannessen J-A (2020b) Artificial intelligence, automation and the future of competence at work. Routledge
Johannessen J-A (2020c) Knowledge management for leadership and communication: AI, innovation and the digital economy. Emerald, London
Johannessen J-A (2021a) China's innovation economy: artificial intelligence and the new silk road. Routledge, London
Johannessen J-A (2021b) Artificial intelligence, automation and ethics in the innovation economy. Routledge, London
Johannessen J-A (2022a) A systemic approach to continuous change in the innovation economy. Routledge, London
Johannessen J-A (2022b) The new silk road and the innovation economy in China: four driving forces. Routledge, London
Johannessen J-A, Sætersdal H (2020) Automation, innovation and work. Routledge, London

Kanbur R, Zhang X (2009) Which regional inequality? In: Fan S, Kanbur R, Zhang X (eds) Regional inequality in China. Routledge, London, pp 15–31
Kissinger H (2012) On China. Penguin, New York
Knight J, Sicular T, Ximing Y (2013) Educational inequality in China: the intergenerational dimension. In: Shi L, Sato H, Sicular T (eds) Rising inequality in China. Cambridge University Press, Cambridge, pp 142–197
Kroeber AR (2020) China's economy. Oxford University Press, Oxford
Kwan KR (2021) Confucian sentimental representation. Routledge, London
Li, C. (2021). Middle class Shanghai: reshaping U.S.-China engagement. Brookings Institution Press, Washington, DC
Liu Y (2016) Higher education, meritocracy and inequality in China. Springer, London
Liu S (2021) Neoliberalism, globalization and "Elite" education in China, becoming international. Routledge, London
Løfstedt JI (1980) Chinese educational policy: changes and contradictions, 1949–1979. Almqvist & Wiksel International, Stockholm
Ma W (2016) China's mobile economy. Wiley, London
Ma W (2021) The digital war. Wiley, New York
Mahbubani K (2020) Has China won? PublicAffairs, London
Mandel E (1972) Introduction. In: Marx K (ed) Capital, vol II. Penguin Books, London, pp 11–80
Mandel E (1977) Marxist economic theory. Merlin Press, London
Mandel E (1990) Introduction. In: Marx K (ed) Capital, vol I. Penguin Books, London, pp 11–87
Mandel E (1991) Introduction. In: Marx K (ed) Capital, vol III. Penguin Books, London, pp 9–91
Mantoux P (1961) The industrial revolution in the eighteenth century: an outline of the beginning of the modern factory system in England. Routledge, London
Mantzopoulos V, Shen R (2011) The political economy of China's systemic transformation. Palgrave, London
Marx K, Engels F (2020) The communist manifesto. Wordsworth, New York
McGraw TK (2007) Prophet of Innovation: Joseph Schumpeter and creative destruction. Belknap Press, Cambridge
Miao Y (2019) Being middle class in China: identity, attitudes and behaviours. Routledge, London
Ning K (2016) Institutional innovation in higher education resource allocation in China's transitional economy. McGraw Hill, New York
Orlik T (2020) China: the bubble that never pops. Oxford University Press, Oxford
Pan Z (2020) Strategic linkages: China's belt and road initiative and power capture through global value chains. In: Chay YW, Menkhoff T, Low L (eds) China's belt and road initiative: understanding the dynamics of a global transformation. World Scientific, London, pp 221–241
Rahim E (2009) Marx and Schumpeter: a comparison of their theories of development. Rev Polit Econ 21(1):51–83
Reinert H, Reinert E (2010) Creative destruction in economics: Nietzsche, Sombart, Schumpeter. In: Backhaus J, Drechsler W (ed) Friedrich Nietzsche (1844–1900): economy and society. Springer, Berlin
Reves RV (2018) Dream Hoardes: how the American upper middle class is leaving everyone else in the dust. Why that is a problem and what to do about it. Brooking Institution Press, Washington, DC
Rocca J-L (2018) The making of the Chinese middle class: small comfort and great expectations. Palgrave, London
Rosenberg N (2000) Schumpeter and the endogeneity of technology: some American perspectives. Routledge, London
Ryan J (2019) Education in China: philosophy, politics and culture. Polity, London
Saich T, Hu B (2016) Chinese village, global market: new collectives and rural development. Palgrave, London
Schuman M (2015) Confucius: and the world he created. Basic Books, London
Schumpeter J (1951) Theory of economic development. Harvard University Press, Boston

Schumpeter J (1954) History of economic analysis. Oxford University Press, Oxford
Schumpeter J (1989) Business cycles. Porcupine Press, New York
Schumpeter J (2010) Capitalism, socialism and democracy. Routledge, London
Shi L, Sato H, Sicular T (2013) Rising inequality in China: key issues and findings. In: Shi L, Sato H, Sicular T (eds) Rising inequality in China. Cambridge University Press, Cambridge, pp 1–44
Smith NR (2021) The end of the village. University of Minnesota Press, London
Thøgersen S (1990) Secondary education in China after Mao: reform and social conflict. Aarhus University Press, Aarhus, Denmark
Vangeli A (2019) A framework for the study of one belt one road initiative as a medium of principle diffusion. In: Xing L (ed) Mapping China's one belt one road initiative. Palgrave Macmillan, London, pp 57–89
Vogel EF (2011) Deng Xiaoping and the transformation of China. Harvard University Press, Cambridge, Mass
Wedeman A (2012) Double paradox: rapid growth and rising corruption in China. Cornell University Press, Ithaca
Xing L (2019) Understanding the multiple facets of China's "one belt one road" initiative. In: Xing L (ed) Mapping China's one belt one road initiative. Palgrave Macmillan, London, pp 29–56
Xinyu L, Zukosky M (2022) The future of China: three critiques of neoliberalism. Palgrave, London
Yu H (2020) Motivation behind China's one belt, one road initiative and establishment of the Asian Infrastructure Investment Bank. In: Zhao S (ed) China's new global strategy. Routledge, London, pp 3–19
Zhang J (2015) China's new foreign policy under Xi Jinping: towards peaceful rise 2.0? Glob Change Peace Secur 27(1):5–19
Zhao Y (2014) Who's afraid of the big bad dragon: why China has the best (and worst) education system in the world. Jossey-Bass, New York

Chapter 4
China's Progress in Artificial Intelligence: A Synthesis

Core Idea
China's 'grand strategy' can be operationalized in the following way: China will be able to strengthen the periphery through the Silk Road projects, in order to secure the centre, that is, China. This will enable China to have a dominant regional role.

Key Points

- The 'Chinese Dream' is to raise everyone in China up to a middle-class income.
- The 'American Dream' is focused on the individual; that is, the individual can achieve success as long as he/she works hard enough. The 'Chinese Dream' has a collective focus; that is, everyone in China can be raised up to a middle-class income through collective effort.
- The Chinese leaders need to take into account the fact that any type of armed conflict or social unrest will have a negative impact on the ambitions and expectations of the Chinese middle class.
- The main driver for the development of innovative entrepreneurship in China is artificial intelligence.
- Geo-economic factors influence and change geopolitical relations.
- When the centre is weakened, the periphery will become more assertive, resulting in the centre being unable to resist the pressure.
- The systemic link between the three Silk Roads and the growth of the Chinese middle class can partly explain China's development of artificial intelligence.

Introduction

Geo-economic factors influence and change geopolitical relations. For a long period, China has developed a foreign policy where its 'grand strategy' has been to achieve regional dominance. This regional dominance should not be confused with the type

J. Johannessen, *The AI Battleground Between the USA and China*, Global Power Shift,
https://doi.org/10.1007/978-3-032-10138-9_4

of global dominance that was exerted in the past by Western imperial and colonial powers. For instance, the global ambitions of the British Empire was aptly expressed in the saying "The sun never sets on the British Empire", which expresses the power and reach that the British Empire had, and the fact that its influence was felt all over the globe. Similarly the global ambitions of the German Empire were expressed in the saying, "A place in the sun" (ein Platz an der Sonne), which refers to Germany's imperialist foreign policy adopted by the German Empire, which aimed to transform Germany into a global power. China's 'grand strategy', on the other hand, regarding its foreign policy, is of a completely different nature, as it focuses more on regional dominance based on economic strength and economic reciprocity between countries. This has been evident in the development of the thousands of infrastructure projects that are included in the Belt and Road Initiative (BRI), colloquially called the New Silk Road (Johannessen 2022a), or more specifically, the three New Silk Roads: the land-based, maritime and digital Silk Roads.

The economic corridor between China and Pakistan is just one example of this economic reciprocity. The railway between China and Laos is another example. The development of 5G networks in many countries in the region is a third example. There are thousands of such examples where China has developed regional dominance based on economic reciprocity.

China's global expansion along the three Silk Roads should not be confused with the idea that China's 'grand strategy' is to achieve global dominance. On the contrary. China's global expansion has the strategic aim of strengthening its periphery in order to secure the centre (China), so that it will be able to dominate regionally.

China's global expansion along the three Silk Roads is evident in many parts of the world. Africa is perhaps the best example of how China's global expansion has taken shape (French 2015). However, China and Chinese companies have also invested in many European countries, such as Cosco Shipping's acquisition of a majority stake in the port of Piraeus, Athens, Greece; and the Budapest–Athens railway, a China-CEE project of China's Belt and Road Initiative, a railroad international connection between central and Southeast Europe.

Chinese economic growth has also led to the emergence of a very large middle class of approx. 700 million. This middle class has expectations of a better economic future. If the government is able to meet these expectations then it will be improbable that people will question the role of the Communist Party, as China's only political governing system (Johannessen 2023d).

The middle class provides the Chinese government with leverage to ensure economic growth, and thus also political and military strength. Regional dominance, global expansion and the growth of the middle class have led to the Communist Party having a greater need for both internal and external political alliances. The internal political alliances have increasingly involved the growing middle class, where the new foundation of the Communist Party's thinking is based on meeting the expectations of the middle class. The external political alliances are expressed in various relationships that the Chinese government has developed, such as along the New Silk Road; as well as in relation to BRICS; to RCEP, the world's largest free trade area; relations within the UN; and also relations in the SCO (the Shanghai Cooperation Organization), which is a political, economic and military alliance, which encompasses large parts of Asia. However, it would be a misconception to believe that China's economic expansion is based on a strategic aim of global dominance. China's 'grand strategy' is rather one of seeking to achieve regional dominance.

Professor Kishore Mahbubani asked the following question (which was also the title of his book): "Has China Won?" (Mahbubani 2020). He reaches the paradoxical conclusion. A major geopolitical contest between the US and China is both inevitable and avoidable. It is inevitable because the Chinese competition has created challenges for the American economy that US politicians need to deal with. The US has responded to China's economic growth by imposing sanctions on Chinese high-tech companies, and by launching a trade war with China. It might be said that such a response was inevitable. Moreover, according to Mahbubani, the US needed "a foreign scapegoat to hide the deep domestic socioeconomic challenges that have emerged in American society" (Mahbubani 2020: 253). The paradox can be expressed in the words of the Norwegian philosopher, "It's what you are good at that will be your downfall" (Zapffe's paradox).[1] China became so good at increasing its economic growth and developing its high-tech capabilities, such as in the field of artificial intelligence, that the US could not merely stand by and watch China, a country governed by the Chinese Communist Party, overtake the US economically, without doing something to reduce China's strength. Thus, the answer to Mahbubani's question is: Yes, China has won, but this is precisely what could be its downfall. This is what we may term 'the Chinese paradox'.

China's goal is not to become the leading global economic power and thus the leading global political force, but to dominate regionally, regarding economic growth and influence. The Communist Party has transformed a poor and backward developing country into one of the world's most advanced economies. However, as we have shown throughout this book, China's economic policy has not been a single consistent strategy from 1949 onward, since the creation of the People's Republic of China (PRC). The have been many setbacks along the way, where many 'mistakes' have been made, such as during the economic and social campaign, "The Great Leap Forward", and the period of the socio-political movement, the Cultural Revolution (CR). Nevertheless, China's economic policy has been more consistent from the end of the 1970s up until today, leading to huge economic growth.

Technological development in China from the 1980s onward has shown that using soft-power has been far more effective than the hard-power that was used during the rule of Mao Zedong (Jain 2021). China has developed its technology in the wake of the United States, launched manned space-crafts, developed missile defence systems that can shield the country against incoming missiles, and become a leading developer and user of digital technologies, in particular artificial intelligence.

China has more than 4000 years of recorded history, and is unique among countries in its longevity as a distinct politico-cultural unit (Mahbubani 2018; 2020). Although China is formally a unitary state, it consists of many provinces, autonomous regions,

[1] Zapffe's paradox: https://philosophynow.org/issues/45/The_Last_Messiah

municipalities ("mainland China"), and special administrative regions (SARs). In other words, the various provinces and regions have a relative degree of autonomy. Consequently, governing 1.4 billion people directly from a political centre in Beijing has proven neither desirable nor possible. Therefore, the governance system in China is characterized to some extent by a form of distributed governance, involving a certain degree of administrative decentralization, and a dispersing of authority and power across the various regions and provinces.

The expectations and ambitions of the college-educated Chinese middle class drive economic growth (Li 2021). In other words, the middle class provides the leverage to ensure economic and technological development, as well as drive domestic consumption and demand. In a situation where competition between China and the US is increasing, and technological sanctions have been implemented by the US against China, the Chinese middle class is crucial for China's economic and military development.

The trap that the Chinese Communist Party may fall into seems obvious. China is home to the largest middle-class cohort in the world. If the communist leaders do not meet the expectations of the middle class then this may pose a threat to the leadership of the Communist Party. The Chinese government wishes to avoid the fate of the Soviet Union and the collapse of communism in Eastern Europe (1989–1991). Historically, this can explain the brutal crackdown of the Tiananmen Square protests in 1989 (Vogel 2011; Deng 1994). Against this background, it seems likely that the Chinese leaders will seek to satisfy the ambitions and expectations of the middle class. However, they will only be able to do this if they seek stability in the overall structures, both nationally and globally, while at the same time managing to maintain steady economic growth. Consequently, the Chinese leaders need to take into account the fact that any type of armed conflict or social unrest will have a negative impact on the ambitions and expectations of the Chinese middle class. This constitutes one of the main arguments why China's sabre-rattling against Taiwan will not escalate into armed conflict and the invasion of Taiwan in the foreseeable future. It is not in the interests of the Communist Party to start a war with Taiwan, thereby confronting the United States. Against this background, it is conceivable that China will adopt a different strategy, such as Beijing's plans to develop a training facility in Cuba, which would result in Chinese troops being stationed on America's doorstep.[2] This can well be thought of as a strategy on China's part to create a new 'Cuban Crisis', similar to the one provoked by Khrushchev in 1962,[3] with the aim of forcing the US to withdraw its commitments in relation to Taiwan in exchange for China withdrawing from all its Cuban engagements.

When considering China's future foreign policy strategy, we should take into account China's "Century of Humiliation" and its defeats by foreign powers, such as its defeat in the Opium Wars and the British occupation of Hong Kong; the colonising of Macau by the Portuguese; Japan's brutal conquest of large parts of China during

---

[2] https://www.wsj.com/articles/beijing-plans-a-new-training-facility-in-cuba-raising-prospect-of-chinese-troops-on-americas-doorstep-e17fd5d1

[3] https://history.state.gov/milestones/1961-1968/cuban-missile-crisis

and prior to the Second World War (1937–1945); the takeover of Taiwan by Japan (1905–1945); as well as the period of "Gunboat diplomacy" by foreign powers, such as the United States, European countries and Japan, which opened up China for foreign trade resulting in a period of "unequal treaties". In other words, China's "Century of Humiliation" has become part of its historical identity (Mahbubani 2020; Hong 2021). In this context, every Chinese person wants an economically, militarily, technologically and diplomatically strong China (Brown 2018). This identity is a bond that binds the Communist Party together with most people in China (Brown 2019). The point is simply that the Communist Party must also fulfil people's expectations, if they are to secure the support of most people in China, and especially the middle class. The Communist Party will not be able to do this if they take China into a war with the United States or other countries that have an alliance with the United States. This assumption is the surest argument that the Chinese leaders will for all intents and purposes avoid an open confrontation with the United States or other nations that the United States is willing to support.

China's common identity is embodied in the desire that China will never again experience being degraded and humiliated. This constitutes a common force that binds the population together in a common destiny (Mahbubani 2018). This driving force is also embodied in the 'Chinese Dream', which is to raise everyone to a middle-class income through collective effort (Brown 2018). This is in contrast to the 'American Dream', which is focused on the individual; that is, the individual can achieve success as long as he/she works hard enough. In this context, the Chinese and American cultures can be said to be diametrically opposed to each other (Fig. 4.1).

Based on the above description, we have developed a conceptual model for China's leadership in artificial intelligence.

Geo-Economic Factors

Geo-economics can be defined as: "the study of the spatial, temporal, and political aspects of economies and resources". The distinction of geo-economics separately from geopolitics is often attributed to Edward Luttwak, the American military strategist, and Pascal Lorot, the French economist. Their focus is on how geo-economic factors will play an increasingly important role in geopolitical competition. It is against this background that one can say that Chinese geo-economic realities are influencing its geopolitical positioning, and vice versa (Hass 2021; Allison 2018).

The strategic goal of the Chinese leaders is to develop an economic system that is completely on par with the American economy. In some respects, the goal is to overtake the United States, and become the world's leading economy (Ferdinand 2016; Gungwu 2019). The nations contiguous to China have adopted this strategic objective as a guideline, and are continuously adapting to China's regional and global economic expansion (Jacques 2012; Mahbubani 2020). The countries in the region have already adapted so that they do not come into conflict with what the Chinese consider to be their central interests (Yang 2015). China has a large domestic market

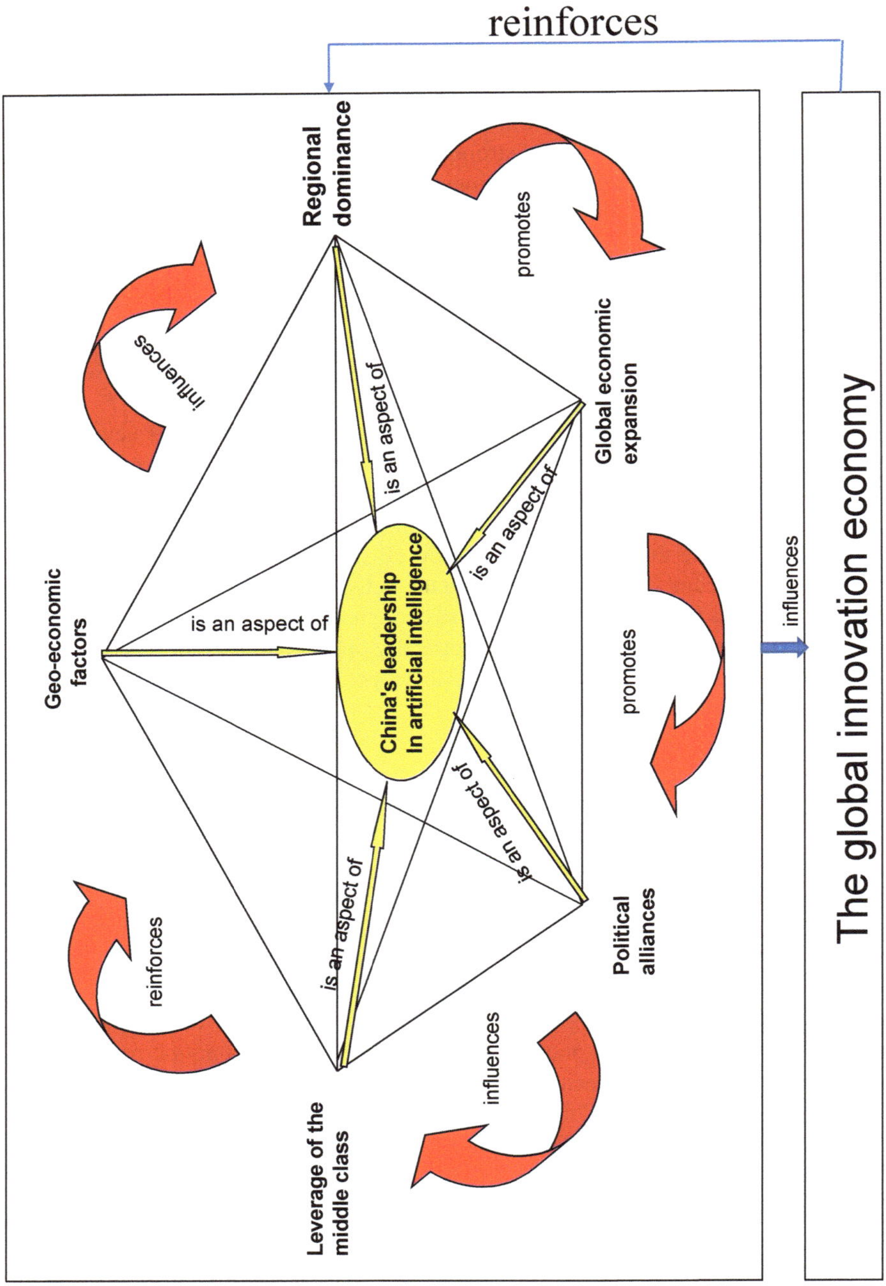

Fig. 4.1 China's leadership in artificial intelligence

of 1.4 billion consumers, including 700 million middle class consumers. For several European countries, this fact is an economic reality they take into account in their relations with China. This particularly applies to Germany and France, which have large revenues from their trade with China. In 2020, China was Germany's most important trading partner; for example, in goods such as machinery and equipment.[4] Eurostat indicates that China has become the EU's main trade partner, taking the top spot occupied previously by the United States. China is the largest market of Germany's automotive industry.[5] This geo-economic reality has already affected the geopolitical situation. The best example is perhaps NATO's 2022 Strategic Concept. The US government wished to define China as a strategic enemy. However, France and Germany wished to moderate this political rhetoric in the drafting of the NATO document.[6]

In order to understand Chinese thinking related to economic expansion, and China's self- identity, it is important to be aware of how the Chinese population thinks in relation to the lands and regions they lost during the period of colonization of China. It was during this period that the lands and regions of China were colonized by countries such as, Portugal, Britain, Japan, the US and France. The return of these lands to China has been, and still is, an exceedingly important issue for the Chinese people and the Chinese government; for instance, this concerned the handover of sovereignty over Hong Kong in 1997 (Mahbubani 2020). In the present day, this applies particularly to Taiwan. Geopolitical tensions between the United States and China have increased regarding the issue of the sovereignty of Taiwan. The period of colonization and the 'Century of Century of Humiliation' still play a role in the thinking of the Chinese leaders and the Chinese people. It is therefore not difficult to mobilize the population against countries that still believe that what was taken from China during the period of colonization does not belong to China. In this context, it should also be mentioned that Taiwan and China together produce most of the world's semiconductors (microchips).[7] In other words, the geopolitical conflict regarding Taiwan, also concerns geo-economic factors.

During the last decade, China has been willing to resort to strict measures against countries that it believes have gone against their central interests. For example, when the Chinese dissident, Liu Xiaobo, was awarded the Nobel Peace Prize, by the Norwegian Nobel Committee in 2010, the Chinese Government responded by freezing diplomatic and economic relations with Norway, and banning the import of Norwegian fish, amongst other things.[8] This type of geo-economic reality can be expected to form a political backdrop in future decisions that go against China's fundamental interests. Another recent case regarding punitive measures implemented by China against countries that are viewed as going against its interests was the 'Taiwan Row'

[4] https://www.globaltimes.cn/page/202112/1241488.shtml

[5] https://www.chinadaily.com.cn/a/202101/14/WS5fffebeda31024ad0baa2a3e.html
https://www.chinadaily.com.cn/a/202103/18/WS6052f45aa31024ad0bab0064.html

[6] https://www.nato.int/strategic-concept/

[7] https://worldpopulationreview.com/country-rankings/semiconductor-manufacturing-by-country

[8] https://www.nytimes.com/2016/12/19/world/europe/china-norway-nobel-liu-xiaobo.html

between China and Lithuania, when China stopped buying beef, dairy products and beer from Lithuania.[9] The move came after Lithuania let Taiwan open a de facto embassy there.

The brief description above shows how geo-economic factors and geopolitical issues can become intertwined. It seems reasonable to assume that geo-economic factors will influence China's future strategy regarding the development of artificial intelligence.

Regional Dominance

Geo-economic factors are primarily something we see developing in the regions bordering China. It is not necessarily correct to assume that China is less innovative than the US, based on the assumption that China has had fewer high-tech breakthroughs. In this context, it seems more reasonable to take a historical perspective. It was first in 1978 that China adopted its 'Open Door Policy', to open the door to foreign investment. On the other hand, European investment in America can be traced as far back to the 1600s. From such a perspective, one can assume that China's progress after opening up to Western capital has shown a great ability to adapt and find innovative solutions to economic and technological challenges. This development is also reflected in China's dominant regional position.

In order for China to have the prerequisites to dominate regionally, it was crucial that the country first developed its own strength, both economically and technologically. This development took many decades, because it required strong competence development. It is precisely this competence development that has enabled China to become the central power in the region. In other words, the development of high-tech expertise has given China an advantage in the region, and also as a future global player. When China's level of competence is on par with that of the rest of the world, its economic position can be strengthened. When human competence is strong, China will dominate both regionally and globally, because the country's 1.4 billion people constitute a force that creates the competence that will move the country economically, technologically, diplomatically, politically, and militarily.

The overall Chinese strategy for dominating both regionally and globally, as we have emphasized in several places in this book, has been to develop human competence in general and high-tech competence in particular. It is through the development of this competence that China has managed to lift itself from a producer of cheap consumer goods for Western consumers, to a producer of high-tech products in general, and artificial intelligence in particular.

[9] https://www.bbc.com/news/business-60343316

China's economic growth has had a profound impact on Southeast Asian countries, not least in the development of infrastructure; it might be said that the Chinese infrastructure development in the region has become a hallmark of China's regional dominance. China has undergone a dramatic transformation of its institutional and business environment since the early 1980s, changing from a centrally planned economy to a socialist market economy. The Chinese investment banks are one example of such institutions that have made it possible for China to become a regional dominant power. The period when China modelled its economy and governance on the institutions of the Soviet Union and Stalinist ideology has long since passed.

China employs several regional development strategies, such as the Belt and Road Initiative (BRI), which focuses on infrastructure development, and enables China to achieve regional dominance. China's regional dominance is also reflected in the economic corridors it has created around its periphery, such as the China-Pakistan Economic Corridor (CPEC), which is a framework of regional connectivity, benefiting both China and Pakistan, as well as other countries in the region. The acquisition and development of ports for the transport of goods is also an important mechanism driving China's regional dominance. China's membership of the world's largest free trade agreement, the RCEP, may also contribute to China strengthening its regional dominance in the future.

Global Economic Expansion

China aims to surpass the United States as the next world leading economic power. This is a strategic goal, and also related to realizing the 'Chinese Dream'. The Chinese Dream is to raise everyone in China up to a middle-class income through collective effort. From this perspective, Chinese global expansion can be viewed as a means of increasing the prosperity of ordinary Chinese people. In this context, it is possibly a faulty assessment when NATO declares China to be a future security challenge.[10] The 'threat' is more probably related to China's economic progress and its development of high technology, including artificial intelligence, rather than its expansionist military goals or capabilities. China has been the fastest growing economy in the world since the 1980s. But it wasn't until 2001 that China was invited by the wealthy, developed countries to join the World Trade Organization (WTO). However, this admission was preceded by drawn-out negotiations and required important changes to the Chinese economy. In the West, this was viewed as China moving towards a more 'Western' form of democratic governance. In China, this democratic governance was framed within the system of Chinese socialism. Since China entered the World Trade Organization in 2001, the US has lost millions of manufacturing jobs to China. The job losses to China can partly explain why Donald Trump was elected US president in 2016. The impact of rising Chinese exports on manufacturing employment in the US is often termed "the China Shock". China's entry into the WTO resulted

[10] https://www.nato.int/strategic-concept/

in trade liberalization in China, and allowed entrepreneurs and private companies greater freedom to operate. Moreover, it also resulted in China adapting to 'Western' methods of production, and to 'Western' economic institutions, such as the free market and intellectual rights, as well as financial institutions, such as banks and insurance companies.

The Group of Twenty (G20), which was established in 1999, includes China. The G20 is a forum for international economic cooperation, and plays an important role in influencing and strengthening global governance on major international economic issues. China's opening to the West, and its participation in international organizations, such as the WTO, G20, the World Bank (WB) and the International Monetary Fund (IMF), contributed to China becoming the fourth largest trading nation in 2002, and the country with the largest direct foreign investment (FDI).[11]

During the last three decades, China has liberalized its economy, and utilized economic mechanisms that could be found in any capitalist country. In contrast, China has not been admitted to the G7, which is a grouping of advanced democracies that meets to address global economic issues. The reason why China is not a member of the important group of seven (G7) is that this alliance consists of an exclusive club consisting of so-called "like-minded people", that is, Western democracies with capitalist economies.[12]

In reality, it might be said that China is being hindered from greater integration into the Western globally led institutions, such as the G7, due to the competition that has developed between the US and China, especially in relation to the development and trading of high-tech products. Both countries play on political alliances in order to develop dynamic blocs, where the economic competition threatens to escalate into military conflict. This is evident if we consider NATO's new "Strategic Concept", from 2022 and 2023, which declares China to be a future security challenge.

China's huge economic expansion from the late 1970s up until today has resulted in China now challenging the United States as the leading global economic power. Moreover, China's leaders have stated that China aims to become a world leader in artificial intelligence and robotics. It is possibly China's technological development that is perceived as the real threat to the USs hegemony, economically, militarily and politically. The adage of "hiding one's strength and biding one's time", advocated by Deng Xiaoping (Vogel 2011), was definitively abandoned in 2012. In 2012, at a conference in Kazakhstan, Xi Jinping launched the concept of the Belt and Road Initiative (BRI), the New Silk Road. Obviously, the Chinese leaders saw that the time was ripe to demonstrate China's resources, and that they no longer needed to "hide their strength". The real 'strength' in China may be said to be the middle class, that provides China with leverage economically and technologically. In other words, the growing Chinese middle class possesses a high degree of competences, and also constitutes a very large market of consumers. Highly competent middle class entrepreneurs are able to start up entrepreneurial businesses based on high-tech

---

[11] https://www.uvic.ca/research/centres/globalstudies/assets/docs/publications/G20andChina.pdf

[12] https://www.uvic.ca/research/centres/globalstudies/assets/docs/publications/G20andChina.pdf

innovation. In this context, it might be said that the main driver for the development of innovative entrepreneurship in China is artificial intelligence.

Political Alliances

China's technological development has promoted what we have termed the "second period of globalization" (Johannessen 2022a). The "Second Globalization" is linked to the increase in the export of high-tech goods from China to the West. These products are produced with relatively lower labour costs than for similar high-tech products in the West, and are therefore cheaper (Johannessen 2023d). The first period of globalization was promoted by political alliances, between the West and China, where Nixon and Kissinger played decisive roles for American policies. It was during this period that Mao Zedong and Deng Xiaoping opened China up to the world, the so-called Open Door Policy. However, Mao had been against such an opening for a long time, but he adopted the new policy for China as a result of the perceived threat from the Soviet Union (Deng 1994). In this way, the new political alliances regarding the relationship between the US and China resulted in a re-orientation of China's foreign policy. However, the political alliances changed character in the 2000s. The change in US foreign policy in the Asia-Pacific region became evident in the article, "America's Pacific Century", written by the former Secretary of State, Hillary Clinton (*Foreign Policy*, 2011). Later, the US's assertive foreign policy materialized when President Trump launched a trade war. The trade war against China was continued by the Biden administration that expressed that China represented the US's greatest challenge in the future.[13] Against this background, the political alliances have changed from the first period of globalization, which was driven by cheap Chinese labour, to the second period of globalization, which is characterized by China's increasing high-tech competence, and its production of high-tech goods using relatively cheap labour. It is this technological competition between the US and China that is fuelling tensions between the two countries. These tensions are also to some extent triggering a reorientation of Chinese trade and policies, where China is now focusing more on the BRICS countries, as well as the countries that are part of the Belt and Road Initiative (BRI). In addition, China became a member of the world's largest free trade agreement on 1 January 2022. It seems reasonable to assume that membership in this organization will also change China's political alliances. In other words, China's political alliances are now moving more towards Asian countries, and to some extent veering away from its alliances with the US and Europe. The explanations for these changes in political alliances may be many, but as mentioned above, the high-tech competition between China and the US has been a driving force behind the changes. Without the alliance with the United States, which was promoted by Nixon and Kissinger in the 1970s, China would most probably not have been able to increase its economic growth to such a great extent. On the other

[13] https://www.brookings.edu/articles/how-biden-could-thaw-us-relations-with-china/

hand, without the new political alliances with the countries along the New Silk Road, and the growing relationships with the RCEP countries, there is much to suggest that China would not have been able to replace the loss of the political alliances with the US and its allies.

The increasingly close relationship between China and Russia can be understood in relation to what we have described above. In particular, China and Russia closed ranks as a result of Trump's trade war against China. The US sanctions policy against China was intensified during the Biden administration. In addition, the Biden administration criticized the government of China for their human rights record, which also contributed to pushing Beijing and Moscow closer together. Moreover, BRICS and SCO also became an increasingly important part of Chinese alliance building.

From an American perspective, it is understandable that the US government focuses on the technological competition with China. In the same way that China exported itself to prosperity based on cheap labour, during the first period of globalization, the high-tech products produced by China today are significantly cheaper than the high-tech products produced in the US and other Western countries, due to lower labour costs. In plain language, this means that the Chinese high-tech products can compete with the Western high-tech products on price. It is against this background that one can understand the technological sanctions that the US has imposed on Chinese high-tech products and technological services. In this context, Huawei was barred from operating in US 5G networks, due to issues about national security. However, there were perhaps other factors than national security at play here; American companies were finding it difficult to compete with Chinese technology on price and quality. But, banning Huawei would breach the principles of market economy, free trade and fair competition, unless other arguments than competition could be given for implementing the ban. In other words, by referring to the issue of national security, the United States has been able to bypass the principle of free competition and free trade as stipulated by the WTO.[14]

As long as the US was the world leader in the development of technological innovations, the US government was not so concerned about Chinese competition. However, the development of Chinese high-tech expertise in recent years, which has enabled China to compete with the US on high-tech products, has brought about a change in US policy towards China. As mentioned above, the US trade war against China, and the banning of Chinese companies, has resulted in the political relationship between the two countries changing character. It might be said that the world may have left the political blocs of the Cold War era, but that it is now again moving into a new era of geopolitical blocs, fuelled by high-tech competition.

The current relationship between the US and China is characterized by the importance of geo-economiceconomic factors that are influencing geopolitical relations. As mentioned above, this is clearly evident in the Huawei case, where the US government used the issue of national security to ban the Chinese company from doing business in the US. It might be said that the national security issue is a more sophisticated argument than the Trump administration's ploy that China "stole American jobs".

[14] WTO: The World Trade Centre, where both the US and China are members.

However, the result and intention are the same; to protect US industry against Chinese competition. Against this background, we can see a transition occurring from open globalization to a greater degree of decoupling, as well as a rise of protectionism and nationalism.

The Chinese Economic Lever: The Middle Class

There have been many empires in the past, and some that also exist in the present day, such as the British, Russian, Spanish, Persian, and Chinese, Hellenic and Roman, and the current American 'empire'. It might be said that these empires all had/have one thing in common, which is that they ignore the interests of the countries or regions that are under their dominion. It might also be said that this way of thinking ultimately leads to their downfall, because they do not build sustainable and mutual political alliances. When the centre is weakened, which always occurs during the fall of great empires, the periphery becomes more assertive, resulting in the centre being unable to resist the pressure. For instance, this occurred during the de-colonization of Asia and Africa during the post-war period, when new states achieved autonomy and independence from their European colonial rulers. In this context, it might be said that the present-day American 'empire' is also in decline. Figuratively, when empires fall, one might say that the peoples who have been colonized by the empires occupy the centre of the empire that had occupied them in the first place. The 'Middle Kingdom' (from 221 BCE to 1912), as imperial China described itself, was also a period partly characterized by trade along the ancient Silk Road (130 B.C.E. until 1453 C.E.). This Chinese empire suffered the fate of other empires—when the centre was weakened, the peripheral states pressed on the empire's borders resulting in its destruction.

It is in relation to the above that the current Chinese leaders focus on strengthening the centre by developing a sustainable and strong middle class. It is this middle class that will act as the strong centre in a future where China becomes increasingly stronger economically and militarily. The stronger China becomes, the greater will be the probability that other nations, such as the US, will try to stem the growing Chinese power. The growing Chinese middle class can be used by the Chinese leaders as an economic lever in order to tackle the political and economic challenges in the outside world. In this context, the Chinese middle class can be utilized in a requisite variety strategy; in other words, the leadership in China should at all times be able to utilize the Chinese middle class so that China can always respond strategically with the variety that is necessary to strengthen the centre, and thus prevent the periphery from taking control.

Put another way, the context is different from the last time China was an empire. The most important difference is that information spreads so quickly that no country can keep its actions hidden, even if the underlying 'grand strategy' is not made explicit. In this context, the others, led today by the United States and its allies, will always be able to counter any Chinese strategic action. It is against this background that we stress the point of a strong centre, because the periphery, which in China's case is the US and its allies, will always react to defend its global position. China is the rising power that is threatening to displace the ruling power, the US, which, according to Allison (2018), will trigger Thucydides Trap, and lead to conflict.

It seems reasonable to say that the Chinese 'grand strategy' to build up and retain a dominant international role in the economic and political system is a strengthening of the centre, which in this context means developing and strengthening the position of the middle class in China. The Chinese middle class can be utilized to initiate many processes, such as using middle-class domestic consumption to counteract the measures and policies enacted by the US and the West, such as trade sanctions and technological containment, against a backdrop of increased Western military presence in the Asia-Pacific region, and the various alliances established by the US and others, such as QUAD; moreover, NATO's 'Strategic Concept' in 2022 is also aimed at China for the first time stating that China's assertive behaviour challenges international order and Alliance security.

If, on the other hand, the Chinese middle class does not feel that their needs, wishes and expectations are being met by the Chinese Communist Party, then this may result in a situation where the middle class will function as a lever ejecting the Communist Party from power in China. It is also in this context that what was China's strength, the Chinese middle class, can also emerge as the force that will lead to the downfall of the Communist Party. Therefore, it is conceivable that although the Chinese middle class can create economic success for China, it may also lead to the fall of the Chinese Communist Party.

References

Allison G (2018) Destined for war: can America and China escape Thucydides trap? Scribe, London
Brown K (2018) China's dream. Polity, London
Brown K (2019) The world according to xi. I. B, Tauris, London
Deng X (1994) Selected works of Deng Xiaoping, vol III (1982-1992). Foreign Language Press, Beijing
Ferdinand P (2016) The China dream and one belt one road: Chinese foreign policy under xi Jinping. Int Aff 92(4):941–957
French HW (2015) China's second continent. Random House, London
Gungwu W (2019) China reconnects: joining a deep-rooted past to a new world order. World Scientific, London
Hass R (2021) Stronger: adapting America's China strategy in an age of competitive interdependence. Yale University Press, New Haven
Hong L (2021) China in one village: the history of one town and the future of the world. Verso, London
Jacques M (2012) When China rules the world. Penguin Books, London
Jain R (2021) China's soft power and higher education in South Asia. Routledge, London
Johannessen, JA (2022a) The New Silk Road and the innovation economy in China: Four driving forces, Routledge, London
Johannessen JA (2023d) De-globalization. Routledge, London

Li C (2021) Middle class Shanghai,: reshaping US-China engagement. Brooking Institution Press, Washington, D.C.
Mahbubani K (2018) Has the west lost. Allen Lane, New York
Mahbubani K (2020) Has China won? PublicAffairs, London
Vogel EF (2011) Deng Xiaoping and the transformation of China. Harvard University Press, Cambridge, Mass
Yang J (2015) China's new diplomacy under the xi Jinping administration. China quarterly of international strategic studies 1(1):1–17

Chapter 5
Concepts

Action

An action is here understood as an actor's intention, intention structure, and manifestation. An action is contrasted to an event, which is evidence of events only to a limited extent within the actor's control.

Boudon-Coleman diagram. This research methodology was developed by Mario Bunge (Bunge 1978:76–79) based on insights made by the sociologists Boudon and Coleman. The purpose of the diagram is to show the relationship between the various levels, such as the macro and micro-levels. For instance, it is shown how changes at the macro-level, such as technological innovations in feudal society, can lead to increased income at the micro-level. However, it was shown that technological innovations could lead to weakening of the semi-feudal structures because dependency on land owners was reduced. Consequently, the landowners opposed such changes especially in the case of technological innovations, which Boudon has shown in his research (Boudon 1981: 100). Coleman (Coleman 1990: 7–12) started at the macro-level, went to the individual level to find explanations and finally ended up at the macro level again.

An important purpose of Bunge's Boudon-Coleman diagram is to identify social mechanisms that maintain or change the phenomenon or problem under investigation (as mentioned above, in Boudon's analysis of semi-feudal society). Bunge's Boudon-Coleman diagram may be said to represent a "mixed strategy"; Bunge says

Part of the chapter are base don the following earlier publications: Johannessen, J-A. (2020). Knowledge Management Philosophy: Communication as a strategic asset in knowledge management, Emerald, London. Johannessen, J-A. (2022). A systemic approach to continous change in the innovation economy, Routledge, London. Johannessen, J-A. (2025). A systemic theory of knowledge management: Knowledge workers in the future of Artificial Intelligence, Emerald, London. Skålsvik, H.; Adriaenssen, D. & Johannessen, J-A. (2016). Leadership aming at innovation: Suggesting and discussing four roles of an innovation leader, Problems and Perspectives in Management, Volume, 14,3:537-548.

J. Johannessen, *The AI Battleground Between the USA and China*, Global Power Shift,
https://doi.org/10.1007/978-3-032-10138-9_5

the following: *When studying systems of any kind a) reduce them to their components (at some level) and the interaction among these, as well as among them and environmental items, but acknowledge and explain emergence* (see the chapter on concepts) *whenever it occurs, and b) approach systems from all pertinent sides and on all relevant levels, integrating theories or even research fields whenever unidisciplinarity proves to be insufficient* (Bunge, 1998:78). The purpose of this research strategy is to arrive at a deeper and more complete explanation of a system's behaviour.

Butterfly Effects

Small, often haphazard and improbable variables potentially capable of having large-scale consequences for social systems and nature.

Calibration

Calibration is here understood as the basis conducive to change in one type of basic relationship to another, e.g. the transition from a symmetrical to a complementary relationship.

Capabilities. Capabilities are for an organization what abilities are for an individual.

An organizational capability may thus be defined as an organization's ability to perform a task, activity or process. Operational capabilities enable an organization to make money in the here and now (Winter 2003: 991–995). Dynamic capabilities, as opposed to operational capabilities, are linked to processes of change. Change and innovation are at the centre of dynamic capabilities.

Simplified, one may say that organizational capabilities are something an organization does well compared to its competitors (Ulrich and Brockbank 2005). These capabilities are intangible and therefore difficult for competitors to imitate (Wernerfelt 1984).

Case Letter

Case letter is a term Mintzberg uses (Mintzberg 2012) for short reports, analyses and discussion of organizations, but which cannot be considered a full-fledged case study. Case letters can be understood as a case example, where you show different sides of a problem, a problem statement, or a research question. A case letter elaborates on some aspects of a problem that you want to have illuminated from a certain perspective.

A case letter is a way of bringing practice into the question being investigated. By using a case letter, practice will be drawn into the investigation, so that the link between practice and theory is made more visible.

You can also say that a case letter is structured like a chronicle, which is organized around the question to be investigated. By constructing several chronicles (case letters) we can examine the question from several perspectives.

A case letter sheds light on the problem so that the question being investigated can be shown in a practical reference text. In this way, the research is made more practical and the learning connects to the experiences of the different readers. The more case letters that are used, the greater the likelihood that the various readers will be able to connect their own experiences to what the researchers want to bring out with their investigations.

Causal Analysis

Making the functional relation and the sufficient conditions between actions and events visible.

Circular Causality

Linear causal explanations are usually contrasted to teleological explanations. Linear causal explanations are normally related to the past, while teleological explanations are linked to the future. In circular causal explanations this distinction is abolished and included in a systemic-oriented integrated model, where cause, effect, and expectations are inter-related entities. All three elements are included in what we choose to call circular causal explanations. Only the relation between cause and effect is of a linear type. If the feed-back between effect and cause is introduced into the relation, a classic cybernetic structure will result. When expectation is coupled into the structure, we will have introduced a feed-forward mechanism, where the entire structure is to be regarded as a circular causal explanation.

Co-creation. Co-creation involves working together to promote knowledge processes and innovation. If knowledge processes and innovation are essential for value creation in the knowledge society, co-creation is an important social mechanism for initiating, maintaining and strengthening these processes. The balance between competition and cooperation, embodied in the concept of co-creation, leads to constructive criticism and the necessary scope of knowledge that exists in the network so as to promote creativity and the innovative. Instead of a zero-sum situation, a positive-sum situation will be developed where everyone wins.

Collective blindness. Collective blindness may be said to be a form of collective arrogance, which results in irrational actions. Minor events slip under the radar, causing the system to not be fully aware of what is happening. Politicians' explanations why voters in a referendum vote contrary to what most of the power elite and the media advocated is an example of collective blindness.

Collective blindness is understood here as some very special mental models (Bateson, 1972:159–338). These mental models have a strong tendency to narrow our perspective. This means that we only see a few aspects of reality. In this way, collective blindness limits our choices. It is possible that other mental models could have worked better for us. For various reasons we are blind to these models. The flock of sheep that follows the leader off the cliff is the picture of collective blindness.

Collective blindness is framed by ideology, Group Think and blind spots.

Collective blindness is a new concept, a form of "missing link" between group think and ideology. One could say that the basis of collective blindness is how our mental models are developed. The core of understanding collective blindness is to engage with our mental models. These mental models are determined, among other things, of an interaction between ideology, groupthink and blind spots.

A larger meta-analysis shows that people with moderate self-esteem have a greater influence on others than people with low and high self-esteem (Rhodes and Wood 1992:156–171). There is also another side to this hypothesis. The other side literally consists of the others who are affected. Their self-esteem also affects how easily they allow themselves to be dominated or influenced by other people. One must assume that this relationship is linked to a superior and inferior relationship in relation to self-esteem. This means that the people who have a lower self-esteem than the people who influence, the greater the probability that they allow themselves to be influenced. The rationale for this assumption is given by Brinol and Petty (2005:591): "—they may be more likely to reason that their own opinion was as good or better than that of the source".

We see that self-respect as a consequence of self-confidence directly and indirectly affects the development of collective blindness. In order to get the full picture, however, one must always bring the self-confidence and self-respect of the other person(s) into the equation, when assessing how simple or complex it is to understand and possibly apply collective blindness in a specific situation. This situation can be similar to what is called "The Endowment Effect". In short, this effect means that we will spend more energy on maintaining an object or similar that we already have, than trying to get something we don't already have. Transferred to our phenomenon of collective blindness, one can say that those people who themselves have a higher self-esteem than those who want to influence, will seek to preserve the opinion they already have, rather than being dominated by others to change their opinion (Kahneman et al.; 1991:193–206).

Conceptual Generalization

Research falls into two main categories: conceptual generalization and empirical generalization (Bunge 1998:3–50, 51–107, 403–411). Conceptual generalization is an investigation whereby the researcher uses other researchers' empirical findings in conjunction with his or her own process of conceptualization in order to generalize and identify a pattern. This contrasts with empirical generalization, where the researcher investigates a phenomenon or problem that is apparent in the empirical data, and only thereafter generalises in the light of his or her own findings (Bunge 1998:403–411). The starting point for the researcher in the case of both empirical and conceptual generalization will be a phenomenon or problem in the social world.

Conceptual generalisation and empirical generalisation are strategies that are available for answering scientific questions. Which of these strategies one chooses to use will be determined largely by the nature of the problem and "the subject matter, and on the state of our knowledge regarding that subject matter." (Bunge 1998:16).

Conceptual generalisation, which is the subject of our investigation here, is "a procedure applying to the whole cycle of investigation into every problem of knowledge." (Bunge 1998:9).

Conceptual generalization is not statistical or mathematical rigor. The method is an attempt at exemplification through narratives, description, analysis, theorizing, presentation of practical utility, and often systemic connections, through the use of analogy.

The approach is to develop a conceptual model and then discuss each element in the model. An analytical scheme or model is a general sociological analytical tool (Turner 1987:162), which may be used to illuminate and organise a phenomenon, event, action or process. The purpose of an analytical scheme is "the construction of abstract systems of categories that presumably denote key properties of the universe and crucial relations among those properties. Explanation of specific events is achieved when the scheme can be used to interpret some specific empirical process" (Turner 1987:162). Often an analytical scheme will take the form of an analytical model, precisely, as Turner suggests, to show relationships between properties.

An analytical scheme may be used methodologically in two ways, says Turner. One way is when an empirical event can be placed in a category in the scheme: "then the empirical event is considered to be explained" (Turner 1987:162). The other way is "when the scheme can be used to construct a descriptive scenario, of why and how events in an empirical situation transpired, then these events are seen as explained" (Turner 1987:162). Both these methods may be used in conceptual generalization. In addition to Turner's approach, conceptual generalization draws on Deleuze and Guattari's ideas concerning how a concept can be studied (Deleuze and Guattari 2011: 6–9; 15–17). Adriaenssen and Johannessens (2016) and Johannessen and Olsen (2023) have elaborated on conceptual generalization.

Core Competence. The concept was popular in the strategy literature of the 1990s. Core competence may be defined as: "*a bundle of skills and technologies that enable a company to provide a particular benefit to customers*" (Hamel and

Prahalad 1996:219). More recently, core competence as a concept has been given less attention in the research on dynamic capabilities, and now there is more focus on the concept of *fitness*. The term *evolutionary fitness* is also used in the research literature in connection with technology, quality, cost development, market development, innovation, and competitive positioning (Helfat et al., 2007: 7).

Creative Competence Destruction

Creative competence destruction is a central concept in innovation economics. It tells us something about the fact that technological innovation, specifically in the fourth industrial revolution, artificial intelligence, destroys the competence of many, at the same time that this technology demands the creative new competence that is compatible with the new technology.

Evidence. This may be results, such as research results, that can be relied on. However, it is also important to be aware of the fact that other evidence may be available without having to refer to figures and quantities, such as evidence that emerges from observations and good judgement without the assessment being quantified. Evidence-based research is research results that are based on approved and accepted scientific research methods.

Emergent. An emergent occurs if something new turns up on one level that has not previously existed on the level below. With emergent we mean: *Let S be a system with composition A,* i.e. *the various components in addition to the way they are composed. If P is a property of S, P is emergent with regard to A, if and only if no components in A possess P; otherwise P is to be regarded as a resulting property with regard to A.* (Bunge, 1977:97).

Entrepreneurial spirit. The entrepreneurial spirit may be described as follows (Roddick, 2003: 106–107):

- The vision of something new and belief in this that is so strong that belief becomes reality.
- A touch of positive madness.
- The ability to stand out from the crowd.
- Creative tension bubbling over.
- Pathological optimism.
- To act before you know!
- Basic desire for change.
- Creative energy focused on ideas, not on explicit factual knowledge.
- Being able to tell the story you want to sell.

Feedback Giving the other person feedback, for instance with regard to their behaviour, attitudes, and the like, is the most important element in the area of interactive skills and emotional intelligence (Goleman 1996; 2007). Analysis of feedback is a sure way to identify our strengths and then reinforce them (Wang et al. 2003).

Failure to give people feedback on their behaviour in some contexts may even be considered immoral.

Feed-forward. Feed-forward is regarded here as an expectation mechanism. It seems reasonable to assume that our expectations influence our behaviour in the present. It is therefore important that we make explicit to ourselves the expectations we have of a situation. By making expectations explicit, we have a greater opportunity to learn from our experiences and thus improve our performance.

Global competence network. These competence networks may be divided into political, social, economic, technological and cultural patterns. It is when these five patterns interact that one may perceive the overall pattern. In the global knowledge economy it seems reasonable to assume that those who control this pattern set the conditions for economic development. These global competence networks will most likely make an impact on HR departments in companies competing for this kind of expertise in national markets.

Global competence networks are also emphasized as crucial for economic growth by OECD (2001), although they use the term *innovative clusters.* The purpose of innovative clusters and global competence networks is the development, dissemination and use of new ideas that promote wealth creation.

There is much to suggest that a greater degree of integration and cooperation between private and public sectors at the national and regional levels is an important prerequisite for initiating the innovative locomotive effect. The global competence networks are metaphorically the energy source that sustains the motion of this locomotive. It would be counterproductive to replace the locomotive once in motion. Conversely, the individual carriages of the locomotive (read: organizational level) can be changed depending on their competitive position. The individual passengers on the train create ideas and knowledge through the processes that may be called *creative chaos.* In this way we will arrive at a tripartite of the prerequisites for global competence networks. At the individual level, creative chaos occurs. At the organizational level, there will be creative destruction. At the social and global levels, creative collaboration takes place. These three processes create innovation and economic growth as an emergent, not as a *future perfectum*, i.e. a planned process with given results.

A prerequisite for the reasoning above is that tension and competition at one level requires collaboration at another level. Competition and cooperation are both necessary if one is to develop innovation and economic growth, in the same manner that stability and change are necessary for flexibility. Too much of the one (stability) leads to rigidity, and too much of the other (change) leads to chaos. Understood in this way, emergents cannot be planned.

Hamel's Law of Innovation. The "law" states that only between one and two of one thousand ideas become innovations in a market (Hamel, 2002; 2012). Therefore, an infostructure must be created to ensure that ideas are continuously produced in a business.

Hidden knowledge. Hidden knowledge is what we do not know we do not know. Kirzner (1982) says that hidden knowledge is possibly the most important knowledge domain of creativity, innovation and entrepreneurship.

History's "Slow Fields"

This refers to the fact that norms, values and actions tend to be in operation long after the functions, activities and processes that initially created them disappear, thus generating so-called *slow fields of history*. These norms, values, and actions exist though they have no apparent function, contributing to maintaining a type of behaviour long after the type of behaviour is functional or meaningful.[1] For sociologists and historians it is important to determine whether norms and values have any function, or whether they are part of history's slow fields. By examining history's slow fields, it may be possible to provide better explanations for phenomena.

Infostructure. The infostructure concerns the processes that enable the development, transfer, analysis, storage, coordination and management of data, information and knowledge. The infostructure consists of eleven generic processes.

The eleven processes in the infostructure may be considered as nodes in a social network at different levels, for example team, organization, society, and region, all in the global space. Together, the eleven processes comprise the totality of the infostructure.

It may be said that the *info*structure has the same importance in the knowledge society as the *infra*structure had in the industrial society.

Innovation. Innovation is here understood as any idea, practice or material element, which is perceived as new for the person using it (Zaltman et al. 1973).

Ideas are seen as the smallest unit in the innovation process (Hamel 2002; 2012). However, this refers to the ideas that are in process of development and not fully developed ideas. Before an idea can be characterized as innovative, it must prove to be beneficial to somebody, i.e. the market must accept the idea and apply it. Consequently, the creative process of innovation is here understood as the benefit it has for a market (Amabile 1990; Johannessen et al., 2001: 25). Thus, it is not sufficient that an idea is new for it to be considered an innovation. An idea may have a great degree of novelty, but if it is of no benefit to anybody in the market, then it has no innovative value.

Knowledge. The definition of knowledge used here is *the systematization and structuring of information for one or more goals or purposes.*

Knowledge worker. A knowledge worker has been described by the OECD as *a person whose primary task is to generate and apply knowledge*, rather than to provide services or produce physical products (OECD, 2000 a, b, c, d, e; 2001). This may be understood as a *formal definition* of a knowledge worker.

This definition does not restrict knowledge workers to creative fields, as is the case with, for example, Mosco and McKercher (2007: vii–xxiv). The OECD definition also allows for the fact that a knowledge worker may perform routine tasks. The

[1] Asplund (1970: 55) refers to a similar phenomenon when he discusses Simmel. He points out that the norms that may have had a positive function during a historic phase become in a later phase dysfunctional.

definition also does not limit the type of work performed by knowledge workers to tasks relating to creative problem-solving strategies, unlike the definition provided by Reinhardt et al. (2011).

Knowledge enterprise. This is an enterprise that has knowledge as its most significant output. It is perhaps helpful to think of the process *input—process—output* to separate industrial enterprises from knowledge enterprises. Much knowledge and skills are needed to produce high-tech products such as computers, and there are also many knowledge workers involved in this process. However, the majority of products produced today are high-tech industrial products, and although such products require very skilled knowledge in the production process, they are nevertheless output-industrial products.

On the other hand, law firms, consulting firms and universities are examples of knowledge enterprises.

Knowledge management. Management of knowledge resources in an organization. These resources may be explicit knowledge, implicit knowledge, tacit knowledge and hidden knowledge.

Locomotive effect. This refers to something that generates and then reinforces an activity or development.

Modularization. An extreme fragmentation of the production process in the global knowledge economy. Production is fragmented and distributed according to the following logic: Costs—quality—competence—design—innovation.

Modular flexibility. The modulization of value creation. Modular flexibility may best be understood as an extreme specialization of work processes.

Necessary and sufficient conditions. It may often be appropriate to divide conditions or premises into *necessary conditions* and *sufficient conditions*. Necessary conditions must be present to trigger an action, but these may not be sufficient. The sufficient conditions must also be present to trigger the action.

Non-knowledge

In the process from data via capta to information and knowledge, we continuously select out something. What we select out in this process constitutes non-knowledge.

North's action theory.[2] This action theory may be expressed in the following statement: *People act on the basis of a system of rewards as expressed in the norms, values, rules and attitudes in the culture (the institutional framework)* (North 1990; 1993). North's action theory is also consistent with Asplund's motivation theory (ref. Asplund's motivation theory).

---

[2] North's action theory is a term we use here based on North's research.

Paradoxical Intervention

Doing the exact opposite of what is expected when e.g. a change process becomes a necessity in the organization, can have completely unexpected positive consequences. If people are used to management describing and telling them in plain text what can be expected when a new technology changes their work area, then e.g. doing the exact opposite of what is expected creates a space of opportunity where resistance to change can be reduced. Such a strategy is named by Wazlawick et al. (2011) as a paradoxical intervention.

Proposition. This is an overarching hypothesis. It says something about the relationship between several variables. A proposition relates to a hypothesis in the same way the main research problem relates to research questions.

Punctuation. By punctuation (Bateson 1972:292–293) a distinction is drawn between cause and effect; this is done with a clear motive in mind. A causality is thus created which does not actually exist in the real world, and one is then free to discuss the effects of this cause which has been created through a process of punctuation.

A sequence of a process is selected, and then bracketed. In this way, we de-limit what is punctuated from the rest of the process. Figuratively, we may imagine this as a circle that is divided into small pieces; one piece of the circle is then selected and folded out into a straight line. This results in the creation of an artificial beginning and end. This beginning and end of course cannot exist in a circle, but only through the process of punctuation.

Recursive Thinking

Recursive thinking here means that circular causality must be explained at various logical levels in the system(s) we choose to study. These various logical levels are then inter-dependent and must ultimately be viewed contextual in order to render meaning for the observer.

Social laws. Social laws constitute a pattern of a unique type. They are systemic and connected to a system of knowledge, and cannot change without the facts they represent also being changed (Bunge 1983, 1983a). The main differences between a statement of a law and other statements are:

1. Law statements are general.
2. Law statements are systemic, i.e. they are related to the established system of knowledge.
3. Law statements have been verified through many studies.

A pattern may be understood as variables that are stable over a specific period of time. A social law is created when an observer gains insight into the pattern. By gaining such insight, we can also predict parts of behaviour or at least develop a rough estimate within a short period of time.

Social laws are further related to specific social systems, both in time and space. However, this does not represent any objection to social laws, because this is also true of natural laws (although these have a longer time span and are of a more general nature).

Social mechanism. Robert Merton (1967) brought the notion of social mechanisms into sociology, although we can find rudiments of this in both Weber—with the Protestant ethic as an explanation for the emergence of capitalism in Europe—and in Durkheim, who uses society as an explanation for a rising suicide rate. For Merton, social mechanisms are the building blocks of *middle range theories.* He defines social mechanisms as *social processes having designated consequences for designated parts of the social structure* (Merton 1968:43). In the 1980s and 1990s, Jon Elster developed a new notion of the role of social mechanisms in sociology (Elster 1983, 1989). Hedstrom and Swedberg write that, *the advancement of social theory calls for an analytical approach that systematically seeks to explicate the social mechanisms that generate and explain observed associations between events* (Hedstrøm and Swedberg 1998:1).

It is one thing to point out connections between phenomena. It is something quite different to point out satisfactory explanations for these relationships, which is what social mechanisms accomplish. A social mechanism tells us what will happen, how it will happen and why it will happen (Bunge 1967). Social mechanisms are primarily analytical constructs which cannot necessarily be observed; in other words, they are epistemological, not ontological. However, social mechanisms are observable in their consequences. An intention can be a social mechanism of action. We cannot observe an intention, but we can interpret it in the light of the consequences manifested through an action. Preferences can also function as a social mechanism for economic behaviour. We cannot observe a person's preferences, but we can interpret them in the light of the behavioural consequences that manifest themselves. Social mechanisms are, understood in this way, analytical constructs, indicating connections between events (Hernes 1998).

Bunge says: "*... a social mechanism is a process in a concrete system, such that it is capable of being about or preventing some change in the system as a whole or in some of its subsystems*" (Bunge 1997:414). By 'social mechanism' here we mean those activities that promote/inhibit social processes in relation to a specific problem/phenomenon.

Material resources and technology are social mechanisms of the economic subsystem; power is a social mechanism of the political subsystem; fundamental norms and values are a social mechanism of the cultural subsystem; and human relationships are a social mechanism of the social subsystem. These system-specific social mechanisms interact with each other to achieve certain goals, maintain these systems, or avoid certain undesirable conditions in the system or the outside world.

The difficulty of discovering social mechanisms and distinguishing them from processes may be partly explained by the fact that social mechanisms are also processes (Bunge 1997:414). For the application of social mechanisms, see the Boudon-Coleman diagram.

Social Recognition

Axel Honnet's theory of social recognition can be briefly described with the following hypothesis. The more social recognition the individual receives, the more the person is motivated to give the little extra needed to achieve success (Honneth 2005, 2008, 2012, 2014).

Social recognition can be understood as consisting of five social drivers, or social mechanisms. These are: self-respect, identity, individual freedom, materialization and the struggle for one's own and others' dignity.

Social system. From a systemic perspective, social systems can be conceptual or concrete. Theories and analytical models are examples of conceptual systems. Further, social systems are *composed of people and their artefacts* (Bunge 1996:21). Social systems are held together (in systemic reasoning) by **dynamic social relations** (such as emotions, interpretations, norms) and **social actions** (such as cooperation, solidarity, conflict and communication). None of the social actions have precedence in the systemic interpretation of social systems, such as conflict in the case of Marx, and solidarity in the case of Durkheim.

Systemic thinking. Systemic thinking makes a distinction between the epistemological sphere (Bunge 1985), the ontological sphere (Bunge 1983), the axiological sphere (Bunge 1989, 1996) and the ethical sphere (Bunge 1989). Systemic thinking makes a clear distinction between intention and behaviour. Intention is something that should be *understood*, while behaviour is something that should be *explained*. To understand an intention we must study the historical factors, situations and contexts, as well as the expectation mechanisms. Behaviour must be explained with respect to the context, relationships and situation it unfolds in. What implication does the distinction between intention and behaviour have for the study of social systems?

Interpretation of meaning is an important part of the *intention aspect* in the distinction. Explanation and prediction become an essential part of the *behavioural aspect* of the distinction.

In systemic thinking, it is the link between the interpretation of meaning and explanation, and prediction, which provides historical and social sciences with practical strength. By making a distinction between intention and behaviour, the historical and the social sciences are interpretive, explanatory and predictive projects. According to systemic thinking, many of the contradictions in the historical and social sciences spring from the fact that a distinction is not made between intention and behaviour. The problem of the historical and social sciences is that the actors who are studied have both intentions and they also exercise types of behaviour; however, this isn't problematic as long as we make a distinction between intention and behaviour. By simultaneously introducing the distinction between intention and behaviour, systemic thinking has made it possible to identify, for instance, partial explanations from each of two main epistemological positions, namely, the naturalists and anti-naturalists (Johannessen and Olaisen 2005, 2006), and synthesize these explanations into new knowledge.

Systemic thinking emphasizes circular causal processes, also called *interactive causal processes*, in addition to linear causal processes (Johannessen 1996; 1997). Systemic thinking argues that to understand objective social facts, one must examine the subjective aspects of these. In systemic thinking, objective social facts exist, but they are often more difficult to grasp than facts in the natural world, because social facts are often influenced by expectations, emotions, prejudices, ideology and economic and social interests. *"Aspect-seeing"* is thus a way of approaching these social facts.

Emergents are central to systemic thinking. A pattern behind the problem or phenomenon is always sought in systemic investigations. Patterns may be revealed by studying the underlying processes that constitute a phenomenon or problem, *and the search for pattern is what scientific research is all about* (Bunge 1996:42).

According to systemic thinking it is a misconception to say that the facts are social constructions. The misunderstanding involves confusing our *concepts* concerning facts and our *hypotheses* about the facts together with the facts. Our concepts and hypotheses are mental constructs. The facts, however, are not mental constructs. Social need, for instance, is not a social fact; it is a mental construct of, for instance, starvation. Starvation is a social fact. Social need is a mental or social construction. Not being able to read is a social fact. Illiteracy is, however, a social construction.

A *symbol* should symbolize something, just as a *concept* should delineate something. A *hypothesis* should explain something or express something about relationships. A conceptual *model* should say something about the relationships between concepts. A *theory* should say something about relationships between propositions. Physical or social facts are untouched by all these mental constructions. That one can through constructs change social facts, or that social facts are changed as a social consequence of using constructs, is neither original nor new.

The aim of theoretical research, according to the systemic position, is the construction of systems, i.e. theories (Bunge 1974: v). The order in systemic research is thus: Theory—Analysis—Synthesis.

In the methodological sphere, the systemic position has its main focus on relationships, both in terms of concrete things, ideas, and knowledge. Consequently, systemic thinking encourages interdisciplinary and multidisciplinary approaches to problems or phenomena.

The systemic position thus attempts to bridge the gap between methodological individualism and methodological collectivism, which is considered the classic controversy in historical- and social sciences.

The perceptions that an observer has about social systems will influence his/her actions, regardless of whether the perceptions are true or fallacious. Systemic investigations start, therefore, writes Bunge *from individuals embedded in a society that preexists them and watch how their actions affect society and alter it* (Bunge 1996:241). The study of social systems from a systemic perspective for these reasons always includes the triad: actors - observers - social systems.

The observer tries to uncover a system's composition, environment and structure. Then the actors' subjective perception of composition, environment and structure are examined. In other words, both the subjective and objective aspects are studied. When we wish to study changes in social systems, from a systemic point of view, we have to examine the social mechanisms (drivers) that influence changes; both internal and external social mechanisms must be identified. This study takes place within the four subsystems: the economic, political, cultural and relational. According to systemic thinking, social changes occur along seven axes:

1. As an *expectation* of new relationships, values, power constellations, technologies and distribution of material resources.
2. As a result of our *beliefs* (mental models) about relationships, values, power constellations, technical and material resources.
3. As a result of *psychological elements*, such as: irritation, crisis, discomfort, unsatisfactory life, unworthy life, loss of well-being.
4. As a result of *communication* in and between systems.
5. As a result of an *understanding of connections* (contextual understanding).
6. As a result of learning and new *self-knowledge*.
7. As a result of *new ideas* and ways of thinking.

Historiography, from a systemic perspective, has one clear goal: to investigate what happened, where it happened, when it happened, how it happened, why it happened, and with what results.

Systemic assumptions related to historiography and social sciences may be expressed in the following (Bunge 1998:263):

(a) The past has existed.
(b) Parts of the past can be known.
(c) Every uncovering of the past will be incomplete.
(d) New data, techniques, and systemizations and structuring will reveal new aspects of the past.
(e) Historical knowledge is developed through new data, discoveries, hypotheses, and approaches.

In systemic thinking if changes are to take place, then the material will sometimes be given precedence; at other times, ideology, ideas, and thinking are given precedence. In other contexts, there is a systemic link between the material and ideas that is needed to bring about changes. In such contexts, it is difficult and irrelevant to say what is the primary driver, i.e. the material or ideas; this would be on par with discussing what came first, the chicken or the egg.

The processes that drive social change, according to a systemic perspective, are the interaction between the economic, political, relational, and cultural subsystems. In some situations, one of these four perspectives will prevail, whereas in others it will be one or more of the four subsystems that are the drivers of social change. In many cases, it is precisely the interaction between the four subsystems that leads to social changes.

In this context, the systemic perspective may be described by saying that material conditions/energy, such as economic relationships, may provide the ground from which ideologies develop, but that these ideologies in return influence the development of the material. Whether material conditions/energy or ideology comes first is often determined by a historiographical punctuation process (Bateson 1972:163).

The systemic perspective balances historical materialism and historical idealism. It assumes that overall social changes are the result of economic, political, social, and cultural factors, in addition to the interaction between material conditions/energy and ideas. Furthermore, a systemic perspective views any society as being interwoven into its surroundings (Bunge 1998: 275). When a historian considers a historical situation—such as the massacre in Van in April 1915—from this perspective then he is trying *to throw light upon the internal working of a past culture and society* (Stone 1979: 19).

The systemic position attempts to view the relevant event in a larger context, in order to find *the patterns which combine* (Bateson 1972:273–274), because *change depends upon feedback loop* (Bateson 1972:274). Bunge says about this position: *By placing the particular in a sequence, adopting a broad perspective the systemist overcomes the idiographic/nomothetic duality, as well as the concomitant narrative/structural opposition* (Bunge 1998:275). This means, metaphorically, that the systemic researcher uses a microscope, telescope and a helicopter to investigate patterns over time.

Systemic research strategy is a *zig-zagging between the micro-meso and macro levels* (Bunge 1998:277). Through a systemic research strategy the researcher has ample opportunities to use a Boudon-Coleman diagram.

Systemic thinking examines four types of changes.[3]

Type I change concerns individuals who change history, such as Genghis Khan, Hitler, Stalin, Mao Zedong.

Type II change concerns groups of people acting together who change history. Examples of Type II change include the invasion of the Roman Empire by peoples from the north; and the Ottoman expansion into the Balkans between the late 1400s and when the Ottoman Empire was pushed back partly due to nationalist liberation movements in the early 1900s.

Type III change includes changes in history that are caused by natural disasters, such as the volcanic eruption that destroyed Pompeii. Climate change may also be said to be an example of a type III change.

Type IV change involves a total change in the way of thinking, such as the emergence of new religions, like Islam, or a new political ideology, such as Marxism.

The systemic researcher attempts to explore the relationship between the four types of changes. A single event is in itself not necessarily of special interest to the systemic researcher; rather, the focus is on the *system of events* of which the single event is a part.

---

[3] The four types of changes are related to Bateson's (1972:279–309) work on different types of learning, especially those discussed in his article *Logical types of learning and communication.*

All the social sciences are used in the systemic position to seek insight, understanding and to explain a phenomenon or problem.

Tacit knowledge. Knowledge that is difficult to communicate to others as information. It is also very difficult, if at all possible, to digitize.

Technology

"The scientific study of artefacts" (Bunge 1985a:219–231).

The knowledge-based perspective. The knowledge-based perspective is defined here as creating, expanding and modifying internal and external competencies to promote what the organization is designed to do (Grant 2003: 203).

The Technology System

The innovation economy can be said to be characterized by the technological system (Ellul, 2018:1–21). This technological system can simply be said to consist of five dimensions, which are systemically linked. These dimensions are creativity, innovation, education, competence and technology. By systemically linked, we mean here that the five dimensions influence and are influenced by each other. Creativity affects the development of innovation. Innovation, on the other hand, can also influence and reinforce the development of creativity. Both of these figures influence and are influenced by the education in the population and the competence that is the result of this education. Competence, which is a collective term for the three dimensions of creativity, innovation, and education, promotes the development and use of new technology. The technology in turn also affects the three sizes and reinforces e.g. the innovation processes. These dimensions together and partly also separately promote productivity development. In turn, productivity development also affects the other dimensions mentioned above. In this way, the technological system in the innovation economy operates on different premises than in the industrial economy. In the innovation economy, it is not necessarily only science and technology that create the innovation processes. These are necessary prerequisites for economic development, but not sufficient. The sufficient element may be the technological system mentioned above. In particular, we will emphasize here the role of creativity in the technological system in the innovation economy .

Theory. Here understood as a system of propositions (Bunge 1974: v).

Zappfe's Paradox

You go down by what is your strength.

References

Adriaenssen D, Johannessen JA (2016) Conceptual generalizations, methodological reflections in social science: a systemic viewpoint. Kybernetes 44(4):588–605
Bateson G (1972a) Steps to an ecology of mind. Intertext Books, London
Bateson G (1972b) Steps to an ecology of mind. Intertext Books, London
Bunge, M. (1998a). Philosophy of science: from problem to theory, Volume one, Transaction Publishers, New Jersey
Bunge, M. (1998b). Philosophy of science: from problem to theory, Volume one, Transaction Publishers, New Jersey
Bunge M (1967) Scientific research. In: In studies of the foundations methodology and philosophy of science, vol 3. Springer Verlag, Berlin
Bunge M (1974) Sense and reference. Reidel, Dordrecht
Bunge M (1983) Exploring the world: Epistemology & Methodology I. Reidel, Dordrecht
Bunge M (1983a) Understanding the world: Epistemology & Methodology II. Reidel, Dordrecht
Bunge M (1989) Ethics: the good and the right. Reidel, Dordrecht
Bunge M (1977) Treatise on basic philosophy. In: Ontology I: the furniture of the world, vol 3. D. Reidel, Dordrecht, Holland
Bunge M (1978) A world of systems. Reidel, Dordrecht
Bunge M (1996) Finding philosophy in social science. Yale University Press, New Haven
Coleman JS (1990) Foundations of social theory. Harvard University Press, Belknap Press, Cambridge, Mass
Deleuze G, Guattari F (2011) What is philosophy. Verso, London
Ellul, J. (2018). The Technological System, WS, Eugene, Oregon
Goleman D (1996) Emotional intelligence. Blumsbury Publishing, New York
Grant, R.M. (2003). The Knowledge-Based View of the Firm, i Faulkner, D. and Campell, A. (red.). *The Oxford Hand book of Strategy*, Oxford University Press, Oxford. S.203–231
Hamel G (2002a) Leading the revolution: how to thrive in turbulent times by making innovation a way of life. Harvard Business School Press, Boston
Hamel G (2002b) Leading the revolution: how to thrive in turbulent times by making innovation a way of life. Harvard Business School Press, Boston
Hamel G, Prahalad CK (1996) Competing for the future. Harvard Business School Press, Boston
Hedstrøm, P and S R. Swedberg (1998). Social mechanisms: An introductory essay, In Hedstrøm, P. and R. Swedberg (red.). Social mechanisms: An analytical approach to social theory, Cambridge University Press, Cambridge. pp. 20–32
Helfat CE, Finkelstein S, Mitchell W, Peteraf MA, Singh H, Teece DJ, Winter SG (2007) Dynamic capabilities: understanding strategic change in organizations. Blackwell, Oxford
Hernes, G. (1998). Real virtuality, in social mechanisms: An analytical approach to social theory, Edited by Peter Hedstrøm and Richard Swedberg, Cambridge University Press, Cambridge (pp. 74–102)
Honneth A (2005) The struggle for recognition. Polity, London
Honneth A (2008) Reification. Oxford University Press, Oxford
Honneth A (2012) The I in we: studies in the theory of recognition. Polity, London
Honneth A (2014) Freedoms right. Polity, London
Mintzberg H (2012) Managers not MBAs. Read How You Want, New York
North DC (1990) Institutions. Cambridge University Press, Cambridge, Institutional Change and economic performance
OECD. (2000*a*), *A New Economy? The changing role of innovation and information technology in growth,* Paris
OECD. (2000b), Economic outlook, Paris
OECD (2000c) Education at a glance: OECD indicators. CERI, Paris
OECD. (2000d), ICT Skills and Employment, Working party on the information economy, Paris, 15 November, DSTI/ICCP/IE (2000)7

OECD (2000e) Knowledge Management in the Learning Society. CERI, Paris
OECD (2001) Innovative clusters: driving of national innovation-systems. OECD, Paris
Stone J (1979) The revival of narrative: reflections on a new old history. Past and Present 85:3–24
Turner, J.H. (1987). Analytical Theorizing, In Giddens, A. and Turner, J.H. Social Theory Today, Polity Press, New York. Pp. 156–195
Ulrich D, Brockbank W (2005) The HR value proposition. Harvard Business School Press, Boston, MA
Wang QG, Lee TH, Lin C (2003) Relay feedback: analysis, identification and control. Springer, London
Wernerfelt B (1984) A resource-based view of the firm. Strateg Manag J 5(2):171–180
Winter SG (2003) Understanding dynamic capabilities. Strateg Manag J 24:991–995
Zaltman G, Duncan R, Holbeck J (1973) Innovations and organizations. Wiley, New York

Correction to: The AI Battleground Between the USA and China

Correction to:
J. Johannessen, *The AI Battleground Between the USA and China*, Global Power Shift,
https://doi.org/10.1007/978-3-032-10138-9

The original version of the book was inadvertently published with a few errors. The following corrections have now been made:

- pp. 7 and 100: "Zhengqi (2020)" has been replaced with "Pan (2020)".
- pp. 12 and 110: "Zhengqi P" has been replaced with "Pan Z".
- p. 110: The title of the last reference has been corrected to: "Power Capture Through Global Value Chains".
- pp. 11, 12, 55, 107, and 110: "Wah CY" has been replaced with "Chay YW".

These corrections have been incorporated into the updated version of the book.

The updated versions of these chapters can be found at
https://doi.org/10.1007/978-3-032-10138-9_1
https://doi.org/10.1007/978-3-032-10138-9_3

J. Johannessen, *The AI Battleground Between the USA and China*, Global Power Shift,
https://doi.org/10.1007/978-3-032-10138-9_6

Uncited References

Acemoglu D, Autor DH (2011) Skills, tasks and technologies: implications for employment and earnings. In: Card D, Ashenfelter O (eds) Handbook of labor economics, vol 4. Elsevier, Amsterdam, pp 1043–1171
Aghion P, Antonin C, Bunel S (2021) The power of creative destruction. Harvard University Press, Cambridge, Mass
Allison G, Blackwell AD (2020) Lee Kuan Yew. The MIT Press, Boston
Amabile T (1988) A model of creativity and innovation in organizations. In: Staw BM, Cummings LL (ed) Research in organizational behavior, vol 9, pp 123–167
Amabile T (1996) Creativity XE "Creativity" in context XE "context." Westwiew Press, New York
Appelbaum RP, Xueying Han C-C, Parker R, Simon D (2018) Innovation in China. Polity, London
Armstrong M (2014a) Armstrong's handbook of strategic human resource management. Kogan Page, New York
Armstrong M (2014b) Armstrong's handbook of human resource management practice. Kogan Page, New York
Asplund J (1970) Om undran innfør samhället. Argos, Stockholm
Atkinson RD, Ezell SJ (2014) Innovation economics: the race for global advantage. Yale University Press, New York
Bannister J, Hill K (2004) Mortality in China, 1964–2000. Popul Stud 58(1):55–75
Bartel F (2022) The triumph of broken promises: The end of the cold war and the rise of Neoliberalism. Harvard University Press, Cambridge
Black, J. (2013). Geopolitics and the quest for dominance, Indiana University Press, Indiana.
Bleuer H, Bouri M (2017) New trends in medical and service robots: Assistive, surgical and educational robotics. Springer, London
Bleuer H, Bouri M, Mandada FC (2017) New trends in medical and service robots. Springer, London
Bloom N, Draca M, Van Reenen J (2016) Trade induced technical change? The Impact of Chinese Imports on Innovation, IT and Productivity, Review of Economic Studies 82(1):87–117
Boudon R (1981) The logic of social action. Routledge, London
Boxall PF, Purcell J (2003) Strategy and Human Resource Management. Palgrave Macmillan, Basingstoke
Boxall PF, Purcell J (2010) An HRM perspective on employee participation. In: Wilkinson A, Golan PJ, Marchington M, Lewins D (eds) The oxford handbook of participation in organizations. Oxford University Press, Oxford, pp s. 129–151
Boxall PF, Purcell J, Wright P (2007) Human resource management: scope, analysis, and significance. In: Boxall PF, Purcell J, Wright P (eds)The oxford handbook of human resource management. Oxford University Press, Oxford. pp. s. 1–16

J. Johannessen, *The AI Battleground Between the USA and China*, Global Power Shift,
https://doi.org/10.1007/978-3-032-10138-9

Brinol P,Petty, RE (2005) Individual differences in attitude change. In Albarracin D et al (eds) The handbook of attitudes. Psychology Press, London, pp 575–617
Brockbank W (2013) Overview and logic. In: Ulrich D, Brockbank W, Younger J, Ulrich M (eds) Global HR competencies: mastering competitive value from the outside in. McGraw Hill, New York, pp 3–27
Bruder J (2017) Nomadland: surviving America in the twenty-first century. WW. Norton, New York
Brynjolfsson E, Saunders A (2013) Wired for innovation: how information technology is reshaping the economy. The MIT Press, London
Bunge M (1985) Philosophy of science and technology. Part I: Epistemology & methodology III. Reidel, Dordrecht
Bunge M (1985a) Philosophy of science and technology, Part II. Reidel, Dordrecht.
Bunge M (1997a) Mechanism and explanation. Philos Soc Sci 27:410–465
Bunge M (1997b) Foundations of biophilosophy. Springer Verlag, Berlin
Carney TP (2020) Alienated America. Harper, New York
Cato LAV, Obstfeld M (2019) Meeting globalizations challenges. Princeton University Press, Princeton
Christensen T (2015) The China challenge. Norton, New York, W.W
Clinton H (2011) America's Pacific century. Foreign Policy 189
Drache D, Kingsmith AT, Qi D (2019) One road many dreams: China's bold plan to remake the global economy. Bloomsbury, New York
Duncan R (1976) The ambidextrual organization: designing dual structures for innovation. In: Kilman RH, Pondy LR, Slevin D (eds) The management of organization. North Holland, New York, pp 167–188
Dweck C (2017) Mindset: changing the way you think to fulfil your potential. Robinson, New York
Elster J (1986) Rational choice. New York University Press, New York
Elster J (1989) Nuts and bolts for the social sciences. Cambridge University Press, Cambridge
Farley J (2021) Model workers in China 1949–1965: Constructing a new citizen. Routledge, London
Fewsmith J (2021) Rethinking Chinese politics. Cambridge University Press, Cambridge
Frank T (2004) What's the matter with Kansas? Metropolitan Press, New York, How conservatives won the heart of America
Frank T (2020) People without power. Scribe, London
Fukuyama F (2022) Liberalism and its discontents. Profile Books, New York
Garnaut R, Song L, Yao Y, Wang X (2012) Private enterprise in China. ANY Press, New York
Goleman D (2007) Social intelligence. Arrow books, New York
Goodman DSG (2014) Class in contemporary China. Polity, London
Hewing M (2013) Collaboration with potential users for discontinuous innovation. Springer Gabler, Potsdam
Huang Y (2017) Cracking the China conundrum: why conventional economic wisdom is wrong. Oxford University Press, Oxford
Hurst W (2009) The Chinese worker after socialism. Cambridge University Press, Cambridge
Jakimow M (2021) China's citizenship challenge: labour NGOs and the struggle for migrant workers' rights. Manchester University Press, Manchester
Johannessen J-A, Olaisen J (2005) Systemic philosophy and the philosophy of social science-Part I: transcedence of the naturalistic and the anti-naturalistic position in the philosophy of social science. I Kybernetes 34(7/8):1261–1277
Johannessen J-A, Olaisen J (2006) Systemic philosophy and the philosophy of social science-Part II: the systemic position. I Kybernetes 34(9/10):1570–1586
Johannessen J-A (1996) Systemics applied to the study of organizational fields: developing systemic research strategy for organizational fields. Kybernetes 25(1):33–51
Johannessen J-A (1997) Aspects of ethics in systemic thinking. i Kybernetes 26(9):983–1001
Johannessen J-A (2018) Innovation leads to economic crises. Palgrave, London
Johannessen J-A (2020) Knowledge management philosophy: communication as a strategic asset in knowledge management. Emerald, London

Johannessen J-A, Olaisen J, Olsen B (2001) Mismanagement of tacit knowledge: the importance of tacit knowledge, the danger of information technology, and what to do about it? Int J Inf Manage 21(3):3–20
Johnston AI (2020) Cultural realism: culture and grand strategy in Chinese history. Princeton University Press, Princeton
Kahneman D, Knetsch J, Thaler R (1991) The endowment effect, loss aversion, and status quo bias. Journal of Economic Perspectives 5:193–206
Khana P (2019) The future is Asian, global order in the twenty first century. W&N, New York
Kirzner S (1982) The theory of entrepreneurship in economic growth. In: Kent CA, Sexton D L, Vesper KH (Red) Encyclopedia of entrepreneurship. Prentice Hall, Englewood Cliffs, NJ
Kissinger H, Schmidt E, Huttenlocher D (2021) The age of AI—and our human future. Little, Brown and Company, New York
Krugman P (1994) The age of diminishing expectations. MIT Press, Cambridge
Krugman P (2019) Globalization: what did we miss? In: Catao LAV, Obstfeld M (eds) Meeting globalization's challenges. Princeton University Press, Princeton, pp 113–121
Lampton DM, Madancy JA, Williams KM (1986) A relationship restored: trends in US-China educational exchange, 1978–1984. National Academy Press, Washington
Large D (2021) China and Africa: the new era. Polity, London
Leontief W (1979) Is technological unemployment inevitable? Challenge 22(4):48–50
Leontief W (1986) The future impact of automation on workers. Oxford University Press, Oxford
Lin J, Xiaoyan S (2010) Higher education expansion and China's middle class. In: Li C (ed) China's emerging middle class beyond economic transformation. Brookings Institution Press, Washington. Pp., pp 217–242
Linehan PM (2018) The culture of leadership in contemporary China. Lexington Books, London
Loh C (2010) Underground front: the Chinese communist party in Hong Kong. Hong Kong University Press, Hong Kong
Luhman N (1996) Social systems. Stanford University Press, Stanford
Machiavelli N (1975) The discourses, vol 2, (trans Walker LJ). Routledge, London
Magnus G (2018) Red flags, Why Xi's China is in jeopardy. Yale University Press, New Haven
Mantoux P (1961) The industrial revolution in the eighteenth century: an outline of the beginning of the modern factory system in England. Routledge, London
Mattingly DG (2020) The art of political control in China. Cambridge University Press, Cambridge
Mazzucato M (2013) The entrepreneurial state. Penguin, London
Mazzucato M (2019) The value of everything. Pelican, London
Mazzucato M (2021) Mission economy. Allen Lane, New York
Merton RK (1967) Social theory and social structure, Free Press, London
Miller C (2022) Chip war: the fight for the world's most critical technology. Simon & Schuster, London
Miller JG (1978) Living systems. McGraw-Hill, New York
Mosco V, McKercher C (2007) Introduction: theorizing knowledge labor and the information society. Knowledge Workers in the Information Society, Lexington Books, Lanham
Mukherjee D (2020) Economic integration in Asia. Routledge, London
Naughton B (2010) China's distinctive system: can it be a model for others? J Contemp China 19:437–460
Naughton BJ (2021) The Chinese economy. MIT, Boston
Nelson RR, Winter SG (1982) An evolutionary theory of economic change. Harvard University Press, Cambridge, MA
Nester WR (1989) Japan's growing predominance over east Asia and the world economy. Palgrave, London
North D (1993) Nobel lecture. http://www.nobelprize.org/nobel_prizes/economics/laureates/1993/north-lecture.html#not2, lesedato, 4 May 2012
North D (1993) Nobelforedraget: http://www.nobelprize.org/nobel_prizes/economics/laureates/1993/north-lecture.html#not2. Date of reading: 4 May 2021

North DC (1981) Structure and change in economic history. Norton, New York
Nye JS Jr (2004) Soft power: the means to success in world politics. Public Affairs, New York
O'Reilly CA, Tushman ML (2004) The ambidextrous organization. Harv Bus Rev 82(4):74–81
O'Reilly CA, Tushman ML (2007) Ambidexterity as a dynamic capability: resolving the innovators dilemma. Harvard Business School Press, Boston
O'Reilly CA, Tushman ML (2011) Organizational ambidexterity in action: how managers explore and exploit. Calif Manag Rev 53(4):5–22
Palley TI (2021) Neoliberalism and the road to inequality: A chronicle foretold. Edward Elgar Publishing, London
Patey L (2021) How China loses: the pushback against Chinese global ambitions. Oxford University Press, Oxford
Petras J, Veltmeyr H (2011) Beyond neoliberalism: a word to win. Routledge, London
Petras J, Veltmeyr H, Marquez H (2013) Imperialism and capitalism in the twenty-first century: a system of crises. Routledge, London
Piketty T (2014) Capital in the twenty-first century. The Belknap Press of Harvard University Press, Boston
Piketty T (2016) Chronicles: on our troubled times. Viking, London
Quah D (2011) The global economy's shifting centre of gravity. Global Pol 2(1):3–9
Reinhardt W, Smith B, Sloep P, Drachler H (2011) Knowledge worker roles and actions–results of two empirical studies. Knowl Process Manag 18(3):150–174
Rhodes N, Wood W (1992) Self-esteem and intelligence affect influenceability: the mediating role of message perception. Psychol Bull 111:156–171
Roach S (2014) Unbalanced: the co-dependency of America and China. Yale University Press, New Haven
Roberts D (2020) The myth of Chinese capitalism. St. Martin's Press, New York
Roddick DA (2003) The grassroots entrepreneur, i Elbæk, U. Kaospilot A-Z. Narayana Press, Gylling
Rodriguez-Clare A (2019) The gains from trade in rich and poor countries. In: Cato LAV, Obstfeld M (eds) Meeting globalization's challenges: policies to make trade work for all. Princeton University Press, Princeton
Rodrik D (2011) The globalization paradox. Oxford University Press, Oxford
Rozelle S (2020) Invisible China: how the urban-rural divide threatens China's rise. University of Chicago Press, Chicago
Schumpeter J (2002) Seventh chapter of the theory of economic development, translated by U. Backhaus, Industry and Innovation 9:93–145
Shambaugh D (2016) China's future. Polity, London
So AY, Chu Y-W (2016) The global rise of China. Polity, London
Storey J, Ulrich D, Wright PM (2009) Introduction. In: Storey J, Wright PM, Ulrich D (ed) The Routledge companion to strategic human resource management. Routledge, London, pp 3–15
Tzu S (2014) The art of war. Canterbury Classics, London
Teece D, Pisano, G, Shuen A (1997) Dynamic capabilities and strategic management. Strat Manag J 18(7), 509–533
Teece DJ (2013) Dynamic capabilities and strategic management: organizing for innovation. OUP, Oxford
Thota H, Munir Z (2011) Key concepts in innovation. Palgrave Macmillan, London
Tushman ML, O'Reilly CA (1996) Ambidextrous organization: managing evolutionary and revolutionary change. Calif Manag Rev 38:8–30
Ulrich D (2013a) Forword. In: Ulrich D, Brockbank W, Younger J, Ulrich M (eds) Global HR competencies: mastering competitive value from the outside in. McGraw Hill, New York, pp v–xxi
Ulrich D (2013b) Future of global HR: what's next? In: Ulrich D, Brockbank W, Younger J, Ulrich M (eds) Global HR Competencies: mastering competitive value from the outside in. McGraw Hill, New York, pp 255–268

Vadakkepat P, Goswami P (eds) (2018) Humanoid robotics: a reference. Springer, London
Wang D (2020) Reigning the future, AI, 5G, Huawei, and the next 30 years of US-China rivalry. New Degree Press, London
Watzlawick P, Weakland JH, Fish R (2011) Change. W.W. Norton & Company, New York
Weber IM (2021) How China escaped shock therapy. Routledge, London
White, J. and Younger, J. (2013). The global perspective. In: Ulrich D, Brockbank W, Younger J, Ulrich M (eds) Global HR competencies: mastering competitive value from the outside in. McGraw Hill, New York, pp 27–53
Wilson M (2017) Implementation of robot systems. Butterworth-Heinemann, New York
Winfield A (2012) Robotics. OUP, Oxford
Wolf M (2019) The elites against the people: the crises of democratic capitalism. In: Cato LAV, Obstfeld M (eds) Meeting globalizations challenges. Princeton University Press, Princeton, pp 237–261
Wright P, Dunford B, Snell S (2001) Human resources and the resource based view of the firm. J Manag 27:701–721
Wright PM, Boudreau JW, Pace DA, Libby Sartain E, McKinnon P, Antoine RL (eds) (2011) The chief HR officer: defining the new role of human resource leaders. Jossey-Bass, London
Wright T (2015) Part and state in post-Mao China. Polity, London
Xie Y, Zhang X, Li J, Yu X, Ren Q (2014) China's family panel studies. Beijing University Press, Beijing
Yang Y, Li F (2019) ASEAN-China cooperation under the framework of the belt and road initiative. In: Yang, Li (eds) The belt and road initiative: Asian Countries perspectives. World Scientific, London
Yu L (2014) Consumption in China. Polity, London
Zhao S (ed) (2020) China's new global strategy. Routledge, London
Zhao Y (2014) Who's afraid of the big bad dragon: why China has the best (and worst) education system in the world. Jossey-Bass, New York
Zhongyuan Z (2020) Microeconomic basis for the 21st-century maritime silk road initiative: from the perspective of a value chain. Jianglin, 21st-Century Maritime Silk Road Initiative, Aims and objectives, implementation strategies and policy recommendations. World Scientific, London, pp 101–154

Index

J. Johannessen, *The AI Battleground Between the USA and China*, Global Power Shift,
https://doi.org/10.1007/978-3-032-10138-9

E

F

G

H

I

K

L

M

N

O

P

R

S

T

U

V

W

X

MIX
Papier aus verantwortungsvollen Quellen
Paper from responsible sources
FSC® C105338

If you have any concerns about our products,
you can contact us on
ProductSafety@springernature.com

In case Publisher is established outside the EU,
the EU authorized representative is:
Springer Nature Customer Service Center GmbH
Europaplatz 3, 69115 Heidelberg, Germany

Printed by Libri Plureos GmbH
in Hamburg, Germany